D0573768

# THE OLD WEST SPEAKS

# THE OLD

*Water-Color Paintings by*

# WEST SPEAKS

*by* HOWARD R. DRIGGS

*William Henry Jackson*

PRENTICE-HALL, INC.          ENGLEWOOD CLIFFS, N. J.

LIBRARY OF CONGRESS CATALOG CARD NUMBER 56-9771

PRINTED IN THE UNITED STATES OF AMERICA

63388

# TO MARGARET

My wife, whose artistry and devotion are vibrant through all this book

# TABLE OF

*Chapter one*
*Chapter two*
*Chapter three*
*Chapter four*
*Chapter five*
*Chapter six*
*Chapter seven*
*Chapter eight*
*Chapter nine*
*Chapter ten*
*Chapter eleven*
*Chapter twelve*
*Chapter thirteen*

# CONTENTS

*Foreword*                                          13

THE WHITE MAN ENTERS                                19

MOUNTAIN MEN IN THE LAND OF MYSTERY                 35

OX TEAMS TO OREGON                                  51

OUT OF THE HEART OF TEXAS                           65

CALIFORNIA CONQUEST                                 76

THE DESERT BLOSSOMS AS THE ROSE                     92

HANDCARTS AND WAR                                   107

INDIANS AS THE PIONEERS KNEW THEM                   121

WYOMING WARPATH                                     135

MAIL AND MESSAGES FOR THE FRONTIER                  151

WILD LIFE STORIES OF THE WEST                       170

LONGHORNS AND SHORTHORNS                            182

HOME LIFE IN PIONEER BEGINNINGS                     193

*Bibliography*                                      203

*Index*                                             207

# LIST OF COLOR

*Plate one*

*Plate two*

*Plate three*

*Plate four*

*Plate five*

*Plate six*

*Plate seven*

*Plate eight*

*Plate nine*

*Plate ten*

*Plate eleven*

*Plate twelve*

*Plate thirteen*

*Plate fourteen*

*Plate fifteen*

# ILLUSTRATIONS

SUNFLOWER TRAIL                                     *Facing page 19*

HISTORIC HOMECOMING                          ⎤      *Between pages*
UNDER THE TETONS                             ⎦         *32–33*

RED BUTTES

FORT BRIDGER

WHITMAN MISSION

MOUNTAIN MEN

RENDEZVOUS                                          *Between pages*
                                                       *64–65*
SOUTH PASS

BLUE MOUNTAINS

BARLOW CUTOFF

BIRTH OF OREGON

THREE ISLAND CROSSING

ALCOVE SPRINGS

SUTTER'S FORT

*Plate sixteen*

*Plate seventeen*

*Plate eighteen*

*Plate nineteen*

*Plate twenty*

*Plate twenty-one*

*Plate twenty-two*

*Plate twenty-three*

*Plate twenty-four*

*Plate twenty-five*

*Plate twenty-six*

*Plate twenty-seven*

*Plate twenty-eight*

*Plate twenty-nine*

*Plate thirty*

*Plate thirty-one*

*Plate thirty-two*

*Plate thirty-three*

*Plate thirty-four*

*Plate thirty-five*

*Plate thirty-six*

*Plate thirty-seven*

MARSHALL FINDS GOLD

WESTPORT LANDING

KANESVILLE CROSSING

OREGON TRAIL

*Between pages
96–97*

LABONTE CREEK

ECHO CANYON

SALT LAKE VALLEY

HANDCART PIONEERS

INDEPENDENCE ROCK

OLD FORT HALL

FORT LARAMIE

CALIFORNIA CROSSING

OLD FORT KEARNY

MITCHELL'S PASS

PONY EXPRESS

ROCK CREEK STATION

*Between pages
128–129*

DEVIL'S GATE

BUFFALO STAMPEDE

CHISHOLM TRAIL

VIRGINIA DALE

*Between pages
160–161*

THREE CROSSINGS

UNION PACIFIC

*Between pages
192–193*

# OTHER BOOKS BY HOWARD R. DRIGGS

OUR LIVING LANGUAGE

THE MASTER'S ART

WESTWARD AMERICA

THE PONY EXPRESS GOES THROUGH

PITCH PINE TALES

# FOREWORD

Here once again I start telling stories, as it were, to an eager grandson. Now in my twilight years I recognize the boy perhaps more clearly than before. He is the eternal youth, the boundless energy, the will to dare and do that won the American West, and he speaks with accents known, yet clearer to me by the joy with which I hear him.

For eighty years ago I knew and loved that mightiest province of a mighty nation, even though it had by then developed from its infancy to its robust young manhood. The hands that then I touched had blazed the trails, goaded the oxen of the pioneers, triggered rifles leveled against the savages, guided the plows that turned the deserts and the waste places into fertile fields and gardens. Those hands, too, had grasped others which were the very first to touch the wondering natives', the first to scoop the fish from the untrammeled crystal streams, the first to hew pathways across the mountains and through the virgin forests.

Some of you may have heard my tales before, for history is common property. Yet I have tried to show you freshly the past of your nation in the words and through the eyes of the men and women who made that past possible. To them it was the present, as real as our own daily lives and often more vivid. That they should one day be thought of as heroes was a notion that never entered their minds, perhaps because they were more concerned with making a future possible than with being a part of it. That monuments should rise on spots where they laid their courage down would have appalled them. They did what they had to do. Necessity to them was not a thing to be crowned with wreaths and tributes.

If in reproducing their words—sometimes their thoughts and feelings as well—I shall have seemed to overdramatize their lives, let me assure you that such is not the case. Their experiences were deeply burned into their hearts, too dear and too intimate for them to be falsified. And as they recounted them to me, I also was too imbued by the sacredness of their memories to alter more in their accounts than the laws of communication make obligatory.

Some of the lore of this book I absorbed from my elders—grandparents, parents, aunts, uncles, neighbors—as they sat about our pitchpine fireplace many years ago and related their experiences crossing the plains and settling in the valleys of the mountains. Always I would ask of an exciting tale, "Is it true?" Always I was assured it was. In my father's store I heard the Indians, the hunters and the trappers swap experiences while they swapped their goods for something they needed more. When I was a cowkid in the hills of Idaho I lived among the pioneers and their descendants; and from them too came tales that are the bone and marrow of the West. Through more than my allotted three score years and ten I have searched for the story of the making of the West. Some of it I have found also in diaries, letters, landmarks and, of course, in books based on honest research. I hope that my readers may respond to my words as did once a Ute Indian Chief who replied to a speech of mine: "Me like what you say. You no talk here [pointing to his head]. You talk here [gesturing as if the words had come from my heart]."

This, my twentieth book on a Western theme, has been written with devotion to all the makers of the West: the Indians, to whom it was a beloved homeland; the pathfinders, who charted its trails; the missionaries, who carried the word of Christ across the Rockies; the home-building settlers of the Pacific Northwest; the forty-niners; the pioneers who made the arid desert blossom; the swift couriers and all others who helped join East and West into one great Union.

Others have aided and inspired me in this, another chronicle. Without

# FOREWORD

the help of William Henry Jackson, whose paintings executed from sketches often made upon the spot and realized with painstaking accuracy, illumine these pages, I would have failed as only a writer can fail when compared with a picture-maker. Without the unflagging aid of my wife, my children and my grandchildren, whose memories have revived my own, much might have passed unrecorded here. To them my thanks, and also to my patient editor and his assistants. All these have helped me bring old America to young America, to spread the message that what has made America will keep America.

HOWARD R. DRIGGS

# THE OLD WEST SPEAKS

PLATE ONE

Western emigrants on the Sunflower Trail passing the sandhills of the
Platte River.

# CHAPTER ONE

# THE WHITE MAN ENTERS

In the long days of my fifteenth summer when I was herding the blooded stock of the settlers who had trekked from Utah to Idaho to found the town of Driggs, I used to dream of that beautiful region as it must have been eighty years before when, so far as we know, it had been glimpsed by no man capable of recording its freshness yet untouched by civilization. And from the traces that were left and the stories I heard from our visitors who had been there then, I reconstructed that almost primeval world and in my imagination lived in it.

When I was a boy, few, if any, beavers remained in the valley with its new name of Teton Basin, for the trappers and traders had well-nigh annihilated these animals for their precious skins. But there were still striking evidences of their having been there in great numbers. There was, for instance, the remains of a huge beaver dam, hundreds of yards in length, with which the busy little beasts had made a small lake in which they worked and sported. After the trappers had wiped out the colony, the dam broke down and the lake drained away.

In its place grew up a meadow of luxuriant grasses, covering the thirty acres of the old lake bed, which was a godsend to us pioneer ranchers. For the hay that we mowed from it went far toward saving our cows and horses during the bitter winter of 1888, our first in the snowbound valley. Even so they were pretty lean critters before the snows melted from the flats in late April, and they had to browse among the willows, nibbling bark from the trees, until the new grass appeared.

The buffalo too had gone, though their bones were all over our valley. Once when I was riding after the cattle I stooped to cup water with my hands from a stream just southwest of Driggs. The skull of a buffalo stared up at me through the clear water, and after I had pried it loose and propped it up on the bank with stones, I christened the stream Buffalo Creek. Truly then did I feel like one of the old mountain men whose privilege it was to name for posterity the spots they discovered. Wild life still abounded. Antelope were on the grassy flats, white-tailed deer and moose among willowy retreats along the streams, mule-eared deer and elk farther up the canyons and the grassy highlands during the warmer months. Cougars and bears—brown and grizzly—lurked all through the region. Mountain sheep, now hard to find, roamed everywhere.

Riding along the north rim of Teton Canyon, a pal and I once chanced on a band of bighorn—fifteen of them, mostly ewes with young—led by a stately ram. We were hidden from them by the rocks and trees; they were in the open just below me.

At the ping of the Winchester the ram sprang to the top of a rock by the trail, and stood there turning his head this way and that to discover the source of the danger. His flock clustered around him. Another shot found his heart, and sent his followers scattering and bounding away up the canyon to safety. His horns measured sixteen and a half inches in circumference at the base.

Teton Creek, with its source at the base of the Teton Peaks—or "Pilot

Knobs," as the trappers called them—was a wondrous stream. Hundreds of kinds of wild life lived along its picturesque course through the craggy canyon, the grassy flats, and the willowy meadows as it flowed on to the Teton River. At every turn of its clear, dancing water, was a trout-filled hole. Waterfowl kept the streamside pools and the air alive. Mink and muskrats had their hiding places along the banks. I spent countless hours on my pony learning the secrets of the creek, and I thought nothing of returning to the ranch with a string of ten salmon trout I had drawn from it.

It was in July of that first pioneering summer that I encountered Nick Wilson, the first one I was to meet of those who could put one hand in mine and with the other touch the men who had turned the great American West from a wilderness to a mighty storehouse of historic lore.

That summer day I was grazing our cows by Spring Creek when Chief Lemhi Pete and his band of Shoshones trailed into sight on their pinto and buckskin ponies, some dragging travois, and crossed the shallow ford of Teton Creek as they came toward me. Conquering my first impulse to gallop for safety to the nearest ranch, I sat on my pony and watched them. One of the leaders, possibly the war chief, selected a campsite in the flower-filled meadow and directed the placing of the tepees. Indian women and the older girls unloaded the travois, made of slender lodge poles. Older boys helped to set these up—their bases in a circle, their tips brought together at the top. Coverings, some of skins, some of canvas, were lifted with two other poles over the framework, and secured with buckskin thongs. An opening at the top was left for the escape of smoke from the fire that was to be made inside. A flap was left for the doorway. Robes and extra clothing they carried inside.

While the tepee village was being set up, the children were having their fun. A shout from one of them set others running to a spot among the willows where there was a patch of wild strawberries. Yellow and black currants, plentiful along the stream, were gathered by the older girls in little baskets to add fruit to their evening meal. Several boys went to catch trout.

Four of the hunters, with rifles across their saddles, rode through the willows along Spring Creek casting only a glance at the white herdboy and his cattle. They were after a band of antelope off on the grassy flat, and while I was rounding up my cows to drive back to the fenced pasture, the hunters returned with three pronghorns lying across as many saddles. It was good hunting that day and every day while the Shoshones stayed in the Basin.

When I got back to our ranch I found that Nick Wilson, an old frontiersman, had stopped for the night with us on his way to Eagle Rock, now Idaho Falls.

"Lemhi Pete," he told us, "has led his band into this valley every summer since I first met him. When I was a boy, I used to live with the Shoshones, and I know 'em well. They're good Injuns, but they're touchy about their rights here. Teton Basin and Jackson's Hole, where I live, were part of the great Shoshone region when Lewis and Clark came in 1805. How long before that no one knows."

"When you lived with them—?" I asked.

"Yup. The mother of their chief Washakie got a notion she wanted a white papoose, and they lured me with a handsome pinto pony to leave my pioneer home in Utah, and be her boy. I was with them for two years." He began to unwind the story.

In the arid region where we lived in Utah, he said, the Indians were usually half-naked and hungry. The settlers' cattle were tempting to them, and easier to get than deer or antelope; and often an ox or a cow would disappear in the night. The starved Indians were blamed; some were caught by the settlers, and a few were killed, as a warning to the others. Governor Brigham Young, however, urged a different solution for the problem. "It's cheaper to feed the Indians," he said, "than to fight them."

The Mormon Bishop of Grantsville, south of Salt Lake where the Wilsons lived, further suggested that if the settlers were to feed the Indians they should persuade the red men to help produce the food. Each family should try to get an Indian family to live on their farm and help with the crops and the cattle.

Acting on this plan, Nick Wilson's father went to the tepee of Tosenamp ("White Foot"), one of the Gosiute tribe, and talked the matter over with the good Indian. At length Tosenamp consented to bring his wife and their boy, Pantsuk, to live at the Wilson place. The Wilsons made the granary comfortable for the Indian family and shared food with them. Mr. Wilson and Tosenamp worked together on the farm, while Tosenamp's wife helped Mrs. Wilson about the house.

Nick and Pantsuk, who were each about ten years old, herded the little flock of sheep out on the nearby hills. Alone together, the two boys became fast friends, and learned each other's language, so that Nick was soon talking "Injun" like a native. The plan was working with good results all round.

Then Nick's playmate took a heavy cold, and despite all that the Indian and white parents could do, Pantsuk died.

Nick was lonely. All the joy was gone out of herding the sheep. Some Shoshone Indians came to Grantsville to trade with the settlers. Two or three of the band rode out in the hills to hunt jack rabbits, and happened on Nick with his sheep. When he began to talk Indian language to them, they could understand him, for Shoshone and Gosiute words are much alike.

Interested in a boy who could speak their tongue, the Indians came again the next day, this time leading a beautiful pony. Nick was charmed with the animal and was petting it when one of the Indians said: "Ride him. Pony heap tame."

Nick had never ridden a horse, but he was thrilled to try, and it was not long before he could handle the pinto pony by himself and go galloping along the trails. For several days the Indians kept visiting with the boy, and letting him enjoy the little horse he had grown to love.

Then came the time when the Shoshones told him they were to leave town. Nick begged them to give him the pony. "All right," said one of the Indians, "we give it to you, if you will come and live with us."

"What do you have to eat?"

"Deer, elk, buffalo meat, fish, berries."

It sounded better to Nick than the bacon and beans and bread he generally had, but he asked to be allowed to think about it overnight. He knew his parents would not consent, and so he said nothing to them, but he did tell Tosenamp. The Indian would not take sides, but he did say that the Indians would keep their promise about the pony, and would be good to him.

That was enough for Nick. After dark that night he met two of his new friends in the willows outside of town.

"I wasn't sure yet," he said, "and I was about to turn back. But when I saw the pinto pony, I threw my arms around his neck, jumped into the 'squaw saddle' they had on him, and away we went in the dark."

A long, hard ride through the night, and for two days afterwards, brought them to the Shoshone Indian encampment on a branch of the Snake River, in present Idaho.

Chief Washakie came out of the largest tepee and lifted the boy off the pony, his legs badly punished by the rough saddle. With the chief came his mother. "She put her hand on my head," said Nick, "and cried. I cried too. Then we both felt better. The mother of Washakie, they told me, was to be my mother and I was to live in the big tepee."

Later Nick learned that he had been lured away from his home because of a dream this loving Indian mother had. Her husband had been killed by the Crow Indians, and her only daughter had died from injuries when thrown from a horse. Then two of her sons lost their lives hunting mountain sheep in a canyon where an avalanche had buried them. Washakie, the chief, was the only one she had left.

Day after day, the distracted mother would go out and dig into the snow to find the bodies of her sons, until she fell sick from the exertion, the exposure, and her grief. During her illness, she dreamed that one of her boys came back to her and he was white. She woke with a strange desire in her heart for a white papoose. When the Shoshones found Nick, who could talk their language, they knew he was just the boy for the chief's mother, and they carried through their plans to lure him to their home.

They camped in this very valley most of the summer of 1856. That was when Nick saw a buffalo hunt for the first time. The hunters killed seven of them one day. One on horseback, with a long, sharp knife at the end of a lancelike stick, started the killing. He would dash into a herd other Indians had surrounded, and hamstring the fat younger ones they wanted by whacking through the tendon at the crook of a hind leg so that the crippled animal could not run. Other hunters would dash up and finish it with their arrows. The squaws would skin the fallen buffalo, cut off the flesh in strips, and hang them up in the sun to dry. Then they would pound the meat to tenderness on a flat stone. Finally they packed it in its own fat in buckskin bags for the winter. It was good, nutritious food.

For two years Nick lived with the Shoshones, and no boy ever received better care than the Indian mother gave Nick—or Yagaiki—as the Shoshones called him. Finally Chief Washakie felt it was best that Nick return to his parents and tell his story. Old Tosenamp had told the Wilsons of the boy's confiding in him, so they all felt sure that Nick was among the Indians. It was a glad homecoming when he returned with his pinto pony and two other horses his Shoshone friends had given him, and with a store of buckskin clothing and buffalo robes for the family.

Nick Wilson told me about the many other Indians he had known, but his temporary foster brother held the highest place in his regard. "Chief Washakie," he said, "was more like a just white man in his thinking than any other Indian I knew." Many years later Washakie was one of the Indians who were most co-operative with the Federal Government in its efforts to move the tribesmen to reservations where they would be protected. The Shoshones were assigned to the Wind River Reservation lying mostly east of the Rocky Mountain Divide and southward from Yellowstone Park, which is still their homeland.

As a reward, President Grant sent him a fine saddle horse, and a saddle and bridle of high quality. The Indian agent made the presentation with considerable oratorical flourish. Washakie listened, but said nothing in response.

Thinking the Chief had not understood, the agent repeated the presentation. This time with much emphasis and many gestures. Still the Indian leader was silent.

"Does Chief Washakie savvy?" the agent finally asked. "Great White Father sends horse and saddle and bridle as gift to you."

"Me savvy," Washakie spoke at last. "White man heap talk. Injun let his heart speak."

These first Americans were like other human beings in that they had the same basic needs, and met them as all folk do, with nature's help in getting food, clothing, shelter. They loved and hated, protected their own, and fought for what they believed right. With them, it seemed to be the Biblical rule of "an eye for an eye," just as it has been with primitive peoples through the ages. Most Indians responded to kindness with kindness, and once it was gained, their friendship was lasting.

Explorers, trappers, and home-building settlers of the West generally found the Indians friendly. At times, of course, there were clashes, cruelty, and killing on both sides, unfortunate incidents that have been overstressed. The Indian, having slight means of presenting his side, usually was given the villain's part, though he often deserved a hero's role.

The stories of the pioneers are filled with incidents revealing the true heart of the red men. Sometimes an Indian's heart, as he himself would say, was "bad"; just as often it was good. However, pioneers of understanding and kindliness had little or no trouble with their Indian neighbors.

The attitude of the Indians toward the white settlers varied with tribal leadership. Some chiefs were peaceful in intent; others were haughty and hostile. Naturally the red men did not like the palefaces to take their home land and kill their game, but when they found their rights respected they generally consented to the pioneers' settling among them.

Some of the Indians even had a keen sense of humor and could put a barbed meaning into a few words. Once a pioneer stopped at an encampment for directions and was advised to spend the night nearby.

"Will we be safe here?" his wife asked.

"Heap safe," replied the Indian. "No white man within fifty miles."

Nick Wilson's foster mother had known Sacajawea, "The Bird Woman," a Shoshone, who was of inestimable help to Lewis and Clark in their great expedition and guided them near the Teton Valley. Nick himself had met Old Ocean, the Shoshone who had guided the explorers across the Rockies and the Bitterroot Mountains. And he had heard old Granny Pokiboro tell of seeing her husband killed when the Minatarees stole Sacajawea from the Shoshones.

Sacajawea herself was born in the Salmon River region, where Lemhi Pete, whom I had just encountered, lived most of the year. She too had come on outings like the one I had witnessed, and it was at one of the Three Forks of the Missouri that the Minatarees captured her and later sold her to the Mandan tribe. She was about eleven years old at the time.

Lewis and Clark's winter camp for 1804–05 was made near a village of the Mandan tribe, on the Missouri, near the site of present Bismarck, North Dakota. There by good fortune they found Sacajawea, then the wife of the French trapper, Toussaint Charbonneau, who had won her from the Indians in a gambling game. What was vital to the explorers, this Shoshone girl knew the way back to her home in the Rockies. Lewis and Clark engaged Charbonneau as an interpreter to get the services of Sacajawea as guide.

After dispatching some of their men downstream with first reports for President Jefferson, on April 7, 1805, the captains started up the Missouri in canoes heading farther into the unknown West. With Baptiste, her newborn son on her back, Sacajawea piloted them with all the sureness of a homing pigeon, overjoyed at the prospect of rejoining her own people.

The Indian girl soon won the confidence of the entire party. General William Clark even took upon himself the duty of protecting her from her husband, who had no compunctions about beating her when she crossed him. Not only invaluable as a guide, she was also of priceless service in nursing the sick and finding edible food. On one occasion her quick action saved the expedition's precious scientific equipment from being lost in the waters of the Missouri.

Great Falls, on the main river, held them several weeks while they portaged around the cataract. Then through what they named "Gates of the Mountains," they went on smoother water. Some miles farther west they came to where the Missouri divides into three clear streams, each of about the same size. These they named the Jefferson, the Madison and the Gallatin rivers, after the then President, the Secretary of State, and the Secretary of the Treasury.

"Which of the three streams," they asked Sacajawea, "shall we follow to reach the homeland of your people?"

The Bird Woman pointed to the Jefferson. Up this branch of the Missouri, the explorers went until they reached the point where it divides into what are now called the Big Hole and the Beaverhead River. Their guide advised them to follow the Beaverhead. As the stream narrowed and the waters grew colder, making the work of paddling or drawing the laden canoes harder day by day, dissatisfaction and grumbling increased among the men, especially as their food supply dwindled.

None of Sacajawea's Shoshone tribe had appeared. Canoes would soon have to be left behind. They would need horses badly to get over the Rocky Mountain Divide, not far away. Finally Lewis, with Drewyer, a signtalker, and others, went on ahead to attempt contact with the Shoshones if they could find them. Clark, Sacajawea, Charbonneau and the other men were left to toil on upstream.

A place was named as a rendezvous, but when Clark and the others reached the spot, Lewis was not there. Next morning early, Clark went on ahead with the Frenchman and his wife. As the three reached the top of a low hill they saw an Indian encampment in a vale not far away, where they were to find Lewis.

The Bird Woman danced and began to suck her fingers, a sign that these were her own Shoshone people. Dashing ahead of the men, she came upon an Indian woman about her age, and threw her arms about her. It was the one who had been stolen with Sacajawea, but had escaped and made her way back home. There was a rapid exchange of news, and Sacajawea learned that her father, mother and sister had all died.

"Where is my sister's boy?" she asked.

Upon being told he was at the encampment, she hurried there and took the shy little Indian in her arms, telling him he was now to be her boy. As his aunt, she could adopt him. Indian mothers and other children clustered around her happily.

By this time, Lewis and Clark, the chief and his followers had gathered in a circle to smoke the pipe of peace and hold a council. Sacajawea was called to act as interpreter. As the chief began to speak, she leaped to her feet, ran across the circle and threw a blanket over his shoulders in sign of recognition. He was Cameahwait, her own brother.

Through Sacajawea the explorers were able to get the horses they needed, and a guide to lead them over the Rocky Mountain Divide. Their canoes were left in care of the Shoshones, and they were soon making their way through the Lolo Pass, and over the difficult Bitterroot range, to the Clearwater River. Charbonneau, Sacajawea, and her baby Baptiste went with them. Her sister's boy, Basil, as she named him, stayed with his uncle, chief of the Shoshone band.

In newly made canoes the party set sail again down the Clearwater, the Snake and the Columbia rivers. After portaging around Celilo Falls, and shooting the rapids of The Dalles, they made safe and rapid progress to the mouth of the great "River of the West." On November 7, just seven months to a day after leaving Fort Mandan, Clark recorded in his journal: "Great joy is in camp. We are in view of the Ocean."

Sacajawea and her baby went all the way to the ocean, and when she reached its shore she acted like a delighted child. All that difficult winter she stayed with the party, enduring without complaint the cold, the rain and fog, and the scanty rations—mostly dried salmon and poor elk and deer meat. Then in the spring she journeyed back with the explorers up the Columbia and the Snake rivers, over the Rockies, and down the Missouri to Fort Mandan, where she finally parted with the white captains and their men. During later years, however, she often met Clark in St. Louis. It was to him she entrusted the education of Baptiste and his younger sister.

Basil, the nephew whom Sacajawea adopted, became a sub-chief of the Shoshones under Washakie, and continued the tradition of his people for co-operating with the white men, especially with the efforts of Brigham Young to get the tribe to cultivate farms and develop cattle ranches. Some of the Shoshones settled around Fort Supply, and there at a harvest festival in 1852, Basil showed the beneficent results of that co-operation. Addressing the gathering of whites and Indians he said:

"It is good to see grain growing on the Snake [Shoshone] land. Now our children can get bread to eat, also butter and milk. Before you white people came, our children were often hungry, when we were not fortunate in getting meat. I feel good here" (placing his hand over his heart).

Another parting at Fort Mandan that spring of 1806 was between the captains and John Colter, of Kentucky, one of the best men in the party, who asked to leave on a fur-hunting venture with two trappers from Illinois whom he had met at the fort. Lewis and Clark gave him an honorable discharge, and sent him forth with their blessing.

Colter spent the rest of that year and the winter among the Indians along branches of the Yellowstone River, but the venture did not bring returns worth the risks and hardships he had undergone and that lay ahead of him. In the early spring of 1807 he packed up what few furs he had, with his other belongings, and started for St. Louis.

At the mouth of the Platte River, in present Nebraska, he sighted boats tied up on the shore of the Missouri. Turning his canoe across the river, he landed and learned it was Manuel Lisa's party of fur-hunters on their way up the "Big Muddy." Three of the Lewis and Clark men were there —George Drouillard, John Potts and Peter Wiser—and out of the gay reunion came an urgent invitation for Colter to join the party for another trip along the old Lewis and Clark trail, now familiar to them all.

When they reached the junction of the Big Horn and Yellowstone Rivers, and established a trading post there, John Colter was sent out as a good-will messenger to invite the Absaroka (Crows) and other friendly tribes to come to the new post and trade with the Americans. Through the fall and winter of 1807–8 he carried through this assignment.

Dangers lurked in every part of the untamed region. Yet Colter persisted, following animal and Indian trails for more than five hundred miles through a region of mountains, lakes, rivers, and unbelievable marvels never before seen by white men, and traversing what are now called Teton Basin, Jackson's Hole, and part of Yellowstone Park. Out of this realm of wonders, and also the land around present Thermopolis, Wyoming, he returned with stories of boiling springs, geysers shooting their steaming water high into the air, and thunderous noises rumbling under the earth. But the trappers at the post greeted his tales with roaring laughter and the region he described so vividly they named "Colter's Hell."

More than half a century later, Jim Bridger, whose ventures led through the same region, told his stories of it to a newspaper reporter, whose editor turned them down as imaginary stuff. Later, this same editor printed an apology to Bridger, for further exploration had revealed that the mountaineer hadn't done full justice to the wonderland of the West. It was no longer "Colter's Hell."

Colter's discoveries did not end his adventures in that region. While he and John Potts were trapping along the trail they had followed with Lewis and Clark, and were paddling up the Jefferson Fork, their keen ears caught the sound of hoofed animals. Colter said it sounded like horses with Indians on them. Potts felt sure it was a herd of buffalo. Pushing upstream, they suddenly found themselves among hundreds of Blackfeet Indians on both sides of the river.

The big chief of the band motioned to them to come ashore. When

Colter obeyed, he was promptly disarmed, and stripped naked. Potts, still in his canoe, was shot by an Indian. He had life enough to fire and kill the redskin, but a moment later his body was filled with bullets and arrows by the savages, who proceeded to drag it to the shore and mutilate it.

Colter expected the same fate, but the chief decided to have more sport with the captive. Made to understand that he was to have a race for his life, he was given a start of several hundred yards by a number of the young Blackfeet stripped of everything but their spears. At a signal the trapper was off like a shot, with the howling Indians hard after him. Colter sped like the wind, leaving all but one redskin behind. Turning quickly, Colter grabbed his pursuer's spear and threw him to the ground, where he pinned him with the spear.

With screeching cries, the band again leaped into the chase. Colter dashed on until he reached the Madison River, into which he plunged, and swam until he reached a log jam. Under this he dived and clung, with just the tip of his nose between the logs to keep his breath. In vain the infuriated Indians searched everywhere for him.

With the coming of darkness Colter swam farther down the river, then climbed a cliff to keep off beaten trails. Hiding by day, feeding on edible roots, and following known trails by night, he managed after eleven days to reach Manuel's Post, where the men at first did not recognize him with his tangled hair and badly scratched body. Only the spearhead he kept could convince them of the story of his escape.

Colter did not stay much longer in the wilds, but went back to the Midwest. At St. Louis he met General William Clark, his former commander, then in charge of the Indians of the Missouri region, and presented new data for the maps of the West. The man who discovered the Yellowstone wonderland now lies in an unknown grave in Missouri.

One other of the first white men to enter the wilderness of the West was Zebulon Montgomery Pike, who as a captain in the United States

PLATE TWO

The homecoming of Sacajawea, Horse Prairie Creek, Montana, 1805.

PLATE THREE

Andrew Henry's westbound Astorians, at his trading post on the north fork of the Snake River in Idaho, 1811.

Army was assigned to explore the southwestern part of the territory acquired by the Louisiana Purchase.

A year before he set out on his great expedition of 1806, he had won his spurs as an explorer by leading a detachment of soldiers up the Mississippi, making successful explorations of its headwaters, and later along the Osage and the Arkansas rivers. On a detour northward from the Arkansas, he met with the powerful Pawnees near the present Kansas-Nebraska line and held a "Grand Council" with leaders.

Over the tepee of the head chief was a Spanish flag, for a few weeks before the arrival of Pike and his men, some three hundred soldiers from New Mexico had visited the Pawnees and other tribes, presenting flags and gifts. The transfer of that territory to the United States was apparently not being recognized by the Spaniards, and Pike had come not only to explore the region but to establish American authority over it.

His detachment of twenty-five soldiers in their plain uniforms was not so impressive as the larger Spanish force in their more colorful array. Nevertheless, the young captain rode up to the big chief's tent and firmly delivered his message—the Pawnee leader could not have two "White Fathers." If the chief wanted the Spanish to rule over him, he must take his people into their country; if not, he must haul down the Spanish flag and raise the American.

There was a brief period of strained silence. Then the chief turned and took down the banner of Castile. Pike passed him the Stars and Stripes, which was soon waving over his tepee. A good-will powwow followed, with an exchange of presents, and an Indian feast.

Pike's explorations of the region that later was called the "Colorado Rockies" were made during the fall and winter of 1806. Starting from St. Louis two months before the return of Lewis and Clark, he made an encampment on the Arkansas, near present Pueblo, Colorado, his base of operations. With three companions he climbed to the top of one of the high ranges to the north. There, almost waist-deep in snow, they gazed on a "grand mountain" which since has borne the name Pikes Peak.

That was on Thanksgiving Day—November 27, 1806. Before making the hard climb, they had killed and dressed a deer. What the ravens had left was still hanging in the tree. The nearly stripped bones of venison and a partridge they killed served as a Thanksgiving dinner for the four hungry explorers.

Winter had begun in earnest, yet Pike and his men persisted in exploring the snowy region around the headwaters of the Arkansas and the Platte rivers. Some of them went down the deep, icy "Royal Gorge" of the Arkansas, losing two of their horses in the adventure. After that, there were bitter experiences in store for them. Two men froze their feet. In attempting to find the Red River, they came to the headwaters of the Rio del Norte—or Rio Grande. Unknowingly, they built another camp on New Mexican soil.

A detachment of Spanish soldiers found the cold, ragged and hungry Americans there. When told they had overstepped their American boundary line, Captain Pike explained it was in error, and apologized for the invasion. The Spanish, however, took the exploring party to Santa Fe, where fortunately they received no unfriendly treatment. On the contrary, they were entertained as visitors, and through several months were escorted around the towns of New Mexico and finally to Natchitoches, in Louisiana, where American soldiers and citizens gave them a joyous welcome.

The Americans who first set foot in the West were scarcely older than the young nation they served. Small wonder that as a boy I felt akin to them and thrilled to the true stories I heard of their discovery of the wonders of the West I loved.

# CHAPTER TWO

# MOUNTAIN MEN IN THE LAND OF MYSTERY

Pink cliffs, vermilion cliffs, white cliffs. Red sands, purple sagebrush, green waters. Caves, canyons, crags like giants congealed in writhing agony. These were the apparitions that met the astonished eyes of two men of God who were the first white men to sight the weird wastes of southern Utah.

The men were Father Escalante and Father Domínguez; the year, the same as heard the Liberty Bell two thousand miles east in Philadelphia proclaim the birth of a free and independent country.

The priests with a band of Indians were searching for a route from Santa Fe to Monterey, a trail that would link the two outposts of the Spanish empire in the new world. Mile after weary mile they had pushed northwestward from Santa Fe until they came to the Green River in eastern Utah. Following this tributary of the Colorado, they moved westward across the Wasatch Mountains, over the rim of the Great Basin into Utah Valley.

Here they came upon the mountain-rimmed region, nearly five hundred miles in diameter, that lies between the Sierras on the west and the Utah ranges on the east. So far they had kept to the old rule of explorers—"Follow the waterways." Somehow they must run to the sea, to the Spanish coast of California. But the rivers of the Great Basin do not.

The Indians the fathers had brought along helped them make friends with the shy and frightened Utes of the valley. Gifts were made, and assurances that no harm would come to these simple primitives. And some information was gathered, but none that would help the party find a route to the Pacific. They had reached what might well have seemed to them the end of the world. Here everything stopped.

Baffled, they named this desolate *ultima Thule* the "Land of the Northern Mystery," and turned southward again with the sad awe of men who have looked on final things and found no answer to their quest.

The days were growing shorter as 1776 drew to, for them, an inglorious close. Once again in southern Utah, on what has since been named the Escalante Desert, they were stopped by an early snow storm. Their food supply was low, and no sign could they discover of other human beings who might succor them, out of a sense of common mortality. Now and then a jack rabbit would leap across the snow and fall prey to their weapons, but a single rabbit was small comfort to the band of tired, starving, beaten men.

Father Escalante examined the store of provisions. Little remained for the men themselves, less for their indispensable beasts of burden. Push on to California they knew not how. Return to New Mexico they might with God's help.

Rousing his little band, Father Escalante asked them to kneel with him in the frozen sagebrush and pray for guidance; then they would cast lots, as Jesus' disciples did, and abide by the Heaven-directed outcome. The lots directed them to return to their mission home in New Mexico.

Nearing the mighty Colorado River close to the present Utah-Arizona line, they hacked steps, still visible in the steep cliffs, for their mules to get down to the river. Then they made what is still known as the "Crossing of the Fathers," and retreated past the painted cliffs that rose in beautiful and fantastic forms, leaving the Land of the Northern Mystery for others to puzzle out.

Ten years after the semi-failure of these heroic pathfinders, some now nameless Spaniards, profiting from the sketchy knowledge the priests had gained of the mysterious realm, opened a horseback way from Santa Fe to Los Angeles. It was a route of dishonor, used mainly by Spanish slave-traders for their raids on the Paiute and other desert tribes to capture Indian women and girls whom they sold into bondage at either end of the line. The operation must have been successful; by 1850 bands of Paiutes frequently had no women among them. The practice continued until Brigham Young, as governor of Utah territory and United States Indian agent, put an abrupt end to it in 1853. This old Spanish trail along the southern boundary of Colorado, over Southern Utah, the toe of Nevada and the Mohave Desert in California, was eventually followed in part by the railroad.

It was nearly fifty years, however, before more secrets of the enigmatic region that had eluded Escalante and Domínguez were solved by white men. The northern edge of the Great Basin was found to be a treasure house of furs by the Englishman Donald Mackenzie during the War of 1812; and in 1823 a band of American trappers got through the South Pass of the Rockies into what is now called Cache Valley, Utah, where they established a camp in its well-watered, meadowy stretches swarming with otter, muskrat, beaver and mink.

These fur-hunters, led by General William Ashley and Andrew Henry, were to search every nook and cranny of the unknown realm for the wealth that its furs would bring. It was almost their only source, for the British had largely taken over the old Oregon country, forcing the American mountain men to find new fields.

Like most great discoverers they succeeded in doing so by breaking a rule, the rule of "Follow the waterways." Lewis and Clark, eighteen years before, had gone up the Missouri River and down the Columbia, and had missed the mystery land completely. For the Great Basin has no streams flowing out to the ocean, and no one could get into it by following the waterways.

The hunters had learned from Spanish maps of earlier days that the region contained an inland sea, but the cartographers, relying more on hearsay and imagination than on observation, had indicated a river, the Buenaventura, flowing out of it into the Pacific.

Now they were over the rim of the Great Basin the same question perplexed them as had the Spaniards. Why did no water run out to the sea?

One night as Ashley and his men sat about the fire in their camp by the beautiful mountain stream now known as the Bear River, they wondered where the stream could run. Was it perhaps a part of the fabled Buenaventura? Some thought it must reach the Pacific; others guessed it flowed into the Missouri and on to the Gulf of Mexico. They fell to betting, but there was no way to settle the question.

I heard the story of the campfire argument from Josh Terry, who had it straight from the mouth of Jim Bridger, then a youngster of twenty, and the freshman of the trapper band. For it was to Bridger that the others turned.

"Jamie, how'd you like to find out where this bloomin' river runs? Take a day or two off. Get in our old dugout canoe and go explorin'."

Jim had hoped they would nominate him. He was too self-confident to reflect that their selection indicated they thought him the most expendable of the party. Older in experience and more widely traveled than most men twice his age, he had not left his native Virginia in search of adventure and fortune only to turn down an opportunity like this one.

"I'll do it," he said, "if one of you will tend my traps."

Early the next day Jim Bridger loaded his blanket and some jerked buffalo meat, put one foot into the canoe, and shoved off into the stream. For over a mile he paddled with its slow current, the stillness of morning in the virgin land broken only by the plash of a muskrat slipping into the sparkling water, and the notes of the waking birds. The rising sun checkered the surface of the river with the cool green shadows of fir and birch and aspen, and the fragrance of the primeval forest quickened in the warming air.

Then from ahead of him came the rustle of swifter water. The craft moved faster. The rustle became a roar, and the almost glassy surface swirled and rushed. Crags rose on either side, and presently the eager explorer was struggling to keep a straight course in the white water that crashed through the canyon he had entered.

Quickly and vigorously paddling to the shore, Jim Bridger tied the boat to a sapling with a buckskin thong. Then he scrambled to the top of the cliff that towered above him.

Over the tops of the trees he could see a long, wide valley stretching splendidly for twenty miles beyond the canyon. The river smoothed out and ran placidly through meadows backed by low hills till it ended in a body of water that glistened in the sunlight almost beyond the range of Jim's eyes.

He hurried back to the canoe, and walking along the bank, guided it by a line through the foaming waters of the short canyon. Then re-embarking, he paddled swiftly downstream till he shot into the shining water he had seen.

Cupping his hand, he scooped some water into his mouth. He gagged, coughed, spat it out. It was salt, saltier than anything he had ever tasted. Clearly the river ran into the ocean, of which this was a bay. He was at what is now called Bear River Bay.

He caught his breath and paddled back to the mouth of the river where he had noticed a spring trickling down the bank. Kneeling by its fresh, cold water, he rinsed the bitter taste from his mouth and drank deep. When he rose, the sun was dipping into the western reaches of the bay. Jim gnawed a supper out of the jerked buffalo meat, wrapped himself in his blanket and slept soundly.

The stars were paling when he awoke. After stowing the canoe safely on shore he headed straight across the hills toward the trappers' camp.

The mountain men were too used to hearing and telling tall tales—of trying to shoot elk through glass mountains, and of streams that ran so fast they cooked the trout in them—to believe young Bridger at once.

But he persisted in his story so earnestly that the men decided to take the trail over the divide and see for themselves.

Even then they were not fully convinced.

"The water's too damned salt," said one. "Not a sign of a fish, only these bits o' shrimp."

"Don't look like the ocean to me," said another. "I've seen the Pacific."

Jim was vindicated, but there was neither time nor equipment then to learn more about his discovery. Like all business men the trappers were too occupied with their perilous livelihood to afford more than a day's jaunt. Further exploration was to wait for another year.

Then some of the trappers in "bullboats" paddled clear around what proved to be an inland sea, the one the Spanish maps had indicated. They nearly perished for want of fresh water, but they proved that no stream ran out of that sea to the ocean. The Buenaventura River was a myth. Another riddle of the Land of the Northern Mystery had been solved. Jim Bridger had discovered Great Salt Lake.

Jim Bridger lived fifty-seven more years, most of them as a mountain man or trader and guide, watching the West turn from wilderness into civilization. As a mountain man he won a high reputation, for he knew intimately all the region over which American fur-traders and trappers roamed, and he carried on even after the palmy days of the fur trade.

The decline of this industry, which had so greatly influenced American history and the spread of the young nation, was due to a change of fashion. In the late 1830's the beaver hat went out of style and silk toppers took their place. As a result the price of beaver pelts dropped to such a low point that it was no longer profitable to pursue the intense struggle of extracting the diminishing supply of animals from hidden streams of the West. Even with good prices, it had been a hard way to earn a living. Some of the trappers remained as squatters on little farms in the West, where they made a scanty living for themselves and their Indian wives and halfbreed children by trapping and swapping, and by hunting the few deer and other game remaining along the wooded streams. But most of them drifted back East to the towns they had left along the Mississippi.

A few lingered, living as best they could on the rugged land; and still fewer became scouts for the westward-moving wagon trains of emigrants and the soldiers who protected them, or guides for wealthy buffalo-hunters.

Jim Bridger stayed on in the mountain realm he loved, but he changed his work. He had sensed the change that was coming to the West and in a practical way he prepared for it. The scattered covered wagons that pushed relentlessly westward he foresaw were heralds of a tremendous stream of migration into the region beyond the Rockies. These later pioneers would need help and supplies. By December 10, 1843, he could write to his friend Pierre Chouteau, Jr., head of a thriving fur-trading firm in St. Louis:

> I have established a small fort, with a blacksmith shop and a supply of iron in the road of the emigrants which promises fairly. In coming out here they are generally well supplied with money, but by the time they get here they are in need of all kinds of supplies, horses, provision, smithwork, etc. They bring ready cash from the states, and should I receive the goods ordered, will have considerable business in that way with them, and establish trade with the Indians in the neighborhood, who have a good number of beaver with them. The fort is a beautiful location on Black's Fork of Green River, receiving fine, fresh water from the snow on the Uintah Range. The streams are alive with mountain trout. It passes the fort in several channels, each lined with trees, kept alive by the moisture of the soil.

His fort, which had probably been established there, in the southwestern corner of Wyoming, a year or so before this letter was written, was planted advantageously at a point where the first trail to Oregon and the later Mormon trail parted. The increasing stream of emigrants, as Jim had anticipated, did generally arrive badly in need of such help as a way station could provide. Furthermore, the Indians of the surrounding country were usually to be found in varying numbers camped in their tepees and wickiups among the trees and willows that bordered the limpid branches of Black's Fork. These streams were alive with mountain trout; moreover, the hills round about were at that time swarming with sage-hens, while deer by the thousands still were to be found in the not far distant Uintahs. It was altogether a goodly place that Bridger chose for his fort.

Four years later Josh Terry met Jim Bridger for the first time. A vigorous youth, Josh had started West with a neighbor in the first Mormon emigration, ahead of his parents who were planning to set out from their home on the Mississippi the following year. The boss of a wagon train gave Josh a job driving the loose stock of the caravan as they traveled from Salt Lake City by way of Fort Hall on the Snake River, over the Humboldt Route to the California coast. At Fort Hall, the caravan was prevented from proceeding by the commander at the post, for the Paiutes were on the warpath and the train was insufficiently manned to cope with an Indian attack. Josh lost his job.

The wagon boss gave him a piece of dried buffalo meat and an old overcoat, and advised him to go back to Salt Lake, but instead he walked the old Oregon Trail to Fort Bridger, hoping he there might strike a wagon going back to Iowa.

The first night of the journey he spent in a cave of lava rocks, curled up in the old overcoat. Dark overtook him the second day on a snow-covered ridge, but he managed to get a fire going and melted a place in the snow, on which he again rolled up in his overcoat and got some sleep before daylight. Better luck came the third night when he reached the camp of Peg Leg Smith, a mountain man, whose Indian wife gave the lonely, hungry youth roasted venison, and a buffalo robe for sleeping in the tepee—a kindness he never forgot.

"After that good rest," Josh Terry told me nearly sixty years later, "I was up early, and kept up a steady walk all that day and the next. Then the buffalo meat I had set out with was all gone. I met an Indian who had just killed an antelope, and traded my gunpowder for a piece of the meat. He made signs for me not to eat too much of it, but I was so starved I didn't take his advice. As a result I became so sick I could hardly walk. I slept by the dusty trail. Next morning, I was a little better and plodded on until I saw Fort Bridger in the distance.

"A man was walking out to meet me. It was Jim Bridger. He had the habit of getting up on one of his cabins every morning and scannin' the country around his post with a long telescope. Seeing me wobblin' along, he came out to help."

In response to Jim's questions, Josh told of his plan to try to get back to his family in Iowa and return with them the next spring.

"That don't make sense," said Bridger. "You'll only add a burden to them. Stay here and work for me. I'll give you mountaineer wages."

"How much is that?"

"Three dollars a month and your keep. Besides, when your parents come, I'll trade them fresh, fat oxen for the tired, lean ones they'll be likely to bring."

Josh Terry agreed and became Bridger's hired hand, taking care of the horses and cattle, and hauling firewood on a wagon he fitted with running gears for that purpose. He even stayed on after his parents arrived, and they continued on their way west without him.

In the middle of a bitter January night in 1848, Josh was awakened by a violent banging at the big wooden gate of the fort. Opening it, he found Joe Meek, a former mountain man, with bad news.

"The damned Cayuses," he said, "have killed Dr. and Mrs. Whitman."

Marcus Whitman had come into the region as a missionary from the American Board of Foreign Missions, acting for the Congregational and Presbyterian churches, in 1835. Then after a visit to his home in Pratts-burg, New York, he returned the following year with his bride Narcissa. A year later they established their mission at Waiilatpu, near present Walla Walla, Washington. Whitman worked devotedly with the Indians, and also as a guide for many caravans. Eventually the mission became a place of refuge and comfort to weary emigrants. Narcissa Whitman also opened a school for Indian and white children, and among her boarding pupils were Mary Ann Bridger and Helen Mar Meek, whose mothers were Indians.

Jim Bridger had been a firm friend of the Whitmans since the time, twelve years before, when Dr. Whitman had cut two arrowheads out of his shoulder.

Jim had run into a party of Blackfoot Indians in the mountains. At first the meeting was peaceful, but there was unmistakable tension between the white men and the red. It was a time for caution, when the slightest untoward incident could act as a spark on a powder barrel.

In Bridger's band was a Mexican named Loretto, who had ransomed a beautiful Blackfoot girl from the Crows who had captured her, and had married her. The Blackfoot girl saw her brother among the group the Bridger party had encountered. Handing her papoose to her husband, she dashed across the space between the two bands and threw herself into her brother's arms.

The chief of the Blackfeet rode forward, peace pipe in hand, to hold parley. Jim advanced to meet him. Both were wary, and the mountain man, nearing the Indian leader, cocked his rifle. Quick as a flash the chief grabbed the barrel of the gun and forced it downward, accidentally discharging it. In the scuffle Jim was thrown off his horse, and two arrows, fired by Indians near the chief, struck the mountain man in the shoulder. Before Jim could get to his feet, the chief had leaped on Bridger's horse and dashed back to his followers, who sprang behind rocks and trees and began shooting.

Bridger, though wounded, had also leaped with his men to sheltering places, and kept firing at the Blackfeet. Suddenly the Mexican Loretto, seeing his wife frantically trying to get back to their baby, dashed with the papoose in its Indian cradle across the line of battle and placed it in the mother's arms. The Blackfeet and the mountain men, respecting the act of courage, stopped their shooting until the father of the child was back with the Americans. His wife and babe were not allowed to return.

Hearing that a real doctor had come into the wilderness and was holding a "swapping bee" on the Green River, Jim Bridger came to the young missionary to have the torturing barbs cut out. Whitman made him lie face down on the grass. Then, with a circle of deferential Indians and mountain men observing, he deftly cut out the arrowheads from

Jim's shoulders. The operation was successful and the mountaineer was deeply grateful.

Now, twelve years later, Marcus Whitman and his lovely wife Narcissa were dead. An epidemic of measles had broken out among the Indian children about the mission, and the treatment the red men used most was to put the patients in a sweat house with hot stones, then pour cold water over them when they were sweating. Many of the children died as a result of this inevitably fatal method of cure, and though he had protested against it, Whitman was blamed. Resentment grew against him, his wife, all his mission helpers. Led by Jo Lewis, a treacherous halfbreed, who spread the story that Whitman was giving the Indians poisonous medicine, some two hundred of the Cayuses fell upon the mission and killed Dr. and Mrs. Whitman and all the boys and men. The women and girls were abducted by the savages, and little Helen Mar Meek and Mary Ann Bridger died from exposure and cruelty.

In his old age Jim Bridger moved back to Westport, Missouri, now part of Kansas City. Just before he died in 1881 he was asked: "Of all the mountain men you knew well, who do you feel was the greatest?"

"Jed Smith," came the prompt, decisive reply. "He had all the grit and courage of the best of the mountaineers, could outtrap and outshoot most of 'em. But he had something more—school learnin'—and he believed in God and the Bible. Damn shame the Injuns finally got him."

Next to Lewis and Clark, Jedediah Strong Smith contributed most to the opening of the West. He was the first to lead Americans the full length of the Salt Lake–Los Angeles trail, the first to take white men through central California, and the first, with his companions Evans and Gobel, to cross the Great American Desert.

A God-fearing man from New York State, he carried his Bible with him when he left home in 1815 at the age of seventeen to make things easier for his hard-working parents and their large brood of children. In

St. Louis he joined as a partner the Ashley-Henry expedition of 1823 that journeyed in search of new fur territory up the Missouri River and established the South Pass route across the Rockies into the Green River valley of Wyoming. This expedition, in whose employ was young Jim Bridger, was one of the forerunners of the Rocky Mountain Fur Company.

Now at a distance of over a hundred years it is hard for us to see the mountain men as they really were. We think of them as dauntless and intrepid explorers, and indeed they were. But they were after wealth first —at one time Gen. William Ashley sent 700 pack animals laden with furs back to Missouri—and the thought that they were making history came to them second, if at all. They were men of action, and alone as they were in these early days of the West, they were motivated by the need for survival. Whatever customs and ideals they had acquired in that part of their lives when there was a need for them to consider the survival of their social group as well as of themselves, soon disappeared in a primitive world where self-preservation and basic human needs were their only consideration. Romantics and sentimentalists have glorified and ennobled them, as they have the savages against whom the mountain men strove; but for us truly to understand them we should remember that it was competition rather than idealism that drove them on.

Few of them have left any record of their thoughts or their feelings. One who did was Jedediah Smith—different also from the majority in his magnanimity. On Christmas eve of 1829 he wrote to his beloved brother Ralph back home:

> It is that I may be able to help those who stand in need that I face every danger. It is for this that I travel the mountains covered with eternal snow. It is for this that I pass over the sandy plains, in heat of summer, thirsting for water where I may cool my overheated body. It is for this that I go for days without eating and am pretty well satisfied if I can gather a few roots, or better satisfied if we can afford ourselves a piece of horse flesh, or a fine roasted dog, and most of all it is for this that I am deprived of the privilege of society, and the satisfaction of the converse of my friends.

The letter was written after his return from California. Three years before, Smith had seen the necessity for his company to find new fields for trapping fur-bearing animals. The competition was increasing, not only from the English to the northwest but also from the Americans who were following in ever-increasing numbers the paths that Ashley, Henry and Smith themselves had already marked. The Company had originated the fur-traders' rendezvous, a yearly gathering held at some place easy of access to friendly Indians and trappers, and a spot where water, wood, grass and game were plentiful.

In 1826 the rendezvous was held at Ogden's Hole at the junction of the Ogden and Weber Rivers near Salt Lake. To it, in answer to the invitations sent by runners, came fur-hunters from points as far distant even as New Mexico to match their skill at shooting and riding as well as at trading. It was clear that the Rocky Mountain Fur Company must expand its activities.

From this rendezvous Jed Smith struck southwestward with a band of his men, following to a great extent the old Spanish Trail across the deserts to San Diego. After the torture of the burning wastelands, where even lizards have a tussle to exist, the Los Angeles country was as inviting as the Garden of Eden. But the Spaniards were not.

Polite on the surface, the rulers of the region were suspicious of these intruders. Subtly they confiscated the maps and notes Smith had made of his route, and then suavely invited the Americanos to vamoose.

The trappers did so with alacrity, breaking trail north to where Sacramento afterward was founded. Here they wintered, gathering furs, on the banks of a stream the Spaniards named after them Rio de los Americanos. It was the same river on which James Marshall found the gold nuggets in January 1848, that started hundreds of thousands rushing for the rich diggings.

The following spring, Smith grew anxious about his men in Utah and eager to rejoin them. Two barriers lay between him and his objective—the snow-capped Sierras, which he could see, and the unexplored Great American Desert, which he was not aware of.

With Robert Evans and Silas Gobel, whom he chose as companions,

Smith set out. Twice they tried to get themselves, their saddle horses and their pack animals over the mountains, and twice snow storms drove them back. But Smith was determined to conquer the mountains. Later in the spring they tried a third time, and succeeded.

From the crest of the high Sierras they descended to what is now the Carson Valley of Nevada. Ahead of them lay the vast, empty and mysterious desert. How far it stretched they had no notion.

Twenty days after they plunged into the desert they reached, with one horse and one mule left of their original nine, Skull Valley at the south end of Great Salt Lake.

Evans dropped to the ground exhausted and refused to go on despite the pleadings of Smith and Gobel. Reluctantly the two abandoned him and staggered on till they found living water. Revived, they filled their hats with the cooling drink and went back to Evans, who soon recovered enough life to get up and push on.

Finally they came to a camp of Gosiute Indians. The men were away, and the only human being in the camp was a girl. She had never seen a white man before, and when the three ragged explorers staggered to her wickiup and half crazily besought her for water, she ran screaming away.

By signs they entreated her to return and conveyed to her that they intended no harm. Finally she brought them water in a tightly woven wicker basket and they drank and drank until their maddening thirst was slaked. Three days later they reached the camp of the mountaineers.

Smith wrote a report of his explorations to the superintendent of Indian Affairs in Washington. Then duty called him back to the trappers he had left in California on the banks of the American River. With a larger force than previously he followed his first trail, fearing to risk an east-west crossing of the desert, a shorter route.

A tragic reception greeted him in California. Mojave Indians, instructed by the Spanish to let no more Americanos pass, ambushed and massacred ten of his men. The rest fled to the Mission San Gabriel, where they bought supplies and hastened on to find the other Americans they had left in the springtime. When Smith made an appeal to the father in charge of the San Jose Mission for more supplies, he was thrown into prison for daring to cross into Spanish-controlled California. Then he was released only to go to the governor at Monterey.

Here also the courageous leader was imprisoned, and it took the combined influence of four captains of American ships anchored in the Bay of Monterey to effect his release. Even then the governor of the province made Smith sign a bond for $30,000 to back his promise to leave the territory ruled by the Dons. Finally set free, he went northward into Oregon, which by rights of discovery and exploration was American territory, though temporarily dominated by the British fur-traders.

Again massacre struck. Most of his men went down before Indians, but Smith and a few escaped.

Doctor John McLoughlin—the fine factor of the Hudson's Bay Company—proved a good Samaritan in this emergency. Smith and the men who had survived the Indian attack were brought to Fort Vancouver, and cared for. Some of the furs they had lost were recovered and purchased by McLoughlin. Finally Jedediah Strong Smith left the mountains in 1830 with something of a fortune for the hard work and the dangers he had undergone.

Smith was ready to quit the frontier, but he took one more trip into the wilds to help his younger brothers Austin and Stephen get a start in trading. Joining with William Sublette and Thomas Fitzpatrick in a new venture, he set out over the Santa Fe Trail.

At the Cimarron Crossing of the Arkansas, they took the dry short cut for Santa Fe. The streams en route had become arroyos, and men and animals suffered for want of water. Smith and Fitzpatrick rode ahead to find it. To widen their search, they separated. Riding up a dry river bed, Jed Smith disappeared over a sandy ridge. That was the last ever seen of him.

Later in Santa Fe, Stephen and Austin Smith found in an Indian trader's store the gun and revolvers their brother was carrying when he left the caravan to search for water. The Indians who had sold the weapons to the trader told him how Comanches had waylaid the explorer and shot him, on May 27, 1831, when he was digging in the wet sands of the Cimarron to get water for his horse and himself. Smith had killed two of the Indians before he himself was overpowered and killed. No trace was ever found of his body. It seemed as if the desert had taken to itself the man who had done so much to solve its mysteries.

# CHAPTER THREE

# OX TEAMS TO OREGON

I t was the same Joe Meek, whose midnight visit at Fort Bridger with the news of the Whitman massacre awakened Josh Terry, who first demonstrated that wagons could be driven across black rocks, sand and sage, and over the Blue Mountains into the valley of the Columbia River. From Josh Terry's reminiscences of this pioneer, I first learned of the opening and settlement of the vast Oregon Territory out of which were to be carved the present states of Oregon, Washington and Idaho, and the western parts of Montana and Wyoming.

The region had, of course, been reached by the sea long before, first by Captain Robert Gray, of Rhode Island, who had sailed into the mouth of the great "River of the West," and named it after his ship, the *Columbia*. Lewis and Clark, too, had later pushed through the territory. Then some years afterward John Jacob Astor had founded Astoria as a fur-trading post on the Pacific. But the trail from the East into the untamed region which had first been traced by buffalo and other wild animals, then by the Indians and the trappers, did not become a roadway for covered wagons drawn by plodding oxen, until some thirty-odd years later.

By that time trapping and fur-trading had grown unprofitable for reasons that will be discussed later. Trading posts replaced the trappers' rendezvous, and a rising tide of travel spurred up new business opportunities on the frontier.

Once the South Pass of the Rockies, through which ran the famed highway known as the Oregon Trail, was discovered, probably in 1811, a channel was found for this tide, hitherto dammed by the mountain wall. Credit for the discovery probably belongs to scalpless Edward Robinson, who had lost his headpiece to the Indians when he fought with Daniel Boone in Kentucky. Though left for dead, he recovered from his wounds, tied a kerchief round his head and pushed farther west with his companions John Hoback and Jacob Rezner.

Astorians, going overland to Oregon on the Missouri River route, came upon these three Kentucky hunters floating downstream on a raft. Blackfoot Indians had robbed them of furs, traps and weapons; but they had escaped with their lives and were heading back for St. Louis. They accepted an offer to serve as guides across the Rockies for the Astor party, and led the fur-traders back to where Andrew Henry had built his trading post on the Snake River, in present Idaho.

After receiving guns, traps and horses for their service, they set forth again to trap the streams for furs. Joseph Miller, one of the Astorian party, cast his lot with the Kentucky hunters. Robinson and his two companions gathered furs and headed eastward with their packs for St. Louis. In this two-hundred-mile trek they came upon the South Pass. Then they ran into Arapahoes, who robbed them of everything they had, even stripping the clothes from the captives' backs and leaving them naked to survive if they could in the wilds. They lived.

Robert Stuart and party, heading eastward in 1812 with a message of disaster concerning Fort Astoria on the Pacific, came upon the three Kentucky hunters and Miller on the bank of the Snake River, catching fish to keep themselves alive. Had he missed them, South Pass might have remained unknown years longer, for shortly after the three Kentuckians were killed by savages on the Boise River. Miller stayed with Stuart.

History-making South Pass is the pass south of the Wind River Mountains in western Wyoming, and the Colorado Rockies to the southeast. Later, however, during the years of the westward migration, it came to mean the upland over which all the pioneer trails ran from the head of the Sweetwater valley across the Continental Divide into the Green River valley.

But to map a way, as the Kentuckians did, is one thing; and to open it as a sure route for home-building pioneers is something more. From 1812 on, a series of events led to Joe Meek's final blazing of a route for wagons, for the lava lands of the West were hard on wheels.

General Ashley, in 1825, marked the trail with wheels of a cannon he took with a span of mules through South Pass into the Great Basin. Five years later the Rocky Mountain Fur Company took a wagon train, laden with goods for Indian trade, to the eastern base of the Wind River range. In 1832, Captain Bonneville led his covered wagon train through the Gateway of the Rockies to the fur-traders' rendezvous on Green River. In 1836, Dr. Marcus Whitman and Dr. Henry Spalding, with their wives, tried hard to get a wagon to the mission they planned to establish beyond the Blue Mountains; but they got only as far as Fort Boise, after remodeling the wagon into a cart.

Finding, like so many others, that trapping and fur-trading was a losing game, Joe Meek, from Virginia, and his friend Bob Newell, another mountain man, had decided in 1840 to try farming or ranching in Oregon. Rigging up some wagons left at Fort Hall, they made harnesses out of rawhide and buckskin, and trained "squaw ponies" for the pulling. Then with their Indian wives and papooses, skin tents, buffalo robes and other equipage, they set forth. Joe had one mule, to hitch on as leader of a "spike team."

With this ragtag outfit of wobbly wagons and ponies, Meek and Newell managed to get the first wheeled vehicles over the beautiful Blue Mountains. At the Whitman mission they had a brief visit, and it was then that Joe left Helen Mar Meek, his little daughter, with Mrs. Whitman to go to school.

The wagon trip ended at Fort Walla Walla, a few miles farther west on the Columbia River. Thence the mountain men took boats down that stream to the valley of the Willamette.

In 1843 the "Great Migration" followed the trail left by Meek and Newell. On May 13 of that year, about one thousand Americans gathered at Fitzhugh's mill near Independence, Missouri. Peter Burnett, one of the leaders, told of the free land in Oregon, the healthful climate, fertile soil, fine timber, and abundance of fish and game. There was to be no round trip to this country. Any faint-hearted ones had their chance to turn back. All accepted the challenge of the long trip with its difficulties and dangers.

An organization was effected with Burnett as captain. Later on the trail, a so-called "cow column" for slower wagons and herds was made, with Jesse Applegate as its leader, who left a moving word picture of a day with the cow column.

Sentinels fired their rifles at four o'clock in the morning to wake the camp. Fires were lighted and the herders drove the oxen into the circle of wagons to be yoked for the day's journey. This corral of the plains was made the night before by parking the wagons in a circle. The rear wagon was connected with the wagon in front by its tongue and ox chains. It was strong enough to keep the oxen from breaking out, and also served as a barricade in case of an Indian attack.

Five to seven o'clock were busy hours, with breakfast to be eaten, teams yoked, tents folded and wagons loaded. Promptly at seven the bugle sounded, and the wagon train was on its way. Women and children often walked beside the trail, gathering wild flowers and odd-looking stones. Boys and young men on horseback kept the loose stock from straying too far, as they trailed along behind the wagons.

At noon, the emigrants stopped to eat. Oxen were turned loose with their yokes on, so they might graze and rest. Sometimes the officers of the train got together at noon to consider the case of someone who had violated the rules or had committed a crime. He was given a fair trial and, if found guilty, was sentenced according to the nature of his offense.

At one o'clock the bugle sounded, and the wagons were once more on their way. All through the afternoon the oxen plodded, and when the wagons arrived at the spot chosen by the guide as a camping place, preparations were made to spend the night. Livestock were driven out to pasture, tents were pitched, fires built, and supper was on its way. Perhaps hunters came in with choice parts of buffalo or antelope, and everyone enjoyed a feast.

After supper, the children played their favorite games; the elders gathered in groups and talked, perhaps making plans for the new homes to be built at the end of the Oregon Trail. Some of the young folk danced to the music of fiddle or accordion; while those more seriously minded sang their favorite songs, some religious, some sentimental. "Old Hundredth" was a favorite, and as the music and words of that grand old hymn floated on the evening breeze, many paused to listen and ponder.

> "Praise God from Whom all blessings flow;
> Praise Him all creatures here below;
> Praise Him above ye Heavenly host:
> Praise Father, Son and Holy Ghost."

But youth was not to be denied, the trek was a great adventure, and life stretched far ahead. Many a troth was plighted at the impromptu gatherings along the trail, beside a dim campfire.

Guard duty commenced at eight o'clock at night and continued until four o'clock in the morning. Various companies took turns at guard duty, one night out of three. Fires were dimmed at an early hour, and everyone retired to rest for tomorrow's march. Some slept in tents, some in wagons, some on the ground, under the stars. Usually their sleep was undisturbed save perhaps by the sharp yelp of a coyote on a nearby hill, and the challenging bark of the camp dogs.

By following the streams these ox-team caravans were assured of fresh water most of the way to Oregon; for they journeyed along the Kaw, the Big and the Little Blue, to the Platte. The last named river, flowing almost due eastward across present Nebraska, made a comparatively easy route for the westbound pioneers, and the good grass along its banks gave them pleasant campsites. Buffalo by thousands roamed over the rolling hills near the trail, while bands of lithe antelope in tan and white added touches of color to brighten the scenes. These wild animals were a source of good meat. On the treeless plains the dried dung of the bison—"buffalo chips"—provided fuel for the campfires. Robes from the buffalo warmed the beds of the pioneers.

Indians on their pinto and buckskin ponies, some of these dragging laden travois, frequently trailed by, gazing curiously at the ox-drawn wagons. Often they stopped to swap robes, buckskin, Indian-made moccasins, fringed shirts and leggings, for whatever the pioneers had to offer. There was parleying between chiefs and leaders of the caravan, and good-will offerings were made to the tribesmen over whose lands the road ran. This trail-breaking caravan to Oregon had no serious difficulty with the red men, though in later years warfare at times broke out and added tragedy to toil.

At the junction of the South and the North Platte streams, the vanguard of 1843 was overtaken by Dr. Marcus Whitman and his nephew Perrin Whitman. The Doctor, who had made several trips over the trail, traveled with these pioneers nearly to his mission on the other side of the Blue Mountains, and his guidance cheered them on the way. His first practical counsel was, "Keep traveling! If it is only a few miles a day, keep moving." Thus they would come to new feed for the animals, and steadily shorten the way to the journey's end.

Dr. Whitman's medical skill, freely given, was also of vital worth to the mothers, children, and even some of the men who fell ill, and brought most of them back to health. Despite all he and others could do, however, death came. Yet in seeming compensation, babies were born to bring happiness and new courage.

Think of an ox-team caravan as a moving community. These earnest folk, old and young, with dreams of a new homeland, had the same basic problems as in the towns they had left, and met them on the march and afterward with courageous spirit. In the beginning of their trek, they chose their leaders by vote and made their own rules of the trail, which were administered fairly yet firmly. There were unruly, selfish ones with any group that took the ox-team way West; but there were also more law-abiding, generous, co-operative ones. Folk soon found out who were the tricky, undependable characters, and who the upright and helpful. "You never know a man 'till you travel with him," is a sound saying of the pioneers. They had ample opportunity to prove its truth while the ox-team trains were making their long way West at about twelve miles a day.

The vanguard of 1843 left the Missouri River on May 22. According to Captain Peter Burnett's reckoning, it took 147 days for this caravan to travel the 1,691 miles to Fort Walla Walla, on the Columbia. At the time, that was one end of the wagon road. Some hundreds of miles, on the Columbia or along animal and Indian trails on either bank of the stream, had still to be traveled before they reached the other end of the trail, nearer the Pacific.

One group decided to take their wagons as far down the south side of the Columbia as they could. It was tough going, but they managed finally to reach the Methodist mission established about ten years before by Jason Lee at The Dalles, Oregon. Then they took smoother waters down the great river, while part of the cow column was driven around Mt. Hood. This group started with 108 animals, and finally reached the Willamette valley with only 68, for the mountain way exacted a heavy cost.

Eighty others of the vanguard—Jesse and Lindsay Applegate and their families among them—took the river route from Fort Walla Walla. Not enough boats could be procured at the fort to carry all the party, so more were made from driftwood.

Sailing down the picturesque river was a welcome change from trudging through the dust of the wagon trail. Yet the old stream, tumbling over its lava-strewn bed, took its toll. Some of the boats were overturned, and several of the emigrants lost their lives, among the victims being the son of Jesse Applegate and the son of his brother Lindsay.

The tragedy turned these pioneers to opening what is commonly called the Applegate Trail, which followed the Raft and Humboldt rivers over what is now parts of Idaho and Nevada, and crossed the difficult Black Rock Desert northward into southern Oregon. While it avoided the dangers of the Columbia, it was too dry and rough a route to be used by many.

Captain Kimbrough Barlow finally opened a better wagon way. Asserting that "God never made a mountain without leaving a pass through it," the Captain persisted until he found one south of Mount Hood and developed it into a practical wagon road. During the later rush of emigrants for the fertile lands of western Oregon, large numbers of them took the "Barlow Cutoff" from above The Dalles to Oregon City.

Whence came these home-building pioneers?

George Himes, who as a boy of ten years was among them, once showed me the collection of the Historical Museum of Portland, Oregon, of which he was curator.

"In this corner," he said, "I have a relic brought from every state east of the Mississippi. Here is a clock that used to tick time in Vermont. This old Franklin stove warmed a Quaker home in Pennsylvania. This scythe has mowed blue grass in Kentucky. And here is a cradle in which a pioneer mother rocked her baby as the family crossed the plains from Indiana."

The West became a transplanted East. Another proof is the names sprinkled over the West by the pioneers. Folk from Massachusetts brought the name of Salem. New Yorkers carried the name of Albany. The flip of a coin decided that the present largest city of Oregon should be called Portland, after the older city in Maine, rather than Boston.

What this ten-year-old noted best about his trip in the covered wagons was the prairie-dog villages, sometimes covering acres, and the comical little animals barking at the travelers as they passed by. There were thousands of buffalo too, which gave them good meat. Once the Indians stampeded a herd of the big, brown animals through part of the wagon train, upsetting wagons and crippling some of the oxen. Otherwise the Indians gave them little trouble.

Their worst hardships were the stifling dust on the long, long trail, and the sickness and deaths that came to many who couldn't stand the gruelling test. Yet there was always the lift of new experiences, new scenes, and the heroism of their leaders—men and women—who never gave up, even in the face of insurmountable tasks. One of these came, like the darkest hour before dawn, near the very close of their journey.

When they had got over the Blue Mountains, the decision was made to break a wagon road through the Natches Pass. They followed the Yakima River, crossing the stream, as one teamster recorded with notches on his whipstock, fifty-nine times. Then it was a fight through virgin forests until they reached the crest of the Cascade range, just north of Mount Rainier.

Before them was a precipice hundreds of feet down to its base. To turn back would mean starvation. Forests on both sides blocked any passage for ox teams and wagons. What was done exemplifies the remark of one of the stalwart pioneers: "Yes, we had difficulties—some were pretty hard to overcome. Those that were impossible took more time."

Go round this precipice they could not. Go down it with logs trailed to their wagons, as they had done in other places, they dared not, for the logs would be a menace instead of a help. The leaders held a council. Then came the orders:

"Get your chains and ropes to make a cable."

"Women and children take all the things out of the wagons, and find a trail to carry them to the base of the cliff."

Meanwhile men made the cable. It was not long enough.

"Kill one of the oxen," ordered James Biles, captain of the train. The order was obeyed. The hide, cut into strips, lengthened the cable, but still it was short.

"Kill two more oxen," directed Biles. Hides of these, spliced to the cable, brought one end to the bottom of the cliff. The other was secured around a tree at the top so that it could be payed out in lowering the empty wagons down the precipice.

Then, one after another, with strong men to make the descent slow and safe, twenty-nine of these wagons were lowered to the place where they could be reloaded and driven on to the plains west of the Cascades. Only one, probably not well tied, broke away and went crashing into the rocks below.

The pioneers had come into a land which was not yet under the jurisdiction of any one government, for owing to a provision in the Treaty of Ghent, which concluded the War of 1812, the territory was to be jointly possessed by the Americans and the British. Until the wagon trains began to pour Americans into the region, the British, through the powerful Hudson's Bay Company, had done most of the possessing through their fur brigades and trading posts.

The American missionaries and mountain men and the few settlers from the states who preceded the first great movement into the territory naturally opposed the authority of the Hudson's Bay Company. On May 2, 1843, these Americans met to pass resolutions and take steps to meet a need for civil action that had arisen.

Ewing Young, who had come from California driving a band of horses and cattle, had established himself as a rancher on the Willamette River, where he built a sawmill and was thriving until he died of a sudden illness. No heir was known. Something legal had to be done to administer his estate. This and other matters of moment to the colonists led to the question of organizing Oregon on a provisional basis of American pattern. It was put to a vote. Joe Meek jumped up, drew a line on the ground where 102 men had assembled. All who favored the proposition to set up a government of American type for Oregon were invited to get with him on his side of the line.

Fifty-two men stepped across with Meek. Two Hudson's Bay men at outs with the company also voted with the Americans. In this group of fifty-two there were fourteen states represented. Eight of the men were from New York, and New York law was the first law of American code to be administered in Oregon.

At the beginning the organization was simple, and only a few officials were chosen. Joe Meek was appointed sheriff. First attention was paid to the estate of Ewing Young; other matters were dealt with in turn. Hudson's Bay leaders in England may not have liked the new turn of events, but Dr. McLoughlin, the wise and understanding factor of the company at Fort Vancouver, accepted the new regime, and co-operated with the Americans, who he believed would in short time be the real possessors of Oregon.

Four years after the birth of the provisional government, at Champoeg on the Willamette River, all Oregon was saddened by the Indian massacre at the Whitman mission.

As soon as the word reached Fort Vancouver, Peter Skene Ogden, one of the stalwarts, with Dr. McLoughlin's full co-operation, loaded canoes with Indian goods and set out with trappers to ransom the captives. He was not long in making contact with the Cayuse tribe, some of whom were directly involved. All the girls of the mission who had survived the shock and treatment by their captors were ransomed and brought back to the white settlements.

The massacre at the Whitman Mission spurred the establishment of the Oregon Territory, for the protection and support of the nation was clearly needed. Joe Meek was selected to go to Washington as a representative from the frontier realm, and with four other men he struck out on January 4, 1848, to fight his way east through cold and snow over mountains and plains. No one could have been better fitted for such a journey than this mountain man, who knew how to avoid or deal with hostile Indians. Peg Leg Smith and Jim Bridger, old friends, helped him and his men along the way.

He arrived at St. Joseph, Missouri, without food or funds. Yet in mountaineer costume he soon won new friends. Aboard a steamboat, in hotels, on trains, folk flocked about him, and the way was opened for him finally to reach Washington. Happily for Meek, he was a relative of President Polk, who welcomed him warmly and opened the doors of the White House to him. He did not avail himself of the hospitality he might have shared there, however, but procured new quarters, and new clothing in which to carry forward his mission—to win territorial status for Oregon.

Congress that same year passed the law bringing that far northwest territory securely under the American flag. President Polk signed the measure; and appointed General Joseph Lane, of Indiana, as governor of Oregon, and Joseph Meek as marshal. Meek was requested by the President to proceed at once to General Lane with the official word. The two were then to go with all speed to their new duties. The President's expressed hope was that Oregon officially would become part of the United States during his administration.

A long, hard journey Lane and Meek made together—first to Fort Leavenworth, then via Santa Fe over the southern trail to California. From there they went by ship up the coast to the Columbia, and managed to get to Oregon in time for Governor Lane to take office on the last day of President Polk's administration.

One of the first acts of Lane's administration was the punishment of the Indians who had perpetrated the Whitman mission massacre. Some two hundred of the Cayuse tribe were implicated in the murders and the captivity of the women and children.

Determined to bring the criminals to justice, Oregonians were ready to make war on this tribe. To avert such a calamity falling on the settlers as well as on the Indians, guilty or innocent, Governor Lane gave the Cayuses the alternative of delivering the chiefs who had led them in the cruel affair, to be tried and punished according to the law of the white men. Five of these were named.

They might have escaped by fleeing to the mountains, but they made no effort to do so. Early in 1850, they were delivered to Governor Lane at the territorial capital, Oregon City. Joe Meek was given charge of them. With stoicism they accepted their fate, only one declaring his innocence to the last. The others expressed no remorse for what they had done.

A formal trial was held, with judge, jury and lawyers to prosecute and to defend the Indians. The jury brought in a unanimous verdict of guilty, and sentence of death by hanging was passed upon the five chiefs. When one of them was asked why he had permitted himself to be taken, he replied: "Your missionaries tell us that Christ died to save his people. We die to save ours." Joseph L. Meek carried through the sentence. His admiration and affection for Dr. and Mrs. Whitman, his love for his little daughter Helen Mar, all of whom had met death at the hands of savages, made this an intensely personal, as well as a stern official duty. It was another dramatic moment in the story of the West.

This American instinct for fairness and a hearing for everybody was another of the great contributions of the East to the building of the West. Ezra Meeker, who crossed the country in a wagon train in 1852, from old Iowa to Oregon, told me of the right and justice that existed on the plains, even in country outside the pale of the law. It was by no means true, as evildoers soon discovered, that each man was a law unto himself, free to do his own will so far as his physical prowess could enforce his self-made rules. There was no individual do-as-you-please, nor was there mob rule. Social preservation was a necessity to the emigrants, and the counsels of the level-headed older men usually prevailed.

An incident on Meeker's trip of 1852 illustrates the point. One night a murder was committed and the slain man's outfit taken by the killer, who was afterward found to be a man with a wife and four children. Twelve men of the train were called together to act as jurors. A judge was appointed. The case was tried under the open sky, with witnesses, and others to act as prosecutor and to represent the defense. A verdict of guilty of murder and robbery was decreed. The sentence, death by hanging, was pronounced, and despite pleas that it be waived for the sake of the dependent family, it was carried out after arrangements had been made for the care of the condemned's wife and children. The wagon train solemnly and silently passed by the gallows made from three wagon tongues run together, which was left standing with the rope dangling from it as a reminder to the rest of the emigrants and to those who would follow them.

The establishment of justice in this once untamed region, and the passage of the Land Donation Act of 1850, by virtue of which a settler of the territory could get 320 acres of fertile farm land practically as a gift from the government, brought hundreds of thousands of families over the westward trail. After all, it is the mothers and children who stand first in the shaping of the destiny of states. Where they go, homes are built and schools and churches. Villages grow into cities and civilization and culture thrive.

PLATE FOUR

Red Buttes, where the returning Astorians built a winter quarters. Later they abandoned the post and went down the Platte to a safer region.

PLATE FIVE

Fort Bridger, in the southwestern corner of Wyoming, built by the mountain
man in 1843 at the division of the Oregon-Mormon-California trails.

PLATE SIX

Whitman mission, established in 1883 near present Walla Walla, Washington, by Marcus Whitman and his wife.

PLATE SEVEN

Mountain men leaving St. Louis in April 1830 to open a wagon road to Oregon.

PLATE EIGHT

A trappers' rendezvous on the Green River in Wyoming.

PLATE NINE

South Pass, "Gateway of the Rockies," in central Wyoming.

PLATE TEN

The Blue Mountains, the pioneers' last barrier before they reached the valley
of the Columbia River in Oregon.

PLATE ELEVEN

The Barlow Cutoff, road built by Captain Kimbrough Barlow, south of Mount Hood, which allowed the pioneers to complete their journey into Oregon with their wagons instead of going down the Columbia River in boats.

PLATE TWELVE

The pioneers vote to organize Oregon as an American territory, at Champoeg on the Willamette River, May 2, 1843.

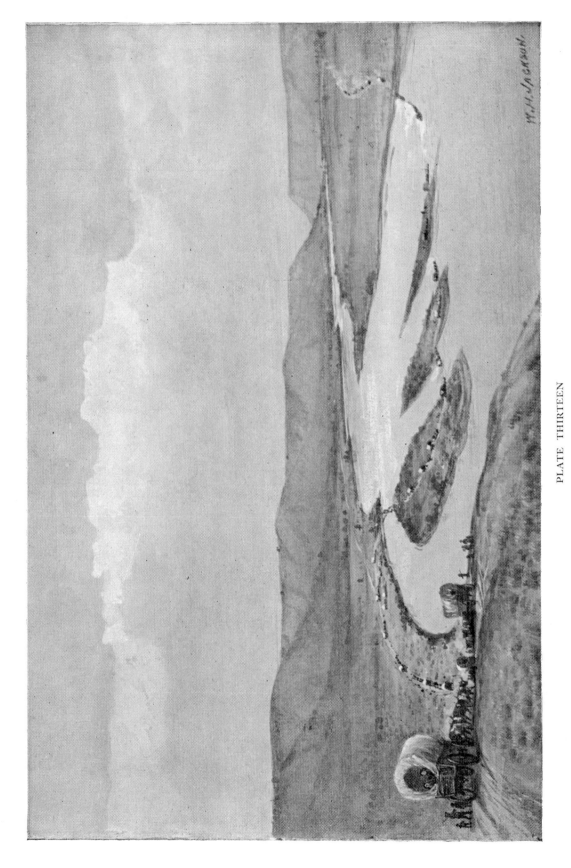

PLATE THIRTEEN

Three Island Crossing, a natural ford in the Snake River, where thousands of covered wagons crossed on the trail to Oregon.

PLATE FOURTEEN

Alcove Springs, near present Marysville, Kansas, where the Donner Party, and many others, crossed the Big Blue River.

PLATE FIFTEEN

The fort built by John August Sutter in 1839, on the site of the present city of Sacramento.

# CHAPTER FOUR

# OUT OF THE HEART
# OF TEXAS

The same expanding movement of Americans from all the original thirteen colonies, and from the newly born states east of the Alleghenies, that had brought the customs and traditions of the fighters for liberty into the West and the Northwest sections of America, also was responsible for winning freedom for Texas and adding to the Union its largest state. Among these colonists was Charles F. King, whose daughter Sarah preserved many stories of the building of Texas and passed them on to me.

Charles King had been born in New Hampshire in 1820, of a family which on both sides had fought for the Colonies in the Revolution. When only sixteen years old he had followed New England friends into Texas, arriving in time to take part in the Revolution of 1836 against the Mexican domination that resulted in the independence of Texas.

65

Even before the people of Mexico threw off their Spanish yoke in 1821, Moses Austin, a far-seeing son of Connecticut, had won approval from the Spanish-dominated government of Mexico for his plan to establish colonies of Americans on Texas soil. Dying before his enterprise could be fully realized, he bequeathed it to his son Stephen, who rose to the heritage and became known as the "Father of Texas." Its capital city now bears his name.

Thousands of home-building folk responded to Austin's invitation to join in the development of the rich lands of Texas. Lovers of freedom all, they soon found to their disgust that their new homeland, though constitutionally protected by the now independent Mexican government, was actually subject to the tyranny of Santa Anna, the president of liberated Mexico. Naturally they challenged the actions of this dictator and were joined in their rebellion against Santa Anna's usurpation of power by Spaniards who years before had come into Texas, and also by native Mexicans who had become loyal Texans. When Stephen Austin, who had gone to Mexico City to plead the cause of liberty, was held in prison there for two years by Santa Anna, the Texans prepared to fight.

A skirmish on the outskirts of San Antonio ended with the defeat of the Mexican garrison, and the victorious Texans charged into the town, where they forced General Cos, Santa Anna's brother-in-law, to surrender. After solemnly promising not to fight Texas further, Cos was permitted to leave the town with his troops. But at the Rio Grande he met the enraged President, who ordered Cos' troops to join his own, and returned to San Antonio to battle it out at the Alamo.

San Antonio then, as Charles King recalled it, was still a frontier town in which life was simple, friendly and colorful. Dangers, however, lurked beyond the town, and it took constant vigilance and courage on the part of the rangers to keep wild Indians—and wild whites—from attacking the law-abiding citizens.

Sometimes there would be fighting with such outlaws close to the town, and for safety's sake the windows of the houses were iron-barred, and all but the entrance door opened on a patio. The floors were of adobe clay, kept hard and also cool by frequent sprinklings with water. Candles and soap were homemade, and the weaving was done mostly by Mexican women, who were expert craftsmen and imaginative designers. Milk was delivered straight from the cow by a milkman who extracted just what the housewife demanded as she stood in her doorway. Vegetables were scarce, but venison and other game were plentiful. Sweets—molasses candy and popcorn balls—were made by the white children out of sorghum imported from New Orleans, and there was also the Mexican candy-man who wandered through the town calling *"Carmencillo—deleche—dulce, dulce!"*

The Alamo itself was then already gray and old and tumbling into ruins, many of its fallen stones having been removed to the walls of newer buildings. It had been built long before by the Franciscans who had followed the conquistadores into the new world, inspired by the saintly Mary Coronel de Agreda, who longed to see the gospel light carried to the Indians of America. Led by Father Massanet, these friars pioneered north of the Rio Grande to minister to the Tejas tribe, from whose name Texas is derived. Later their work extended over other parts of the region, particularly along the old Spanish trail; and several of their missions, the Alamo included, were built around San Antonio, where, worn down through the long years, they still stand as memorials to their founders.

In one of the *jacalitas* built against the wall of the Alamo lived Gregorio Esparza who, as an old man, told of life in the childhood of the Lone-Star State.

"My father would hunt and fish and farm," he said, "and my mother sold tamales and beans to the Texans."

The boy would carry the jars full of this food for his mother to sell. Once as he was crossing the San Antonio River on the single log that served as a bridge, he slipped and fell into the current with the heavy jar he had been carrying. Standing nearby was James Bowie, whose prowess in a fight had caused his name to be attached to the one-edged bladed knife—actually made by his brother—which all soldiers and frontiersmen in the Southwest used. Bowie jumped into the stream and pulled the young Mexican boy to shore, later becoming very attached to the lad and hoping to adopt and educate him.

Esparza and his mother were among the civilians who took refuge within the outer buildings of the Alamo when Santa Anna and Cos led their four-thousand-odd Mexican soldiers into the town and besieged the old mission which the Texans had converted into a fort by mounting cannons on the thick walls. Santa Anna ran up a blood-red flag over the cathedral, but the Texans did not care. They were ready to fight, and at night they would sing and dance. Gregorio and the other children loved to watch their defiance.

Gregorio was nine years old that March of 1836, yet he could still remember how the noise of those big guns terrified him and the other children. Once inside the protecting walls, he sought out his rescuer Bowie, then sick in bed, who ordered the men to give the family beef and corn. "We were too scared," he said, "to care much about eating, but mother made some *atole*, or mush, and almost poured it down our throats. Father told her she had better go away from the Alamo, but she said 'No,' she wanted to be near him, so we stayed all through the days of terror. Some of the time we hid in the corners of the rooms, sometimes under the hay. Mrs. Dickerson, wife of one of the Texas officers, and her baby were with us. She did not know what to do, and I heard mother say, '*pobrecita*,' and saw her take the lady some food.

"One night father captured a Mexican, one of Santa Anna's soldiers, who was prowling around, and kept him prisoner. During the battle he would tell the Texans what the bugle calls of the enemy meant."

Owing to the illness of Bowie, the Texans' leader, Lieutenant Colonel William Travis was given command of the fighting force of fewer than three hundred men. Every effort to rally reinforcements had failed, for the men who had beaten Cos were mostly scattered and could not be reassembled in time. A demand made by the Mexican leader for surrender was answered by a cannon shot from Travis. The battle was on.

Fortunately for the heroic fighters at the Alamo, just before the shooting began, into their midst had walked three frontiersmen—volunteers in the fight for freedom. These were Davy Crockett and two companions he had picked up on his way from Tennessee to Texas, one a bee-hunter, and the other a colorful character called Thimblerig. All three were experts with a rifle.

"There was great cheering when Señor Crockett came with his friends," Esparza related, "wearing a buckskin suit and a coonskin cap. He made everybody laugh and forget their worries. I was told he had killed many bears, and I knew he would kill many of Santa Anna's soldiers.

"Then came days of terrible fighting, but all we could do was watch and wait. The roof of the old Alamo was off, and along one wall there was a dirt embankment up which the Texans would run to fire over the wall.

"Davy Crockett seemed everywhere, shooting from the wall or through portholes. Then he would run back and say something funny. Sometimes he tried to speak Spanish. Now and then he would run to the fire we had in the courtyard, and make us laugh."

Travis, however, was sad and stern, yet he kept hoping for reinforcements. Esparza heard him say to Bowie, "Help will come." But it did not come.

When he knew they had to fight the battle alone, he gave his men a chance to decide whether to stay by him to the end. "I saw him draw a line with his sword, and heard him say: 'All who are willing to die, cross this line.' I think all jumped across. Bowie said: 'Boys, lift my cot across that line.' "

On the last day of the fighting, Esparza was wakened from a deep sleep by the guns firing as soon as it was light enough to see. He ran into the courtyard, where terror rooted him to the ground. The Mexicans were swarming over the walls, and although many were being killed by the Texans, more kept coming. He saw his father killed, fighting by the side of Travis; and a moment later Travis himself was shot down while firing a cannon.

"Santa Anna's men broke down the outer wall and poured into the courtyard. The Texans retreated to the second wall and fought them back, clubbing them with their rifles, and stabbing them with their Bowie knives. At last the few Texans left drew back into the monastery and shot the enemy as they came on. The women and children hid themselves where they could. I crawled under the hay, but I could not keep myself from looking and hearing.

"The soldiers of Santa Anna came on, thick as bees. Inch by inch they gained ground, but for every Texan they killed, five of them fell. Fourteen of the enemy were lying dead around Davy Crockett before he too died fighting.

"When my good friend Bowie was killed, panic seized me, and I hid with the other children and the mothers. Some of the Mexicans shot into the room, and one boy was killed, but the rest of us escaped. Then some of the Mexican soldiers came searching through the rooms.

"One of them put his bayonet against my mother, demanding: 'Where is the Texans' money?'

" 'If they had any money, find it,' she said.

"The soldier struck her, and I screamed. An officer ordered the soldier to go and leave the women and children alone.

"When it was broad daylight, the families were sent to the home of Don Musquiz at the Plaza, and given coffee and tamales; for we were very hungry. That afternoon we were taken before Santa Anna, whom we found sitting behind a table covered with a pile of silver.

"He asked the women: 'Why do you fight your countrymen?'

" 'They are not our countrymen,' answered my mother. 'We are Texans.'

" 'I suppose if I let you go, you will raise your children to fight Mexico.'

" 'Yes.'

" 'You ought to have your ears cut off.'

"At this all of us children screamed.

" 'Get the mob out,' he ordered. 'Give each woman two dollars and a blanket. *Vamanos*.' "

The night of March 6, 1836, fell upon the Alamo with a strange quiet. In San Antonio, the victors were reveling over their costly triumph, but the stillness within the ruined walls was broken only by the wailing of the Mexican mothers and children whose husbands and fathers had fallen by the side of the Texans. Afterward the dictator spared these, sending

Mrs. Dickerson, the one white mother, and her child, to tell what had happened to those who defied Santa Anna. The others were ordered out of his sight. As for the bodies of the heroes, they were heaped upon a funeral pyre and consigned to the flames.

It took three days for the soldiers of Santa Anna to gather up their dead and bury them.

Dark days came in the wake of the Alamo. Santa Anna's unleashed forces were spreading terror throughout the land. After cutting to pieces a small force under Grant and Johnson, an army under General Urrea marched on Goliad and forced Colonel Fannin to surrender for lack of food and ammunition. A few days later, on Santa Anna's order, Urrea marched his prisoners of war out of Goliad and had them shot down without mercy. Only a handful escaped. "Remember Goliad!" was added to the battle cry of "Remember the Alamo!" as the Texans rushed to arms.

Among the homeless people who were fleeing for safety from Santa Anna's soldiers was Gail Borden, who had emigrated from Massachusetts to San Felipe, where he set up a printing office. In his flight he carried his press and paper, and kept on printing leaflets consisting of diatribes against the Mexican tyrant, which cheered the escaping colonists.

Everywhere along the route of the refugees was the sound at night of babies crying for milk. When Borden found one mother whose baby was not crying, but contentedly sucking its supper from a bottle, Borden asked the woman how she managed to keep the milk fresh and sweet.

"Oh," she said, "I just use enough sugar to preserve it."

From this incident Borden caught the idea of preserving milk for young and old, and made his name famous by producing the new invention. Borden County, Texas, and Gail, its county seat, were named for him.

Edward Miles, a veteran of the fighting that followed the battle of the Alamo, related many stories of the almost hopeless days and weeks that the Texans endured. The guns of the men who fought with Sam Houston were poor, the ammunition was scanty, clothes turned to rags and boots to shreds of leather. They had to forage for food, and often were on scanty rations. Only patriotism and a determination to crush Santa Anna kept the meager army's spirits high.

For ten days this straggling army marched from San Antonio toward the most populous part of Texas to get reinforcements and supplies, the enemy sometimes no more than two miles behind them. But once they had crossed the Colorado River they were joined by volunteers who increased the ranks to twelve hundred men.

At the same time, however, a few men who had escaped at Goliad came into camp with stories of the massacre, and started a panic that caused many men with their families to flee on toward the Sabine River. For days it rained, and they floundered through mud and water. Smallpox, measles and pneumonia broke out in the camp. Men and women died and were buried without coffins. Women grew hysterical, laughing, crying and even fighting, until after a time a quiet of desperation came over them and they faced the situation. Rich and poor, refined and coarse, became sisters together, sharing and helping one another and taking care of themselves.

The refusal of Houston to stop the retreat and fight Santa Anna caused grumbling and even desertions, especially as he turned the retreat southward again toward San Jacinto. The spot he eventually chose as a battle ground was a prairie bounded by Galveston Bay and its marshland, Buffalo Bayou, San Jacinto River and Vinces Bayou. With arrogant confidence Santa Anna took his position in front of the marshlands. Houston chose the higher ground near Buffalo Bayou. Deaf Smith, one of the Texans' scouts, played the part of the Roman Horatius by cutting down the bridge across Vinces Bayou to keep reinforcements from getting to the dictator.

"April 21, 1836," said Miles, "dawned clear, and the Texans took that as a good omen, for they were only eight hundred against double that number. At three o'clock they formed their battle lines. General Houston on his horse shouted 'Follow your leader!' and we leaped into the fray. 'Remember the Alamo!' 'Remember Goliad!' burst from all our throats."

The enemy was taken completely by surprise, as the Texans charged into its ranks like fighting demons. Down they went under the fire of the

American rifles and cannon, and there was not time for them to send many return shots. They had bayonets, but Houston's men clubbed the blades aside with the butts of their guns. Santa Anna's soldiers could not stand against the terrific onslaught. Their lines broke and they fled in every direction with the Texans hot on their heels. Within twenty minutes, 630 of the enemy went down.

"What an outburst came from our little army over this triumph!" Miles said. "We wept and danced. We hugged one another. We swore and prayed. We yelled and kept running and killing relentlessly those who had fought our men to the death at the Alamo, and shot them down in cold blood at Goliad. All our hate and hunger found vent in those maddened moments when we crashed through to victory at San Jacinto."

By nightfall the enemy was completely in their power. Besides the hundreds of dead and wounded, 700 had surrendered. Mexican money amounting to $12,000, together with arms, ammunition and equipment had been taken. Against all this, the Texans had sustained a loss of only 2 killed and 23 wounded. Sam Houston had been shot in the ankle.

Santa Anna himself was not to be found among the slain, the wounded, or the prisoners. Scouts were dispatched in all directions to find him and bring him to punishment. Then a Lieutenant Sylvester, out with a party including Miles to round up enemy stragglers and also to bring some water to camp, stopped at noontime to rest and to shoot at some deer they saw in the distance. Sylvester dismounted and began to creep toward the deer. Suddenly they bounded away, but the Lieutenant knew he had not scared them, for their heads had been turned from him. It was something else that had alarmed the deer. Calling his men, Sylvester led them in a search. Not far off they found a man hiding in the grass.

"Get up," commanded Sylvester.

The fellow did not obey. Sylvester jumped from his horse and gave the man a light kick. At this, the fellow stood up and said something in Spanish. Robinson, one of the men who spoke that language, asked, "Are you an officer?"

"No," he replied. "I am a soldier, but I want to speak to your General Houston."

Just then Miles caught sight of a diamond stud on his shirt front, and exclaimed: "Look, that man is an officer and rich."

"I am an aide to Santa Anna," he said.

"Where is Santa Anna?" asked Robinson. The fellow shook his head.

The men scanned him closely. He had on a glazed leather cap, a striped jacket, country-made cotton socks and coarse white pants. His shirt, however, was fine linen; his shoes, pointed and elegant. Later it was learned that he had picked up the coarser clothing in an abandoned house.

They started back toward camp. After trudging a little way the captive asked Robinson how far it was, and when told it was about eight miles, said, "I can't walk far."

Robinson took him behind him on his horse. Afterward he rode behind the Lieutenant. When the party reached camp, the Mexican prisoners saluted and said, *"El Presidente!"*

"Straightway," Miles said, "we took the prisoner to General Houston, who was lying under the shade of a tree with his wounded leg bandaged."

"You ought to be generous to the vanquished," Santa Anna began.

"You should have remembered that at the Alamo, and at Goliad," returned Houston.

"I was acting under orders of my government," Santa Anna replied.

"You were the government of Mexico. A dictator, sir, has no superiors."

The prisoner was taken away and placed in irons under guard while General Houston and the other Texas leaders discussed the terms to be meted out to him. Feeling among the men rose high, some being eager to give the tyrant the death penalty. The leaders of Texas, however, felt that Santa Anna was worth more alive than dead to the newborn nation. They drew up a treaty that made him acknowledge the independence of Texas, cease all hostilities, and withdraw the Mexican troops to the south of the Rio Grande. Santa Anna signed the compact.

"That night," Miles concluded, "we gave ourselves to the wildest of joy. We built bonfires and danced like Indians. The Mexicans who had stood by Texas through all the fight for freedom were just as overjoyed as we, for a goodly share of the praise for victory was due to these patriots, led by Captains Sequin and Menchaca, and Lieutenant Flores, who had plunged into the fight at San Jacinto like tigers. The thunderous voice of Menchaca could be heard above the din of battle, yelling, 'Give no quarter!' Some said Menchaca's booming voice probably gave Santa Anna the scare that made him run for life."

The victorious soldiers soon turned their serious thoughts to getting home. As soon as they could be released, the Texans hastened to find their scattered loved ones, though many of their wives and children would never return. The difficult days ahead called for sustained heroism, but with victory came new hope and courage. Texas became a new and independent nation.

# CHAPTER FIVE

# CALIFORNIA CONQUEST

In the afternoon of a late summer day, fifty-five weary, famished men stood at last on the high crest of the Sierras and gazed more in despondency than in wonder at the precipices and gorges that lay ahead of them. A single Indian caught sight of the strangers, the first white men he had ever seen, dropped the acorn-laden basket he had been carrying, and fled howling with terror. Then men fell greedily upon this abandoned treasure and crammed the nuts into their mouths. It was the first real food they had had since starting their ascent of the mountains.

Only one of these rugged mountain men seemed to observe the scene before them. "Here and there," he was to write in his journal of the expedition, "small streams would shoot out from high snow banks, and after running a short distance would precipitate themselves from one lofty precipice to another until they were exhausted in rain below. Some of the precipices appeared to be a mile high."

It was the first glimpse a civilized man had had of the splendid valley of the Yosemite and of the continent's highest waterfall tossing its wondrous rainbow-tinted spray into the air. The man was Zenas Leonard, clerk of the party led by Joseph Reddeford Walker, from Tennessee, which had set out in high spirits from the Green River–Horse Creek rendezvous in distant Wyoming on July 24, 1833.

There one of the greatest of the explorers of the West, Captain Benjamin Louis Eulalie de Bonneville, of the United States Army, had established the previous year what the oldtime fur-men called Fort Nonsense, after blazing a wagon way over South Pass. Bonneville had appointed Walker ostensibly to find new streams for trapping, as he was on a so-called fur-trading venture in the West on leave from the Army; but actually he had been instructed by his government to keep a watchful eye on the tottering Spanish regime in California. Andrew Jackson had already made an offer to Spain to purchase the northern part of this province, and had been refused. The British also were interested in the region, so full of potential wealth of all kinds, and maintained their Captain Stuart, in the guise of a big-game hunter, as an ever-present spy on the American rendezvous both east and west of the Rockies. It was a critical time for the expansion of the United States across the continent to the Pacific.

Walker had led his men across the Sierra Nevadas, following, in the tradition of the explorers, the waterway of the Humboldt River across what is now Nevada to its sink in the thirsty desert. At the present Battle Lakes they found themselves being followed by a band of desert Indians, and taking no chances, fired into them, killing thirty-nine. Then they pressed on across seemingly endless stretches of barren wasteland until they reached the snow-capped Sierras, which Jedediah Smith, the "Puritan Pathfinder," had traversed some seven years before. Their food had dwindled, and they had been forced to slaughter and eat seventeen of their horses. Now at last at the summit of the mountains, they faced the serious problem of getting down the rugged western slope of the range.

Fortified by the acorns, they took courage again. One of the men shot a deer which, Leonard reports, "was dressed, cooked and eaten in less time than it takes a hungry wolf to devour a lamb." And at last they found a way leading into the spectacularly astonishing valley so far below them.

Reaching the level plain, they hurried across it to discover the oldest living things in the world, the giant redwood trees. "Incredibly large," recorded Leonard, "some of them would measure from sixteen to eighteen fathoms around the trunk at the height of a man's head from the ground." Those who first found and told of the giants were laughed at by the men in the camp, and everyone had to see the marvels before he could believe that they existed.

As they lay down in the forest of redwoods to sleep, a roaring came to their ears. When it did not cease, fear seized some of the men, for it sounded as if it might be an earthquake. Then Captain Walker "suggested that the noise came from the Pacific rolling and dashing against the shore," wrote Leonard. The thought of being at the end of the Far West inspired all the men. Soon afterward they were watching the great ocean lashed by a stormy gale. Patriotic feelings rose in their hearts. With something of a prophetic spirit Leonard wrote:

> Most of this vast waste of territory [over which they had come from the Mississippi] belongs to the Republic of the United States. What a theme to contemplate its settlement and civilization! Will her hardy, free-born population here plant their homes, build their towns and cities, and say, here shall the arts and sciences of civilization take root and flourish?
>
> The Spaniards are making inroads on the South—the Russians are encroaching with impunity along the seashore to the North, and further Northeast the British are pushing their stations into the very heart of our country, which even at this day resemble military forts to resist invasion more than trading stations.

Then Leonard added a code for the nation, which soon was to be echoed over the East:

> Our government should be vigilant. She should assert her claim by taking possession of the whole territory as soon as possible. . . . For we have good reason to suppose that the territory west of the mountains will some day be equally as important to the nation as that on the east.

This sounds as if fur-hunting had been somewhat forgotten by these explorers.

Walker, with Captain Baagshaw from Boston, whose ship the *Lagoda* the explorers had found, as it were, waiting for them, made friends with the Spanish governor at Monterey and gained permission for the Americans to winter near that town.

The life that they found there was still leisurely and tranquil, for nature had provided an easy survival. Bear, deer and other valuable wild animals abounded. The lakes and bays were alive with waterfowl, the streams filled with fish and their banks haunted by fur-bearing creatures. Birds made the groves and meadows vibrant with their colors and the sound of their wings and their voices. The realm seemed waiting for adventurous souls to awake its valleys and desert reaches and plunder their hidden treasures.

The native Indians had been trained already to work with wool and leather, and to make simple furniture. Orange and olive trees had been planted, and vineyards too. Flocks of sheep and goats, and herds of cattle, grazed on the hillsides.

It was the pastoral period of California history which had been ushered in a half-century before by the mission-building Franciscan padres. Led by Father Junipero Serra, the kindly friars had followed the Spanish politicos bent on checkmating the fur-hunting Russians, who had begun to extend their activities southward down the Pacific. These officials, appointed by the King of Spain, and supported by Spanish soldiery, ruled rather independently and autocratically, for, as one put it: "Madrid was far away, and heaven was high."

Walker's men were entranced by the superb horsemanship of the *vaqueros* as they handled the longhorned cattle that provided beef, hides and tallow for a widely flourishing export trade. Old Spain was there with its bull-fighting, contests between bulls and captured grizzly bears, its fiestas, and beautiful women. It was hard for the American adventurers to leave and face once more the rigors of the mountains and the desert, and some chose to remain.

Most of them, however, reported for duty. Walker traded furs they had gathered for ammunition and other supplies, and purchased new horses from the California ranches. They made their way eastward over the snowy range through what was afterwards called Walker's Pass, taking less time than on their westward trip. The desert, however, was just as tough going as before, and exacted a serious toll of dogs and horses. Some men, too, came close to dying of thirst before they reached the Humboldt River, where Indians, probably remembering the massacre at Battle Lakes, made an attempt to even the score against the palefaces with their "fire sticks." Again some of the red men were shot down. Angered, stealthy Indians through later years took revenge on emigrants and gold-seekers who followed the Humboldt Trail.

Walker and his men had opened this subsequently famous and well-traveled route to California, but they had little to show in the way of pelts. It became established that there were no truly promising fur-bearing streams flowing eastward from the Sierras. Their stories of the alluring land they had found, however, were a challenge to those who saw opportunities in the undeveloped region, and who took the trail to wealth.

Others there were who, as a pioneer wag once put it, "went willingly because they had to." One of these was John Marsh, of Massachusetts, of whom my great-uncle, a member of Kearny's Army of the West, told me, and who was to play a significant role in the drama that finally brought California into the Union.

John Marsh's parents had intended him for the ministry, but his prankish disposition at Harvard closed that profession to him, and the college authorities felt that he should be very grateful for the simple bachelor's degree they reluctantly granted him. Armed with his impressive, Latin-inscribed diploma, he accepted a position as teacher of the post at Fort Snelling, Minnesota, where he began to study medicine. This was long before years of post-graduate study and internship were required for medical practice, and so after a short apprenticeship to an experienced doctor, Marsh began to tend the sick on the frontier and to exert considerable influence in the region.

His activities brought him into close contact with the Indians, and he fell in love with a beautiful girl of French-Sioux parentage named Marguerite. Indian troubles soon crashed into their happiness, and to protect Marguerite and their son, Marsh took them to live with a pioneer family in Illinois while he attended to his duties at the Indian agency at Prairie du Chien, where he was sub-agent. Marguerite was desperately unhappy living among strangers, and when one day the pioneer mother slapped little Charley Marsh, Marguerite fled back on foot to John, leaving the boy behind. She planned to return for him later, but fate prevented. Shortly after she reeled exhausted through her husband's door and into his arms, she gave birth to a girl. Both mother and infant died, leaving Marsh so grief-stricken that friends feared he would lose his mind.

For solace he plunged into the Indian war then raging over Wisconsin and Illinois, and enlisted the Sioux on the side of the whites, who were fighting the combined Sauk and Fox tribes led by Black Hawk. Later, for some infraction of the law against providing Indians with arms, a warrant was issued for the arrest of Marsh. Warned by friends, he escaped and fled to Independence, Missouri, then the jumping-off place for the farther West. A trip with trappers to the Rocky Mountains was followed by a trading adventure back in Independence. Then another flight over the Santa Fe Trail, capture by the Comanche Indians, escape, and a longer trek southwestward finally brought him to Los Angeles.

By using his Harvard diploma, Marsh was able to win approval from the California authorities to set himself up in a medical practice that consisted mainly of setting broken bones, delivering babies, administering quinine for fevers, vaccinating for smallpox, and occasional amputations. The practice proved lucrative, though the pay was almost wholly in cattle or hides and tallow. His back yard often was full of the longhorns, and out of this stock the vigorous and enterprising Yankee doctor was able finally to establish himself solidly on an extensive ranch near Mount Diablo, not far from the scene of the great gold discovery that was soon to break upon the nation and the world.

Sensing that the control of California, which had passed from Spain to Mexico after the Revolution of 1821, was fast slipping, Marsh turned his influence toward bringing the rich realm under American control. Letters extolling California were written by him to former Governor Cass of Michigan and were published in the East. Marsh also played rather shrewd politics in the far-western province to help bring it under the American flag, and turned to advantage the events that were shaping swiftly to this end.

Another adventurer of more generous heart and spirit had meanwhile come to California to carry forward an ambitious plan of colonization and development for the tottering, Mexican-ruled province. This was John August Sutter, who had been born in Switzerland and had emigrated to America. After giving up a plan to go into farming with a friend in Indiana, Sutter went on to St. Louis and thence on a trip with traders to New Mexico. The Gobernador of Taos, who had been to California, gave him an alluring description of that far-western realm, and Sutter decided forthwith to make it the scene for the colony he dreamed of establishing in America.

The year 1838 he spent getting to California. Acting on the advice of Sir William Drummond Stewart, the British buffalo-hunter, he took a long, hard way to get there—first, with a band of American traders to Fort Hall, in present Idaho; then on to the Hudson's Bay Post at Fort Vancouver, in old Oregon; after that, a voyage to the Hawaiian Islands; then to Sitka, Alaska, where he got to know Russian fur-traders; and finally down the Pacific Coast in a Russian vessel to the Mexican village of Yerba Buena, near which San Francisco was soon to spring up into a thriving city. These months of delay in getting to California, however, were not without their advantages to Sutter, for they brought him contacts important for carrying out the ambitious plan he had made for his "New Helvetia."

The one basic thing he needed was a generous grant of land on which this dreamed-of colony could be promoted, with John August Sutter as its beneficent ruler. To win this he went to see Governor Alvarado, at Monterey. Introduced by a friend to his Excellency, Sutter presented so many letters of recommendation that the Governor was astonished.

Convinced that Sutter was honest in his intentions to help California, Alvarado granted his request. On becoming a citizen of Mexico—a requirement for a landowner—the Swiss leader was allowed to select a site for his proposed colony from an unoccupied region, covering eleven square leagues of land, where three rivers, the Sacramento, the San Joaquin, and the American, flow together into the Bay of San Francisco.

In 1839 New Helvetia was begun on the site of California's present capital, Sacramento, with Sutter's Fort as the center of the new colony. It was soon humming with activities—building, farming, ranching, trading. The proprietor was tactful in handling the Indians who flocked around, and dealt with them with a firm yet kindly hand. Among his hired men were already a number of faithful Yankees, and Sandwich Islanders, and a welcome was out for all others who would come to help. Americans in increasing numbers found succor and employment at the fort after fighting their way westward across the deserts.

One of the first of such groups to arrive was the Bartelson-Bidwell party, in 1841, who had staggered out of the Sierras after abandoning their wagons, first to the Diablo Ranch of John Marsh, where they received some aid doled out with an ungenerous hand; then on to a real welcome from John Sutter. John Bidwell was to become a right-hand man for the Swiss leader.

A first important assignment passed on to Bidwell was to take a party of helpers to Bodega Bay, where Sutter had purchased a post from the Russians, along with their Fort Ross to the north of San Francisco, with its herds and equipment. These were to be transferred to Sutter's Fort. The Russians, for whom also fur-trading had become a losing game, had made their new neighbor a bargain offer for $30,000, on a kind of pay-as-you-go basis, and Sutter took it.

Among the things that went with the purchase, Bidwell recorded, were "forty-odd pieces of rusty cannon and one or two small brass pieces, with a quantity of old French flintlock muskets, pronounced by Sutter to be of those lost by Bonaparte in 1812 in his disastrous retreat from Moscow." These were used to protect the new fort on the American River, and to arm the nondescript forces of Mexicans, Indians and others whom Sutter had organized to defend his frontier post.

Soon, despite efforts to keep out of Mexican politics, Sutter found himself in a tangle of them. Alvarado was displaced, and President Santa

Anna of Mexico appointed Manuel Micheltorena as governor of California. The change was resented. John Marsh and other Californians didn't want a Mexican over them, but Sutter supported Micheltorena "to secure good land titles," as he said, "and protection for the immigrants." In appreciation, the new governor gave Sutter a military commission. From this time forward, he was General Sutter.

Armed conflict ensued between the two factions, and the ruler of New Helvetia marched to reinforce Micheltorena with a force of eighty-five riflemen under Captain Gantt, formerly of the United States Army, and about one hundred Indians, besides some native Californians. In addition, Sutter drafted John Marsh, and forced him to march as a common private from his Diablo ranch to the final scene of action in San Fernando. Marsh, however, took his revenge by sowing disaffection among the troops.

When the battle lines were being formed, Captain Gantt gave the men a chance to vote, and most of them decided against fighting. Sutter's forces and Micheltorena's melted away. The Governor was captured and sent back to Mexico. Sutter was permitted to make his way with a few followers northward over the hard trail to his post on the American River. A new governor, Pio Pico, was appointed, who held office until Mexican rule had finally ended in California.

Another force in the passing of the old regime appeared at Sutter's Fort in 1844. John C. Frémont, American Army officer, under the guise of leader of a scientific exploration, came to the frontier post with Kit Carson and a few other mountain men who had guided them out of the Klamath country in Oregon.

"We were about as naked and in as poor a condition as men could be," says Carson, "but were well received by Mr. Sutter, and furnished in princely manner everything we required." Thereafter they continued their explorations to the north.

Another type of trouble was about to break over New Helvetia when a group of California officials came to buy Fort Sutter and its surroundings. Sutter refused their generous offer. Too many people were involved —folk he had gathered around him, for Americans had continued to straggle into the hospitable rendezvous.

Then in June 1846 Frémont paid a second visit, and left again for northern California. No one seemed to know exactly where he went, but Lieutenant Gillespie, of the United States Marines, bearing the news that war with Mexico had been declared, was not long finding the leader and his men in the wilds where, through the alertness of Kit Carson, they had just escaped being massacred by Indians.

Frémont read the secret message Gillespie brought. Off went his disguise as a scientist, and with a small force he was soon heading for Sutter's Fort, gathering mountain men as he went. American mountaineers, who had long held a grudge against Spanish leaders in California for their mistreatment of Jedediah Smith, were ready to strike. War with Mexico was on. Frémont was unauthorized to raise the Stars and Stripes, but he rallied his followers around a "bear flag" and acted. At Sonoma, his force surprised and captured General Vallejo and his few Mexican troops, and sent them under guard to Sutter's Fort, requesting Sutter to hold them there as prisoners. He did so, but treated them as guests; his sympathies were with the United States, but he did not approve of Frémont's impetuous action.

Immediately after the capture of Vallejo, Monterey was taken by Commodore Sloat, who raised the American flag there. Soon afterward, Captain John B. Montgomery, with a United States man-of-war, took possession of the harbor of Yerba Buena, setting the Stars and Stripes waving over the town. There was relief in the minds of both Americans and natives that California was soon to be established on the stable foundation of a free government.

An expression of that feeling came on August 1, 1846, when a group of more than two hundred Mormons, called "The Water Pioneers," sailed through the Golden Gate into the bay at Yerba Buena. They had left New York harbor on February 4 of that year; and while they were on the Atlantic and Pacific, the war with Mexico had been declared, an important battle fought and won, without their knowledge of the trouble. Augusta Joyce Cochran, one of the passengers on this ship, the *Brooklyn*, afterward wrote of their arrival:

From Fort Yerba Buena, a cannon shot boomed a salute, and a gun from our ship responded to the greeting. Then gliding over the waters toward the incoming ship came a sturdy rowboat. In a few moments, uniformed men trod our deck. We knew they were Americans, not Mexicans. In our sweet native tongue the officers in command, with head uncovered, courteously said, "Ladies and gentlemen, I have the honor to inform you we are in the United States of America." Three hearty cheers were given in reply.

Southern California was still to be taken by the American forces. General Stephen Watts Kearny, Frémont's superior, with the dragoons of his Army of the West, was on the way to effect that conquest, unaware of Frémont's unauthorized accomplishments. Neither did Kearny know that the naval forces under Sloat and Stockton had occupied the northern California ports, and that Frémont, still largely on his own, was pushing southward to win other successes. Kearny with his dragoons first reached Los Angeles, where there was hard fighting with Mexican lancers before the American cavalry won. There were casualties on both sides; the General was wounded, and some of his men slain.

In December 1846 Lieutenant Colonel Phillip St. George Cooke brought the Mormon Battalion, another part of Kearny's Army of the West, into California after an excruciating trail-blazing trek from Santa Fe, New Mexico, to San Diego. Baptiste, the son of Sacajawea the Bird Woman, was one of their guides, but not even his keen eyes could find much water or game in the rough desert country they had to traverse. Food was so scarce that the men were ready to boil their boots and eat them. Then suddenly on the San Pedro River they came upon a herd of wild longhorn cattle. The famished men, contrary to Cooke's orders, fired on the animals, who promptly stampeded and injured several of the soldiers before being routed. Over a hundred longhorns were killed, and the expedition was saved.

In his Order Number 1, issued from San Diego on January 30, 1847, Cooke congratulated his men on their safe arrival on the shore of the Pacific:

History may be searched in vain for an equal march of infantry. Half of it has been through a wilderness where nothing but savages and wild beasts are found, or through deserts where for want of water, there is no living creature. . . . With crowbar, pick and axe in hand we have worked our way over mountains—to bring these first wagons to the Pacific. . . .

There was little or no fighting left for Cooke's men, however; for the war with Mexico was all but ended. Consequently the members of the Battalion were set to work helping clean up and improve San Diego by digging wells, paving streets, building a courthouse and schoolhouse, and aiding the *alcalde*—or justice of the peace—to bring law and order of the American pattern to the town. In Los Angeles they built Fort Moore for the protection of the city, naming it for one of the heroes who had been killed in battle with Mexicans.

New Helvetia, meanwhile, was enjoying a more prosperous time under the American rule. A harvest of grain, sold mainly to the Russians, brought Sutter encouraging returns, and his herds of cattle and horses were thriving. American settlers continued to come, generally in need of food and clothing and help, and they found it. Charles Stanton, one of these, late in 1846 brought word of the ill-fated Donner Party.

This band of eighty emigrants to California had set out in the spring of 1846, well-equipped to cross the plains. By May 26 they were at Alcove Springs on the Big Blue River near present Marysville, Kansas; the initials of J. F. Reed, one of the party's leaders, are still to be seen chiseled into a rock there. There, too, died Sarah Keyes, Reed's mother-in-law.

When the emigrants reached mountain land, they encountered ever increasing difficulties, and lost valuable time struggling through Echo Canyon over the Wasatch range into the Great Basin. Further time was lost as they camped on Jordan River to recoup their strength. Crossing an old lake bed on an unmapped route west of Salt Lake they got stuck in the mud and had to abandon many of their wagons. Their cattle strayed away in search of food and water. Men, women and children staggered on over the pitiless desert carrying what food they could. Finally after weeks of this cruel march they were stopped near the crest of the Sierra Mountains by a blizzard that raged for days around their encampment on the shore of the lake now named for them.

The generous Sutter promptly gave Stanton pack mules laden with dried meat, and sent two of his Indian boys back with him to the starving emigrants. Only thirty, mostly women and children, were brought through to safety. The bodies of the rest were found the next spring by the escort led by General Kearny that was returning Frémont to Washington to stand court martial for having exceeded his authority.

Matthew Caldwell, a member of that troop, told me of that appalling discovery. The snow had partially melted away—it was late June of 1847 —and the bodies were found around some log cabins and in them. George Donner's wife, who had refused to leave her sick husband when the other women were saved, lay with her arms around him. Kearny halted there until all the bodies had been buried.

Caldwell also told me of Frémont's uncanny ability as a leader. He knew more about negotiating the plains safely than did Kearny. "Boys," he said, calling the men aside, "if you want to keep your scalps, mind strictly what I advise: First, never sleep where you make your supper fire. Get your meal and pretend you're going to camp there, but soon as pitch dark comes, move on a few miles, for your sleep. Another thing, travel as much as you can in the night. Take a long rest at noontime." The group followed his advice and arrived in good shape at Fort Leavenworth.

Frémont was found guilty of acting without authority, and was given a reprimand. Then he returned to California, whose people held nothing against him for his prompt but irregular action in helping make California American, and in 1850 he was elected one of the first two senators to represent the new state in Congress.

Many of the rest of the Mormon Battalion, when honorably discharged, went northward through California on their way back home to Utah. When they arrived at Sutter's Fort they found its proprietor happy to have them come to him as workers. "I hired about eighty of them," he says, "as mechanics or as laborers. They were very glad to earn money to buy horses and cattle for their new homes at Salt Lake, to which they all longed to go. They were good people. In settling accounts, I never had difficulty with them."

One group of these Mormons was sent under James Marshall, of New Jersey, to dig a mill race for a sawmill Sutter planned to build on the American River, about forty miles from Sutter's Fort. Through the latter part of 1847, and the early part of the next year, the work went on. Then Henry Bigler, one of the Mormons, in January 1848, made this entry in the record he was keeping:

> Monday 24, this day some kind of mettle was found in the tail race that looks like goald, first discovered by James Martial, boss of the mill.

> Sunday 30, our metal has been tride and proves to be goald it is thought to be very rich. We picked up more than a hundred dollars worth last week.

Sutter later told how Marshall had come to him in great secrecy, insisting that they retire to a private room. There the foreman showed him the yellow particles he had picked up in the mill race after water had been turned into it and then turned off. The two men tested it in various ways they knew, and were convinced that it was gold of high quality. There was an attempt to keep the discovery a secret, but it was soon out. Wittwer, one of Sutter's teamsters, seems first to have spread the story. Then Sam Brannan, head of the Mormon "Water Pioneers," who had started a store in Sacramento, got a bottle filled with gold dust, dashed back to San Francisco, and ran through its streets shouting "Gold on the American River!" A local rush for the diggings followed. Sailors, shopkeepers, cowboys and farmers joined in the scramble, and many of Sutter's hired men dropped their work to dig and wash for nuggets.

"Only the Mormons," recorded Sutter in his New Helvetia Diary, "behaved decently at first. They were sorry for the difficulties in which I found myself, and some of them remained to finish their jobs. But in the long run, they too could not resist the temptation."

As Sutter was settling up with these Battalion boys when they were ready to return to their families in Utah, he added a bonus to their pay and presented them with two of the cannon he had purchased from the Russians. These, mounted on wheels, were taken by a group of the Mormons over the Sierras and the deserts to their new homeland in the Salt Lake valley.

One of these cannon is still kept as a storied relic in St. George, Utah. There, in the long-ago days, it was put to a strange, yet peaceful use when its barrel, filled with Babbitt metal, served to tamp the foundation of the Mormon Temple.

Sutter was not unprepared for the discovery of gold in California. Indians and others, it seems certain, had found some of the precious metal. Yet it was not until the discovery by Marshall in January 1848 that the great rush was started for the new Eldorado. Even then it took a full year in those days of slow communication to spread the word convincingly across the United States. Finally when President Polk, in his message of 1849, told of the discovery, the nation was electrified.

The "days of forty-nine" were on, with hundreds of thousands crowding the westward trails and the ships, feverishly struggling to get to the gold fields. There is no need here to detail again the story with all its tragic outcomes—for many of the treasure-seekers were ill-prepared for the journey—and the rewarding successes for those who won riches; but what may be of interest are closing glimpses of the outcomes as they touched characters in this story.

Dr. John Marsh, as the pioneers might have put it, had his plate right side up to catch more than his share of the golden shower. He was quick to stake out rich claims and have his men wash out a store of nuggets. Even more lucrative were his grain fields, orchards, vineyards, and herds, for food brought fabulous prices, and Marsh soon was rolling in wealth.

He had found a teacher from Massachusetts, with friends in California, and had married her. He built a mansion near Mount Diablo, in which they lived happily for a time with their baby daughter Alice. Then the mother died. Marsh found friends to give the little daughter the care she needed, and turned to his duties on the great estate.

One rainy night as he sat by his fireplace, a knock came at the door. His Indian boy opened it to find a stranger in shabby clothes and dripping from the storm, with his foot in the doorway so that it could not be closed.

"What do you want?" demanded Marsh. A recent experience with robbers had made him wary.

"Just to be taken in out of the storm. I'm cold and tired."

Marsh was about to deny help, but changing his mind, said, "Lie down on the rug by the fire."

The stranger did so. Then questions by the Doctor brought out in quick succession that the man's name was Marsh. He had been born in Prairie du Chien—did not know what had become of his mother—had been raised by pioneers in Illinois.

"Take off your shoe and show me your foot—the right one," said the Doctor.

The stranger reluctantly obeyed. Marsh examined the foot, found the toes webbed together, and exclaimed: "You are my son—my own son." With that he took the man in his arms, called to his servants to get food and prepare a bed. The two wept together as their memories unfolded.

Marsh had not seen Charles since he went back from Independence, when the boy was nine. He had begged to go with his father, but Marsh, not knowing then where fate would lead, could not risk taking him. Now Charles had a wife and children. After a short stay with his father, he returned East to bring them to California.

While he was gone, John Marsh was waylaid and murdered by one of his men who held a grudge. The vast estate, by the ruling of a judge of California, was divided equally between the daughter, Alice, and her half-brother Charles. This son, an upstanding citizen, determined to bring his father's murderer to justice, finally found him, and saw him given life imprisonment for his crime.

As for John A. Sutter, he was caught in the torrent of the Gold Rush, and had his vast holdings swept away. Even the home he had built on the Feather River for his wife and family was lost. This courtly son of old Switzerland who had given of his means and of himself so generously to help stranded Americans in California, and who had played a stirring role in its dramatic story, lost all his possessions. He was forced, after the relentless drive of the gold-seekers, to go back with his loved ones, almost penniless, to the peace of the little Moravian town of Lititz, in Pennsylvania, where he built his last small home, and where he is buried.

# CHAPTER SIX

# THE DESERT BLOSSOMS
# AS THE ROSE

"When Joseph and Hyrum Smith and other Mormon leaders were brought to Carthage for trial," Squire Hamilton told me, "I was fifteen years old."

Hamilton and a friend of his named Brown used to drill with the militia of that frontier town in Illinois, called the "Carthage Grays," though they were not yet old enough actually to join the company.

"There was great excitement in the town," he went on, "and most of the inhabitants were out on the streets to see them placed in the old jail with a detachment of the Carthage Grays as a guard.

"On the day of the attack on the jail, the captain of the militia told Brown and me to climb to the tower of the courthouse in the middle of town, and keep sharp watch over the surrounding fields and woods. About three o'clock on the afternoon of that June 27, 1844, we saw a

group of men, some on foot, some on horses, coming out of the woods
to the northwest, and heading over a plowed field toward the jail.

"I told Brown to go tell the captain. He ran downstairs and reported
what we had seen. Then Brown came back as quickly as he could. By this
time the mob, as it proved to be, was close to the jail, and we both hurried
down, but we couldn't find the captain of the Carthage Grays.

"The next thing I heard was the firing of guns, and I rushed to the jail
to see what was happening. I got there just after Joseph Smith had fallen
from the window of the upper story. Some of the mob, with painted faces,
were around him. I got among them, and one warned, 'Look out, kid,
you'll get hurt.'

" 'He's dead enough,' said another. And with that they all broke and
ran away. I was left alone with the body. Then I heard some kind of noise
upstairs, and went to see what it was. It must have been the sound Willard
Richards made when he drew wounded John Taylor back into the cell
room, as I learned afterward had happened. In the bedroom to the front,
where most of the shooting was done, Hyrum Smith lay dead, with some
of the plaster that had been knocked down by the bullets scattered around
him.

"I dashed over to the Hamilton Hotel, kept by Artois Hamilton, my
father. Around the place was a big crowd of excited people. Finally
Father appeared on the porch, but it was some time before he could quiet
the folk milling about. Then he said: 'Now, I'm going to tell you something that some of you won't like to hear. The deed committed here in
Carthage today has left a stain on our town which will never be removed.
I want one of you men to volunteer to go with me and tell the Mormon
people what has happened.' "

Such was the violent end of the prophet of Mormonism. The story had
begun in 1820, when young Joseph Smith received the first of the visions
that led to his founding, ten years later, of the Church of Jesus Christ of
Latter-Day Saints. Immediately following its organization in Fayette
(now Waterloo), New York, Smith sent missionaries of the new faith to
the western frontier. Near Kirtland, Ohio, so many were converted that
the leaders of the church were encouraged to make that town the new

headquarters of the organization. Another group of members was transplanted from New York to Jackson County, Missouri.

Almost at once began a long series of tribulations for the Saints. Mob violence destroyed their property and forced them to flee from town to town until finally they made their way to the Illinois shore of the Mississippi, where they built for their headquarters the first of their cities to reach completion, Nauvoo. The name, of Hebrew origin, implies "beautiful," and in its palmy days in the early 1840's it assuredly lived up to its name. Within five years it became the largest city of the state. Its rise had been spectacular; its fall came with dramatic suddenness after the death of Joseph and Hyrum Smith.

Brigham Young, like the Smiths a native of Vermont, succeeded to the leadership of the church and revived the city that had been paralyzed by the death of the leaders. "Go to work!" was his advice to his followers in Nauvoo. "Though our leader has fallen, the cause for which he gave his life must go forward. Our temple must be completed, even if we must do it with a trowel in one hand and a sword in the other. Take up your duties and carry on."

Even though every house was draped in black because of the tragedy, Nauvoo began again to hum with work. The temple was completed. Farms around the city were tilled with renewed vigor, and bounteous crops were harvested. Worship was carried on with deeper devotion. Outwardly at least, there was promise of progress.

Underneath it all, however, was a spirit of foreboding. Rumblings could still be heard. Some were demanding expulsion of the Mormons from Illinois, and suiting action to their spirit, they began to attack the villages Mormons had built around Nauvoo and to burn the houses of these settlers. Nauvoo, as a city of refuge, soon was overcrowded with families who had fled from violence.

My grandmother often told me of the destruction of her home in the Morley Settlement, twenty miles from Nauvoo, on September 10, 1845, a date she never forgot. The men of the family were out cutting wood in a grove some distance from the house; only my grandmother and her sister-in-law Alvira and the children were on the place.

"Emmeline," called Alvira, "here come some horsemen who don't look good to me. Better get the children into the house."

Presently the horsemen, all carrying guns and all with blackened faces, rode up to the door.

"Get out into the yard," one of them shouted, "and do it quick."

Grandmother, pale but calm, led the trembling children out of doors.

"These cabins are going up in smoke," said the leader of the mob. "If you want to save any of your things, get 'em out."

Grandmother and Aunt Alvira obeyed. Beds, tables, chairs, dishes—everything they could move was piled up in the yard. In nearby homes, other women were doing the same.

Finally, once the house was cleared, the black-faced men piled in straw and set it afire. From the rail fence Grandmother and her brood watched the flames reduce the house to coals and ashes. The mob dashed away on their horses, as they saw the men of the settlement returning.

That night the family slept on the ground. The next day they loaded the belongings that were left into wagons, and drove into Nauvoo, where they were given shelter by a friend in his cellar. In that temporary home, my mother was born on February 22, 1846.

The leaders of the Mormons saw plainly that to have peace and freedom their people must find a new homeland. The unsettled regions of the farther West offered such a realm, and after serious counseling the decision was reached to make an exodus into that wilderness. Just where the trail would lead they did not know, but it was generally felt that it would be somewhere in the valleys of the Rocky Mountains.

Open announcement was withheld until preparations for the long journey into unknown regions could be taken. The Mormons made covered wagons by the hundreds, many under the supervision of my grandfather, a wagon-maker. They hurried the shaping of ox yokes, the making of saddles and harnesses, the preparing of food, clothing and bedding. Every home became a hive of industry.

On February 4, 1846, the same day the Mormon "Water Pioneers" sailed on the ship *Brooklyn* from New York harbor, Charles Shumway drove the first wagon of the overland pioneers across the frozen Mississippi into Iowa. From then on there was a steady stream of "homes on wheels" into Indian Territory. Within the next two years Nauvoo was to become almost a ghost town.

A vanguard of younger men, with lightly loaded wagons, under the leadership of Brigham Young, drove ahead to find the new homeland somewhere in the far West, where Joseph Smith had prophesied his people would find freedom from persecution. Behind the vanguard plodded other trains bearing thousands of Mormon families.

Breaking a wagon road over the rolling hills of Iowa was a cruel task. Mormon journals tell of the bitter cold; the spring rains that turned the trail into a stretch of mud; of wet, chilly camping at night. At first, the animals had to graze on what bushes and scant, frozen grass they could find. Men, women and children had too little food to sustain them in the struggle. Graves marked by buffalo skulls and blazed trees began to line the way.

For help along the trail, way stations were made, with cabins, blacksmith shops and what first-aid stores of food could be provided; then as soon as planting time came, crops were started for the exiles who were to follow later. Garden Grove, Mount Pisgah on the Grand River, and other temporary settlements were established, organized after the church pattern to provide the assistance for the welfare work needed by the exiled Mormons. The largest of these, Kanesville (now Council Bluffs, Iowa), was located on the bluffs of the Missouri River near a ferrying station. It was named after Colonel Thomas F. Kane, who befriended the dispossessed especially by helping them make peace with Indian tribes whose lands they wished to use temporarily.

Owing to Kane's intervention the red men actually extended a welcome to the Mormons. Pied Riche, chief of the Pottawatomies, addressed them in French, a language he is reported to have used with elegance, as follows:

My Mormon Brethren: The Pottawatomi came, sad and tired, into this unhealthy Missouri bottom, not many years back, when he was taken from his beautiful country beyond the Mississippi, which had abundant game and timber, and clear water everywhere. Now you

96

James Marshall finds gold at Sutter's mill, January 24, 1848.

PLATE SEVENTEEN

Westport Landing, at the Big Bend of the Missouri River, where emigrants
disembarked to organize wagon trains for the journey into the farther West.

The tepee of Washakie, war chief of the Shoshones. Washakie is the standing figure, fifth from right. In the background is his tepee village.

(*Photograph by W. H. Jackson*)

Chief Washakie (*center*) fording a stream.

(*Photograph by W. H. Jackson*)

The Three Forks of the Missouri River, where Sacajawea's guidance of the Lewis and Clark Expedition was put to a crucial test.

The framework of an Indian sweat-house.

An Indian sweat-house, used for cur-
ing colds and similar illnesses. Such an
institution led indirectly to the massacre of the Whitmans.

Gosiute Indians of the desert.

A Gosiute Wickiup in the desert, such as the one where Jedediah Smith and his men found help.

Buffalo meat drying before a tepee.

Josh Terry (*seated*) at the age of ninety.

Nick Wilson, showing the scar on his forehead made by a flint-headed Indian arrow when he was a Pony Express rider.

(*Left*) Jim Bridger's name carved by him on the cliff at Names Hill, about twenty miles south of Big Piney.

(*Right*) Monument in South Pass, Wyoming, to the first white women to cross the continent.

A Navajo Indian on the Old Spanish Trail in New Mexico.

A Blackfoot Indian woman, with her papoose in its carrier
on her back, and a travois behind her horse.

The gorge of the Yosemite, discovered in 1833 by Joseph
Reddeford Walker.

(*Ewing Galloway*)

The site of Sutter's Mill near Coloma, California, where gold was discovered on January 24, 1848.

The hill in the Wasatch Mountains that delayed the Donner Party in 1846, and indirectly led to their doom. Over it they had to drag their wagons into Salt Lake Valley.

The Old Oregon Trail, near Guernsey, Wyoming, showing the roadway cut by wagon wheels through solid rock.

William W. Riter a veteran of the
1847 Mormon trek, stands near the
marker on the spot near where Brigham Young envisioned a new homeland for his people.

Freight transportation by ox-team at the time of the Utah War,
about 1857.

Fortifications built on the cliffs of
Echo Canyon for Utah riflemen to
hold back Johnston's army.

Dike built by the Utah militia to flood Echo Canyon if Johnston's army tried to force its way through in the Utah War
of 1857–1858.

Chief Two Moons of the Cheyennes, who led his tribe against
Custer at the battle of Little Big Horn in 1876, shown offering
a prayer at the battlefield forty years later.

Charles Cliff, one of the last of
the Pony Express riders.

William Streeper, pioneer Mule
Mail carrier and stage driver.

Wells Fargo stage coaches in 1862, (*above*) at the company
office in Salt Lake City; (*below*) en route West.

Ezra Meeker with the ox-drawn covered wagon made from three wagons that were driven West over the Oregon Trail.

Mountain buffalo.

The Mormon Tabernacle in Salt Lake City under construction. Resting on 44 stone pillars, the wood construction is held together with wooden pegs and thongs of rawhide.

William H. Jackson (*left*), pioneer photographer and artist, at the age of 97, talking with Martin Garretson (*right*), who played a major role in preserving the American buffalo from extinction.

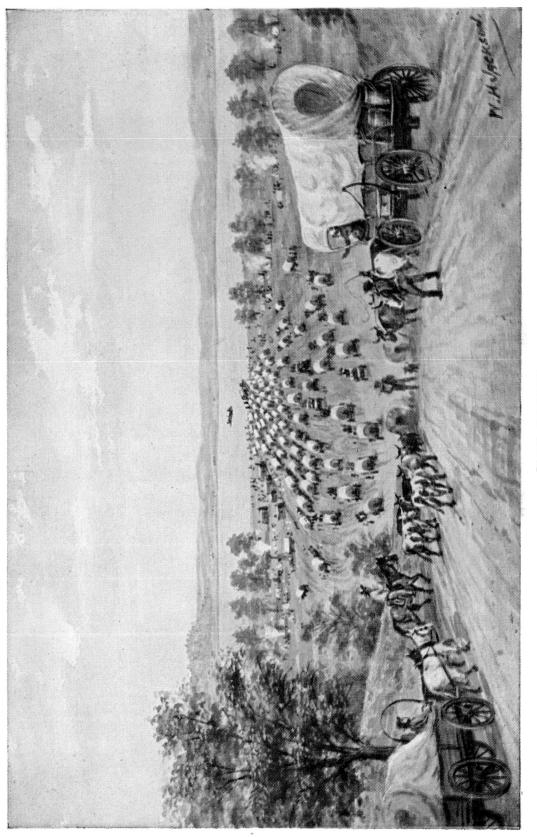

PLATE EIGHTEEN

Kanesville Crossing, near Council Bluffs, where the Mormon vanguard
crossed the Missouri.

PLATE NINETEEN

Emigrants catch sight of Chimney Rock, near Bayard, Nebraska, one of the best known landmarks on the Oregon-Mormon-California trails.

are driven away, the same, from your lodges and lands there and the graves of your people. So we both have suffered.

We must help one another, and the Great Spirit will help us both. You are free to cut and use all the wood you may wish. You can make all your improvements, and live on any part of our actual land not occupied by us.

Here in a western setting was the same spirit of welcome as that given to the Pilgrims by Squanto; and to Roger Williams by Canonicus, Chief of the Narragansetts. So far as we can learn, Indians showed no intolerance to white men or others as to religion.

Beyond the Missouri, in Omaha Indian Territory, the march was halted by the war with Mexico. Troops were needed for Kearny's Army of the West, which was endeavoring to carry through a plan to bring New Mexico and California under American jurisdiction. Meanwhile Jesse Little had gone east to Washington, with introductions from Colonel Kane, to try to get work for his Mormon brethren at improving roads, building forts, or farming. Instead of this came the call for a battalion of volunteers to assist Kearny.

Captain James Allen brought the request from Kearny to Brigham Young, who called the Mormon leaders into council to consider it. There were advantages in granting it: the service, though not without hardships and dangers, would bring pay from the government to help the families of the volunteers; as soldiers in the United States Army they would receive food, clothing and other equipment; by their march to California they might also be brought closer to a hoped-for homeland. On the other hand there were the problems involved in leaving families without adequate food, clothing, shelter and other essentials in untamed Indian Territory.

After deliberation the leaders reached the decision that though their people had suffered, the national government was not to be blamed. The Constitution was still sound and right. A request had come from the President of the United States for volunteers needed to help win a war, and it should be accepted, providing that the Mormons might remain on Indian lands while preparing for their further journeying into the far West. The

Latter-day Saints would respond to the call. At scattered camps back along the trail, the leaders energetically presented the call for volunteers to the people, and five hundred men—mostly young, unmarried ones—soon enlisted and left afoot for Fort Leavenworth, there to be organized and equipped as the "Mormon Battalion," of Kearny's army.

With their young men away in such numbers, the Mormons could not go on to the "valleys of the mountains" in 1846, and they made ready to winter along the Missouri. Camps along the trail were made into villages. Kanesville became a city of refuge for many, while across the Missouri on the Nebraska side of the river, "Winter Quarters" was established for the thousands who had ferried over before the call for soldiers came.

This frontier town was made up of hastily built log cabins, dugouts in the hills with sod sides and dirt roofs, some tents, and wagon boxes with covers over them. Fireplaces fed with wood from nearby groves helped to keep out some of the cold, and served for cooking. Kindness and co-operation added cheer and courage. The whole community of approximately six thousand souls was organized with good leaders to guide the various groups and promote their welfare; yet nearly six hundred died, causing an almost continuous funeral procession from the village to the cemetery on the hill.

"Aunt" Emmeline B. Wells, one of those who spent the winter of 1846–47 there, told me: "Yes, we had our hardships there on the Missouri. There was a great deal of sickness and many deaths, especially of the babies and the older folk. Yet the Lord did not forget us. We had our brighter moments. The brethren built larger log houses in which we could worship, and have our social gatherings to sing our troubles away.

"I taught one of the schools. You see, I was born and reared in Massachusetts, and was trained for teaching when Horace Mann was a leader of our schools there, and I did teach for two years. Afterward I joined the Church of Jesus Christ of Latter-day Saints, and went west to Nauvoo.

"When we left our beautiful city on the Mississippi I was one of those who got over the Missouri River into the land of the Omaha Indians. Then came the building of Winter Quarters. Of course I wanted to help, and seeing a number of barefooted boys and girls running about the town, I asked our leaders to build a schoolhouse and let me teach the lively youngsters the best I could. They were glad to provide the house. It had only a dirt floor and a dirt roof, with just logs for seats. We did not have many books, and mice ate up some we did manage to gather, but the boys and girls were ready to learn. They recited with me, read what they could and sang songs. Best of all, they were out of the cold and were kept busy."

In spite of difficulties and sorrow, preparations for the westward journey in 1847 went steadily forward during the snowy months. Again a vanguard was carefully organized to pilot the way—143 young men, 3 women and 2 children, led by Brigham Young. Leaders were chosen to bring on succeeding caravans. The reports of Frémont were carefully studied. Opportunities to get first-hand information were not missed: Lansford Hastings, returning from California, and Father Pierre de Smet, devoted Catholic missionary to the Indians, were carefully questioned as to western trails and lands. This journey of the Mormons was to be a well-planned movement into a new homeland.

Springtime inspired the weary exiles. On April 4, the first wagons left Winter Quarters for the rendezvous on the Platte, where the vanguard was to assemble. At a conference on April 6, Brigham Young was elected as president of the church, with Heber C. Kimball and Willard Richards as his counselors. Twelve other men were chosen apostles. All except two, who had a special mission to perform in England, were to go with the vanguard in search of the new homeland.

At "Liberty Pole Camp," about forty miles west of Winter Quarters, the vanguard was organized after a military pattern, with Brigham Young as its commander. Two divisions of the expedition were made, with A. P. Rockwood as captain of the first, and Stephen Markham as captain of the second. "Captains of Tens" also were appointed, each to have charge of ten wagons. Another captain was given a detachment to serve as a rear guard, and to take care of the cannon the pioneers had brought along for protection.

Rules were: Up at 5:00 A.M.—on the way by 7:00. Guns always clean and ready for action. Lunch during a brief stop at noon. Wagons to be parked in a circle at night. Evening prayers at 8:30. Fires out, and all except the night guards in bed by 9:00. "Every man is to put as much into . . . taking care of his brother's cattle, in preserving them, as he would his own; No man will be indulged in idleness."

With such regulations this home-seeking vanguard made the journey of a thousand miles into the Salt Lake valley with no casualties to this hand-picked group. The same good fortune, for the most part, attended the succeeding caravans of the Mormon pioneers, though in later years when cholera ravaged the plains they did suffer some deaths.

One of the Mormon vanguard, Orson Pratt, trained in mathematics, and equipped with instruments John Taylor had brought from England, made daily observations of longitude, latitude and altitudes along the trail, and noted varying temperatures. The problem of charting the miles traveled day by day was solved by William Clayton. Measuring a hind wheel of the wagon in which he rode, he found it made just 360 revolutions to the mile. For several days he walked along counting the revolutions. Then with the help of Orson Pratt, a "roadmeter" was devised and made by Appleton Harmon, mechanic, which worked successfully on the westward trip. The distances were verified when some of the vanguard returned that same year to Winter Quarters.

On May 22 they came in sight of Chimney Rock in the North Platte valley, standing sentinel-like at the gate of the mountain region. Clayton, the official historian of the party, records its resemblance to "the large factory chimneys of England." The Mormons rejoiced at the sight, for the landmark meant they had come halfway on their trek.

Fort Laramie, at the junction of the North Platte and Laramie rivers, they reached twelve days later. Here they were welcomed by James Bordeaux, a Frenchman then in command of the fort, who gave them valuable information about the regions that lay ahead. Here, too, they were permitted to set up a forge to mend wagons and shoe animals for the stony road ahead. And they also took time out to write letters which fur-traders going east could take to the folks back on the Missouri.

From Fort Laramie westward, for several hundred miles, the Oregon, Mormon, California trails were one, leading up the North Platte into more picturesque mountain country. On the way were the Labonte River, and La Prele and Deer Creeks—all with good campsites and easy fording, but at the crossing of the North Platte (near present Casper, Wyoming) the vanguard had to do some ferrying. Their *Revenue Cutter*, a large leather boat they had brought along on "running gears," served well in getting equipment and food supplies across the swollen stream, but not the wagons.

A ferry boat had to be made—Brigham Young helped to build it—to carry the pioneer vehicles over. By the time it was in operation other emigrants had come up to the river, who wanted to be ferried across, and were willing to pay for the service in flour, bacon, or cash; so members of the vanguard kept the ferry going to help the emigrants. "The food supplies they gave us," recorded Wilford Woodruff, "were like manna in the wilderness." Since there would be many caravans of covered wagons bound for Oregon and California, and more trains of the Mormon people, it was decided to keep the Mormon Ferry in operation. Thomas Grover, who had run a ferry in New York, was left in charge, with eight men to assist him, and handled it in a businesslike manner, having its schedule of prices and the pay in food, other commodities or cash, listed.

Another high point on the trip came after the vanguard had gone over the South Pass. There they met two mountain men, Moses Harris and Jim Bridger, who knew the West. Both these men advised strongly against their settling in Salt Lake valley. Bridger, who camped with the pioneers overnight, told them they couldn't raise enough corn and other foodstuffs in that arid region to sustain colonies of people; and drought and early frosts, he felt strongly, would ruin their crops. Then while they were preparing to ferry across the difficult Green River, Sam Brannan, leader of the "Water Pioneers," came into the camp. With two companions he had ridden across deserts and mountains to meet the overland, homeseeking vanguard, which showed an interest in the news he brought of the passengers on the *Brooklyn* and their activities in California.

Brannan was enthusiastic about that realm, pictured its advantages in glowing terms, and urged President Young to lead the people there to make their homes. The leaders went into council over the discouraging report the mountain men had given and this brighter one from Brannan. Finally came the decision. In effect it was: We realize that great opportunities are in California. Doubtless thousands will soon be migrating to that rich land; but not the Mormons. We want a realm where we can live in peace—a place which no other people want. The arid region described by the mountain men seems best for our people.

On July 19, Orson Pratt and John Brown, scouting ahead, reached the crest of what they called "Big Mountain." From that point they were the first of the Mormons to get a view of the valley, with the Great Salt Lake in the distance. Two days later Pratt and Erastus Snow followed the tracks of the Donner Party down into a mountain dell, and over "Little Mountain" into what was named "Emigration Canyon." About a mile from its mouth, where the Donners had made their hard pull to get out into the open, the two scouts of the vanguard climbed the same steep hill for another view of what was to be a new homeland for the exiles.

"After issuing from the mountains among which we had been shut up for many days," recorded Pratt in his diary, "and beholding in a moment such extensive scenery before us, we could not refrain from a shout of joy."

The next day nine others of the vanguard, with George A. Smith at their head, carried forward the explorations to find a favorable place where ground might be plowed and planted. Such a spread of land was located between the branches of City Creek.

On July 23 men of the advance company lifted plows from their wagons and attempted to upturn the soil, but it was so dry and hard that two or three plows were broken. Waters from the creek were turned on to the sun-baked plain; then the soil yielded readily to the plowshare drawn by oxen. Two or three acres were plowed, harrowed and planted with seeds of quick-growing vegetables. Success that came even in the short growing season left in 1847 convinced the pioneers that the arid region, through the magic of mountain streams, could be made "to blossom as the rose."

On July 24 the rest of the vanguard drove out of Emigration Canyon into the picturesque valley. Brigham Young, ill from mountain fever, lay on a bed in a lighter vehicle owned and driven by Wilford Woodruff. In later years Woodruff said that as they came from the canyon into full view of the valley, he turned his carriage with one side of its cover open to the west. Young rose from his bed, looked over the scene, and after a few moments, said: "This is the place. Drive on." They went to the encampment of those who had led the way to the new homeland.

Days that followed were crowded with activities. Food, shelter, protection for those who would stay in the valley, and for about two thousand more who would arrive before the end of 1847, posed problems for immediate attention. The plowing and planting went forward with vigor, and within two weeks eighty-three acres had been prepared and sown. A fort was laid out, and within three weeks, twenty-seven log houses had been built along the sides of it.

Four days after his arrival, Brigham Young walked over the site chosen for the city, thrust the tip of his cane into the ground, and said: "Here we will build a temple to the Lord." With the temple as its center, Salt Lake City was plotted.

Josh Terry, who had been among the Mormon vanguard, described to me what was to be Salt Lake City as it looked that first winter—"just covered wagon camps along City Creek, but plenty of work going on, especially along the square laid out for the fort." The people he had come with "lifted the wagon boxes from the running gears, set them on logs, and used them for shelter."

After the pioneer community had been organized with dependable leaders to carry forward through the winter of 1847–48, Brigham Young and most of the members of the vanguard returned to Winter Quarters to bring on their families during the next spring and summer. Meantime other caravans of the Mormons kept arriving at the new haven in the desert.

How to provide enough food was the most serious problem, for what could be carried in the covered wagons was scarcely enough to keep families until harvest time. The turnips, radishes and small potatoes which came from the first planting helped a little, but more as a promise of what a longer growing season would bring. Beef from the cattle brought across the plains was usually poor. Cows gave a little milk for the babies, but butter and tallow were scarce. There was little hunting, except of jack rabbits close by. All in all, it was another winter just above the starvation line.

Fortunately, however, the usually "snowy moons" were mild during that winter of 1847–48. Few Indians appeared. Despite the "pinching time," the pioneers weathered through with little illness and comparatively few deaths. The first spring for them came with sunny skies and promise of better times. A bounteous harvest was the hope of all, and they worked hard.

Every family planted gardens and fields of grain. Though the call had been urgent for food, enough seed was saved to start the crops. About five thousand acres were also plowed and planted to provide food for all. May saw the wheat and other plants coming with promise.

Alas for high hopes! May had not passed before out of the arid stretches around the green fields came a plague of black insects—"army crickets," someone called them. They did not fly, but marched, marched, multi-thousands of them, "gnawing green things down to the sand."

Men, women and children turned out to fight the pest. Herds of cattle were driven around the fields to crush the oncoming crickets. Ditches were plowed in their path, with water turned in to wash the plague away. Rushes gathered from the marshes were piled in their way, and when they crawled into these for the night, fires were set to burn them. Despite all the efforts, it looked like a losing fight.

The people fasted and prayed. Then what seemed to them a miracle happened, when out of the Great Salt Lake came sea gulls—flocks of them. With their cries they circled above, then lighted on the grain fields. At first it looked as if the birds had come to complete the destruction, but to their joy the pioneers saw the birds devouring the cricket horde. Their craws filled, they would fly back to what is now known as Bird Island in the Great Salt Lake, to feed their fledglings in nests on the barren rocks.

For days the gulls kept coming and going until the crickets were cleared away. The fields had been badly dealt with by the plague, but enough of the grain was saved to carry the people through the following winter. A special Thanksgiving was observed that year. First laws passed by the legislature of that territory protected these birds which saved the pioneers. A stately monument by Mahonri Young, placed on the Temple Square, portrays the story of the saving of the pioneers by the gulls of Great Salt Lake.

Within two years after they had settled there, Salt Lake City became the crossroads of the West. With the gold rush to California in 1849, Utah was brought into the current of national activities. Brigham Young had hard work to hold his people from joining in the rush for the diggings, and some did not heed his advice. But a majority stayed in the "valleys of the mountains," raising wheat and potatoes, cultivating gardens and orchards, developing ranches with herds and flocks.

A bounteous harvest in 1849 made Salt Lake City an oasis in the desert for the gold-seekers heading for California. There was double advantage in this for the pioneers: first, food commanded high prices; secondly, to lighten their loads for the last stretch of the long hard road, the Argonauts were ready to sacrifice goods of value to the settlers for something to eat, and for horses and mules to get them to the diggings as fast as possible.

The *Frontier Guardian* of Salt Lake City leaves this record:

> For a light Yankee wagon sometimes three or four heavy ones would be given in exchange. . . . Common domestic sheeting sold from five to ten cents per yard or by the bolt. The best of spades and shovels sold for fifty cents each. Vests that cost one dollar and fifty cents in St. Louis were sold in Salt Lake for thirty-seven and a half cents. Full chests of joiners' tools which sold in the East for one hundred fifty dollars, were sold in Salt Lake for twenty-five dollars. Indeed, almost every article could be bought at a price fifty percent below the wholesale price in eastern cities.

In 1850 the state of California was admitted to the Union. At the same time, Utah officially became a territory of the United States, embracing all the Great Basin and much other land south of old Oregon between the Rockies and the Sierra Nevada Mountains. President Millard Fillmore appointed Brigham Young governor and United States Indian agent over the domain.

Out of this great expanse of mountains, valleys and deserts, Nevada, and parts of Wyoming and Colorado later were carved. The redemption of the arid West went steadily forward, as sons and daughters of the Utah pioneers helped to colonize other parts of the vast region. Now through the magic of irrigation, the waste places have in large measure been reclaimed, the mines have been developed, and a seemingly inexhaustible treasure house added to the nation.

# CHAPTER SEVEN

# HANDCARTS AND WAR

Under the granite peaks of the Wasatch Mountains the trails that wound among the aspens, the pines, and the flower-sprinkled meadows were alive with youthful merrymakers. Around the tents and the covered wagons mothers watched their children with one eye, while they kept the other on the cooking, the domestic organizing and supervising that have been their care since the first picnic long ago. Men with graying hair sat swapping yarns of the old days on the plains. From time to time the steady rustle of talk and laughter was punctuated by bursts of music from brass bands that had come from Salt Lake City, Ogden, Provo, and other towns that the Mormons had built in the ten years to a day since Brigham Young had declared, "This is the place."

They had good reason to celebrate the anniversary, for their hardships, their physical and spiritual suffering, had been well rewarded. Irrigation had brought fields of grain, gardens and orchards. For hundreds of miles to the north and the south, settlements had been planted on life-giving streams. Utah Territory, with Brigham Young as governor, reached from the crest of the Sierras to the summit of the Rockies. Colonies on the borders of the domain had been established: one in fertile Carson Valley, in present western Nevada; and another in the valley of Black's Fork, now southwestern Wyoming. Colonization by Mormon pioneers had also been extended into present Idaho, and into southern California, where San Bernardino was a thriving center.

Preparations for the commemoration had been under way for weeks. From nearby towns and those far away, families had come in covered wagons and lighter vehicles, and had driven up the steep canyon road to this picturesque open place near the mountain top, to spend a week in festivities. The spirit of the occasion filled the scene as the Saints sang one of their favorite songs:

> Let the mountains shout for joy!
> Let the valley sing,
> Let the hills rejoice,
> Let them all break forth into song,
> And be glad before the Lord!
> For the wilderness hath blossomed—
> Blossomed like the rose.

Among the happy reunioners were some of the three thousand men, women and children who had made perhaps the hardest sacrifice of all for their new faith. These were the "handcart pioneers," who had pushed and pulled their laden carts nearly thirteen hundred miles into the promised land that was to be their new home. The trail had led over gentle hills and empty plains and rough mountains, stretching from the terminus of the Rock Island Railroad, at Iowa City, to Salt Lake; and many who had started out now lay forever along the route.

Nearly a hundred years later, at the Covered Wagon Centennial of 1930, the descendants of these pioneers gathered to pay honor to their courageous forebears. The scene was Independence Rock, that huge granite pile that rises out of the plain on the north side of the Sweetwater

River in central Wyoming, inscribed with the carved or painted names of hundreds of westbound travelers who had gazed upon it with awe and uplift. Even as early as 1840, there were so many of these inscriptions that Father de Smet called it "the great registry of the desert."

Near this monument lived an old miner who greeted the Utah folk at the celebration with a question asked with deep emotion: "Why haven't you come before?" Then he led them to a spot on the shore of Rock Creek, the grave of seventeen of the handcart pioneers. He had erected a cairn of stones above it, and every year had brought wild flowers to the simple marker that told of the tragedy of 1856.

The handcart pioneers were converts who had come from across the ocean—mostly from Great Britain and the Scandinavian countries—filled with zeal to join their Mormon brothers in "the valleys of the mountains." Farmers, clerks, weavers, butchers, sailors, musicians, storekeepers, soldiers, bakers and gentlefolk, they had all been galvanized by the preaching of Joseph Smith's new kind of Christianity.

The Mormons who had already settled in Utah had established an emigration fund to help their friends and relatives make the long journey to the "land of Zion." Money had been raised through sacrifice of their own often scanty means, by the sale of heirlooms they had brought along, by gifts of clothing and food. But so great was the cost of covered-wagon transportations that the fund was not able to meet the requests of all those who wished to gather with the Saints. Brigham Young offered a solution which he described in a letter written to Franklin Richards, then in charge of the European mission, in 1855:

> We cannot afford to purchase wagons and teams as in times past. I am consequently thrown back upon my old plan to make handcarts, and let the emigration foot it, and draw upon them [the carts] the necessary supplies, having a cow or two for every ten. They can come just as quick, if not quicker, and much cheaper—can start earlier, and escape the prevailing sickness which annually lays so many of our brethren in the dust. A great majority of them walk now, even with the teams which are provided, and have a great deal more care and perplexity than if they came without them. They will need only ninety days' rations, from the time of their leaving the

Missouri river, and as the settlements extend up the Platte, not that much. The carts can be made without iron, with wheels hooped, made strong and light; and one, or if the family be large, two of them will bring all they will need upon the plains.

Early the following year, Richards launched the handcart movement, and within a short time 1300 had signed up for the adventure. Crossing the Atlantic on the ship *Horizon,* one group railroaded it from Boston to Iowa City, in cars equipped only with hard wooden seats and drawn by a jerkwater engine which would start and stop so suddenly that sometimes the passengers changed seats involuntarily. Then they were forced to wait day after tedious day in an uncomfortable camp on the bank of the Cedar River until the handcarts were ready. They were drenched by the spring rains, and many became so disheartened that they proposed to wait till another year before setting out across the plains. Yet the more ardent prevailed and encouraged the despondent with the marching song:

> ... long before the Valley's gained
> We will be met upon the plains
> With music sweet, and friends so dear
> And fresh supplies our hearts to cheer.
> And then with music and with song
> How cheerfully we'll march along
> And thank the day we made the start
> To cross the plains with our handcart.

It was midsummer before the caravans were ready to roll. Then the weary waiting was forgotten as the pilgrims sang the refrain of the song:

> Some must push and some must pull,
> As we go marching up the hill,
> So merrily on our way we go
> Until we reach the Valley, O!

For a few weeks there was little trouble. If a voyager fell ill he was carried in one of the few covered wagons that accompanied the carters. But thereafter they found that the long delay had shortened the food supply, and in addition the handcarts began to break down. To hurry their completion the wrights had used unseasoned wood, and now that it was drying out it was causing wheels to wobble and progress to be delayed.

The food was rationed to two ounces of flour per person daily. Patience Archer, one of these handcart pioneers, later told me: "Our mother used this flour to make a kind of porridge or gravy, and served this with fairness to each of the eight hungry ones in our family. Then came a day that our brave father, unable to stand the strain, died. All we sorrowing ones could do was to dig a grave in the prairie sod, wrap his body in a blanket, and lay him away. His resting place was dedicated to the Lord, and our courageous mother led us on towards the land of Zion."

George Harrison, another handcart pioneer, said, "We did not reach Fort Laramie until well into September." Meantime, along the Missouri, he had caught a fever which so enfeebled him that the Indians at the fort called him "the white skeleton." Needless to say, he could do little or no pulling or pushing of the family handcart.

By this time the family was down to starvation rations. Harrison's brother enlisted at the fort as a soldier to earn enough money for the rest of the family to buy food, and remained there.

As the pilgrims reached higher altitudes, they became aware that soon winter would be upon them. The carts grew heavier as the ground grew steeper. The loads would have to be lightened so that South Pass could be crossed before storms blocked it. At Deer Creek, a hundred miles west of Fort Laramie, everything dispensable was piled together and burned, as well as all carts with wobbly wheels.

Travelers who had passed the handcart train carried word of their plight to Brigham Young, who immediately sent a rescue party. But it was already October, and as the handcart caravan struggled up the eastern slope of the Rockies, a snow storm caught them. The last of the companies had just forded the icy waters of the North Platte when the snow was churned to blizzard force by a biting wind. That night a goodly number of the weaker ones died from exposure.

At last, however, the rescue party, my own father among them, appeared out of the storm like ministering angels with their covered wagons, and presently the survivors were rolling over the pass into the warm valleys of Utah to the spot where they hoped to find the peaceful life for which they had so gallantly striven.

None of the Mormons gathered to commemorate their first decade in Utah that July 24, 1857, therefore, were more dismayed than these handcart pioneers when, just as the trumpets were to call the throng to the crowning event of the celebration, three travel-stained horsemen rode into the encampment with a message for the Governor. They were Mayor Abram Smoot of Salt Lake City, Porter Rockwell, and Judson Stoddard.

Captain Balloo's band tried to divert the people, but some gathered near the Governor's tent. In after years William Frampton told me: "We knew, when the horsemen rode into camp, that something unusual had happened, but no hint of it came until Governor Young, Mayor Smoot and the others emerged from the tent. I happened to be standing close to them when they walked out, and heard Governor Young say forcefully: 'When we came into this valley, I said if our enemies will give us ten years here, I will ask them no odds. It has been ten years now, and in the name of Israel's God, I ask them no odds.'"

The leaders went to the speakers' platform, and the program was presented. Just before it closed, the message brought by the horsemen was given to the audience of more than two thousand people eager for the news—that an army was on its way to Utah, no one knew why.

While in charge of the Y X Company carrying the eastbound mail and express from Salt Lake, Smoot had seen the advance guard of this army and its supply trains heading west, but he did not learn their destination until he reached the Missouri River. Then, with his swiftest animals hitched to a light wagon, he and Judson Stoddard had driven post haste along the trail to the valleys. At Fort Laramie they found Porter Rockwell, who made the rest of the trip with them—more than five hundred miles—in five days.

Governor Young advised the people to go on with their celebration, then return to their homes the next day to await word as to what would be done. In spite of the approach of an army, and the call to be ready to defend their rights, the Mormons continued the celebration until a late hour. Dawn saw them breaking camp and starting home, confidence in their hearts that all would be well.

Mayor Smoot had joined Mormons and non-Mormons in establishing a regular express and mail service between Independence, on the Missouri, and Salt Lake City. Hiram Kimball, a Mormon, had bid for the mail-carrying at the low price of $26,500 per year, his plan being to join with the Y X Company, organized to carry express only. Express was carried by ox-team. McGraw, the only competitor, had bid $50,000. The contract was awarded to Kimball. On June 2, 1857, Smoot took charge of eastbound express and mail, expecting to receive the westbound shipment of express and mail for the return trip.

At Independence, however, he met with a double surprise. He was told the Army was on its way to Utah, and as for the mail, he found that orders were that none should be delivered to him because the Kimball contract had been cancelled. McGraw, angered at losing the government business to his rival, had written President Buchanan a letter as a "personal and political friend," containing no specific charges, but filled with general denunciations of the leadership in Utah, which he feared would soon reduce that territory to "a howling wilderness."

This letter was probably the principal cause for the withdrawal of the Kimball mail contract. Certainly it was one of the factors that led to the Utah War. But another cogent reason for the costly expedition of 1857 was the scurrilous report of Associate Federal Judge W. W. Drummond about the people of Utah and their officials.

Drummond was a gambler and a bully who openly showed he had come to Utah to make money rather than mete out justice, and had brought with him a woman of questionable reputation, whom he occasionally had sit with him on the judicial bench. Back in Illinois he had left his wife and their children without means of support. Being held in disrespect by Mormons and non-Mormons alike, Drummond resigned his post after a few months and returned east, where he wrote and circulated his report.

Since there was no telegraph, or even prompt mail service, to carry the accusing document to those who had been misrepresented, refutation of the charges and documentary proof of their falsity could not reach Washington in time to stop action in the sending of the army West. There had been no investigation there of the situation in Utah; the order had been given for an army then at Fort Leavenworth to proceed to that territory and, if necessary, install Alfred Cumming in Brigham Young's place, as governor. A move was made that cost the government nearly forty million dollars at a time when the national treasury was almost empty.

The army was halted on the bleak uplands just west of the Rocky Mountain Divide, and held there, suffering cold and hunger, through the bitter winter of 1857–58. Brigham Young, as Governor of Utah Territory, had ordered the troops stopped; and the militia, under General Wells, carried out this executive command.

"Shed no blood, but hamper the movements of the invading army," were Young's orders. "Capture and burn the supply trains, stampede the animals. Do all you can without killing the soldiers, to impede their march into our territory. They must be held back until this unjust, unnecessary conflict is settled rightly."

The pioneers who had settled Utah had been driven from two states of the East, and were determined to defend themselves from injustice. Governor Young had been denied the courtesy of official notice of the coming of the army, and the people of Utah had a right to know why the soldiers were advancing upon them. They had no quarrel with officials of government, leaders of the army, or soldiers, but they were ready to defend their rights.

Captain Van Vliet, advance courier of the United States Army, was the first to reach Salt Lake City. Coming as assistant to the quartermaster, he was courteously welcomed by the leaders and the people, but his request for supplies and a place of encampment was denied.

The people were bitterly opposed to having an army quartered in their midst. They had just suffered tragic experiences from a small body of troops and camp followers who had spent the winter of 1854–55 in the territory near Salt Lake City. Captain Van Vliet was told that to bring two thousand soldiers into the valleys, with all the others that naturally would follow, would mean disastrous consequences to the struggling communities. The newly appointed governor could come with his usual escort, and he would be welcomed, but not with an army.

Van Vliet urged that the officers and soldiers had no hostile intentions against the people of Utah and their leaders. Governor Young replied that the Captain was undoubtedly sincere, but that the people of Utah had suffered too much not to fear an army, however well intentioned. He was told that if the Army succeeded in forcing its way into Salt Lake valley it would find a charred and barren waste. Homes would be burned, trees cut down, fields destroyed. He was taken to see the homes of the city in their flower and garden settings. On being introduced to some of the pioneer women who had helped to bring such beauty and comfort to the arid region, he asked of one: "Madam, would you consent to have your beautiful home burned, your fruitful orchard destroyed?"

"I would not only consent to it," she replied, "but I would set the fire myself, cut down the trees and uproot the plants, if it was deemed necessary."

At a religious service in the Old Tabernacle, the Captain heard the story of the redeeming of the desert, and songs, "Come, Come, Ye Saints," and "Zion," with its lines from the Apocrypha, voicing the spirit of embattled old Israel:

> In our mountain retreat,
> God will strengthen our feet,
> On the necks of our foes we shall tread,
> And their silver and gold,
> As the prophets foretold,
> Shall be brought to adorn our fair head.

From these and other expressions he concluded that the people of Utah were in deadly earnest. He said that they had been lied about—"the worst of any people I have ever seen." Van Vliet's fair and accurate report to leaders in Washington was a turning point in the path to peace.

On his way east the Captain gave sound advice to the troops just emerging from the South Pass, urging them not to attempt to enter Salt Lake valley that winter, as no arrangements could be made for their supplies and they would have to fight their way through. Young officers were all for the fighting, but older ones prevailed, and the troops were kept in winter camp around Fort Bridger, all the log cabins and stockade of which had been burned by the Utah troops. Nearby Fort Supply, with its stacks of hay and its grain, had suffered the same fate.

Meantime three of the supply trains, of twenty-five wagons each, were intercepted and burned one night on the Big Sandy, an east branch of the Green River. All except two wagons loaded with the personal belongings of the teamsters, and supplies to get them back to the Missouri, were set in flames by Captain Lot Smith and his roughriders of the Utah militia. Orin Lee, one of the riders, told me:

"We had watched the troops get across the Green River in early October, 1857. Then under Captain Smith, our red-bearded leader, we scouted eastward, keeping out of sight during the days. At last one clear night we saw the supply trains, great covered wagons, go into camp along the Big Sandy. No escort of troops was with them.

" 'There's our chance, boys, to get beans and bacon,' said our captain. 'We'll ride up together within striking distance; then with a few of you, I'll go up and give my orders to the wagon boss. Now, remember, no shooting—not a bit of it, unless they force the fighting. Understand?' "

Lot Smith rode down to the Big Sandy, where he came upon Lew Simpson and William Cody (later to be known as "Buffalo Bill"), who had led their horses down to give them a drink. As the two looked up they saw the captain and three men.

"What's up?" Simpson demanded.

"Are you the boss of this train?"

"Yes."

"Well," said Lot Smith, "tell your teamsters to draw two wagons aside, put into them all their belongings, and supplies enough to get back to the states."

"By whose orders?"

"By mine, and the men I've got right back here ready for action. We don't want any bloodshed. Just do what I say, and there won't be any."

By this time, some of the teamsters had come up. When Simpson asked whether they would stand by him, one of them exclaimed: "And get shot? Not by a damn sight! We hired out to drive teams, not to fight."

The wagon boss had no other alternative but to follow Lot Smith's orders. While his men were getting the wagons and their things aside, Smith's men chopped up two ox yokes and started a fire. Then, taking burning brands, several of them touched the wagon covers along the train, and they went up in flames. About seventy-five wagons loaded with supplies burned that night along what was afterward called Simpson's Hollow.

It was a blow for the troops who had soon to go into winter quarters on about one-third or one-quarter rations. Lot Smith and his roughriders not only burned wagon trains, but also stampeded the oxen that drew the wagons across the plains and mountains.

Blizzards in the badlands around Jim Bridger's old post kept the soldiers fighting the cold. Solon Robison, one of the mountain boys guarding the trails, told me: "My pal and I had one buffalo robe between us. Through the night we took turns rubbing each other's feet to keep them from freezing." It was often way below zero.

While all this was going on in the far West, efforts were being made in Washington to bring the strange war there to a close. A grievous blunder had been made, and needless suffering, hardships, and anxiety were felt in hundreds of homes. Officials in Washington were straining for a way out of the difficulty.

Though in delicate health, Colonel Thomas L. Kane volunteered to President Buchanan to go at his own expense and attempt to settle the conflict. The President expressed little faith in this self-imposed mission, but gave the Colonel a letter commending him to all officers of the United States he might meet in his travels who could aid in promoting understanding and peace.

On February 25, 1858, Colonel Kane arrived in Salt Lake City, under the assumed name of Dr. Osborne, having made the journey by steamship to Panama, gone over the Isthmus by mule back, up the coast again by boat to Los Angeles, and thence by a heavy spring carriage to the Utah capital. In Salt Lake City he learned of the military situation from Governor Young. His plea was for peace, for relief of the suffering soldiers at Fort Bridger. General Albert Sidney Johnston was ready there to order his troops to march into Salt Lake City, but Kane forestalled any such military action by inducing Alfred Cumming, the newly appointed governor, to accompany him without military escort to the Utah capital. Their route was through Echo Canyon, a main gateway into Utah, which had been fortified to hold back the Army, into Weber Canyon. Emerging from this picturesque gorge into the valley, Governor Cumming had his first view of the Great Salt Lake, shining like a mirror. Then he was taken through a series of Mormon settlements—Kaysville, Farmington and Bountiful—where the people came out to greet him with music, and to present flowers and fruits.

At a public meeting held in the Old Tabernacle in Salt Lake City, the new Governor made a peace-promoting address, in which he said that he had been appointed by the President with the consent of the Senate, to be the chief executive of Utah. It was true that a large body of armed soldiers were on the frontier, but they had come not to destroy but give protection to the people. He was sent to enforce the law. He and his officers had nothing to do with social and religious views. As Americans, all had a right to serve God in their own way. He did not believe his would be a path of roses; in fact, he expected opposition from misguided men. Finally he requested the "brethren," if they saw him go a little astray, not to treat him harshly but to counsel with him as a friend.

One thing that worried Governor Cumming was to see the people of Salt Lake moving out of their homes according to a plan made by officials of their church before Colonel Kane arrived, so that if the Army decided to capture the capital of Utah Territory, it would find Salt Lake City, and perhaps other towns in the Salt Lake valley, in ashes. The Latter-day Saints were ready to burn their homes if the Army expected at any time to take over the city.

Already hundreds of families were in wagons on the roads leading south. Cumming made several journeys along the line of caravans between Salt Lake City and Provo, pleading in vain for the people to return to their homes. He appealed to Brigham Young, who told him that ninety-nine out of every hundred of the Latter-day Saints would rather spend their lives in the mountains than endure the oppression the federal government was heaping upon them. The only way Young saw to get the people to return to their homes was to remove the Army from the territory.

Mail from California brought word that 6,000 more troops were about to be despatched to Utah. Governor Cumming went back to Fort Bridger to bring his wife to the Utah capital, assuring Brigham Young that he would require the Army to remain at Fort Bridger until he had replies from the President to dispatches he had sent by Colonel Kane, who had hurried back east owing to the death of his father.

Sentiment toward an amicable settlement was shaping up in Washington. The suggestion that a commission be appointed to bring the needless Utah War, or "Contractors' War," to a peaceful close, was finally acted upon. L. W. Powell, ex-governor and senator-elect from Kentucky, and Major B. M. McCulloch, a soldier of the Mexican War, were named as a peace commission, and armed with a proclamation from the President offering pardon and amnesty to all who submitted themselves to the authority of the government.

"Pardon for what?" asked those who had helped to halt the Army. They were willing to admit they had burned supply trains and run off with government cattle, but no soldier of the United States had been slain. They felt they were acting within their rights under Governor Young, the chief executive of Utah. Although the proclamation was not satisfactory to either side, it served to open the way to peace.

It was finally agreed that the Army might march into the valley and make an encampment, but not close to Salt Lake City or any of the towns. An oasis on the edge of the desert, about forty miles from the capital, was settled upon. Copies of the presidential pardon were distributed, and the militia withdrew from the canyon fortifications. Meanwhile the Cummings had taken up residence in Salt Lake. When the Governor's lady was brought into the city, it was deserted, and she wept as her husband took her to their home.

On June 26, 1858, the United States Army, under command of General Johnston, marched through the silent streets of Salt Lake City. The General had started early to make sure the troops would reach the west side of the Jordan River, outside the city limits, for their encampment that night. There was no halting within the city. George Harrison, who was with them, told me: "All the people I saw as we passed through town were a man leading a mule, and an old lady who peeped at us from behind curtains. The town was still as a cemetery."

At the end of the long column of infantry came the dragoons, or cavalry, under command of Colonel Phillip St. George Cooke, who in 1846 had led the Mormon Battalion on the two-thousand-mile march from Santa Fe to San Diego. In deference to the Mormon soldiers he had commanded in those Mexican War days, the Colonel rode with his head uncovered through the city.

General Johnston kept his agreement with Governor Cumming and President Brigham Young. A week or two later he established Camp Floyd (named after Buchanan's Secretary of War) in Cedar Valley, west of the Utah lake. Because of the outbreak of the Civil War, this camp was suddenly abandoned three years later. Only a few vestiges of the old post now remain to remind a visitor of the stirring activities that led to its establishment.

# CHAPTER EIGHT

# INDIANS AS THE PIONEERS KNEW THEM

George Catlin, the painter of the early West and friend of the red men, could see no wrong in the Indians. On the other hand, there were plenty of frontiersmen who were rabidly devoted to the opinion that the only good Indian is a dead one. Writing at this distance from the Indians who greeted the first pioneers, it is well nigh impossible to deduce what they actually were like; but my own reminiscences, and the stories told me by old explorers who were close to the unspoiled tribes, have led me to conclude that, as in any society, the leaders of the Indians were the equals in character of any white leaders, while the lesser members of the tribes were no worse than the irresponsible and untrustworthy among the white invaders of the western lands.

Much of the prejudice against the Indians derives from the pioneers' encounters with them after the pioneers had settled into a way of life that aimed to recapture the comforts of the civilization they had left behind. The amenities of such a pattern of life meant little or nothing to the Indians; indeed, they often found such comforts a menace to their health and their survival. Cleanliness, as we understand it, and shelter were harmful to a people used to the open air and its freedom from disease germs. Illness, strange to the natives of the plains and the mountains, seemed to lurk in the relatively elaborate dwellings and clothing of the whites. Often it emerged to attack the unimmunized Indians and decimate their people. As a result the Indians stubbornly resisted attempts to "civilize" them.

Trappers and traders, forced through their work to live close to nature themselves, got on best with the Indians, and truly understood them. In return the Indians treated them with friendship, often with brotherhood, and gave them their daughters for wives.

The loyalty and courage of these women often equaled the fortitude and devotion of the pioneer women. In the eyes of the whites the ideals of the Indians were simpler than their own, and if examples of nobility seem few, the reason is that chronicles of those early days are sadly but understandably lacking in the minutiae of daily life and personal relationships.

One of such stories, however, was told me by Josh Terry, who was born in Canada in 1825, migrated West in 1847, and survived until 1915. When Terry was working as Jim Bridger's hired hand at Fort Bridger he saw a good deal of Mamoots, a handsome Indian girl who was working for Mrs. Bridger. Mamoots had been brought to the fort by Yellow Metal, chief of the Utes, who had captured her from another tribe. Bridger gave the chief a gun to release the girl to him. She proved a good worker, helpful to all, but she was lonely so far away from her own people.

Josh Terry also was lonely. He asked Mamoots if she would care to be his wife and live with him in a tepee of their own. Her answer was: "Ask Jim."

Bridger was glad to give his consent, and also to perform a simple ceremony. "He had us stand before him and his wife," Terry recalled. "Then he asked me if I would take good care of Mamoots. I promised I would. Next he asked Mamoots if she would do the same for me. She smiled and said she would. I took the Indian girl in my arms and kissed her. Jim shook hands with us and wished us the best of luck."

That night there was a feast for Josh and Mamoots. Mrs. Bridger gave the young couple cooking utensils and dishes; Bridger added some good stout canvas to make a tepee; other friends at the post brought beaded moccasins, buckskin clothing and buffalo robes.

For the first few months all was happiness in the new lodge. The young mountain man brought in game, and they bought other supplies. Mamoots was devoted to him. She had been taught to cook by Mrs. Bridger, and she was adept in tanning buckskin and making Indian clothing.

Then Josh fell ill of mountain fever, and all that Mamoots and Mrs. Bridger could do did not stop him from steadily growing worse. His Indian bride was wild with anxiety over him.

"One day," he said, "while I was tossing in my sleep, Mamoots left our tepee for a little while. When she came back, she was strangely excited.

" 'You goin' to die,' she moaned. 'Me no want to live.' With that she held up some poisonous plant she had been eating. Then she fell on a buffalo robe near me.

"I called loudly to some Indian women. One ran to get Mrs. Bridger, who came quickly, and did everything she could to revive Mamoots. But my wife died. We buried her among some aspen trees nearby."

Later Josh Terry married another Indian girl, a Shoshone, with the blessing of Chief Washakie.

Sacajawea, the Bird Woman, had played a significant part in the success of the Lewis and Clark expedition. Another red heroine of the conquest of the West is known now only as Mrs. Dorion, the wife of Pierre

Dorion, interpreter for Wilson Price Hunt and his westbound Astorians of 1811.

Before this French frontiersman accepted the job, he insisted that his wife and their sons, two and four years old, be taken with him. Hunt did not like it, nor did his men, but no other interpreter was available; so the whole family made the long journey from the Mississippi to the mouth of the Columbia.

It was a gruelling, testing trip of weeks with scant supplies of food and little water. On the Snake River, which won from them the name of "Mad River," the party's canoes overturned near the present American Falls, and one of their best boatmen drowned. The rest barely got to shore, where they hid the goods they had brought along for trade, and plodded over sand and sage and lava to Oregon.

The Indian mother withstood the hardships as well as the men. Her husband managed to trade some of his possessions for one horse, and on this she rode with her two-year-old slung in a blanket along the side, while the father and the four-year-old walked beside them. Once when starvation threatened, Hunt demanded that the horse be slaughtered for food, but Dorion refused to surrender it, and the other men supported him, so much did they admire the courage of his wife.

In the Grand Ronde valley of eastern Oregon, the family stopped for a day, and when they caught up with the others, they had a third son. On the way over the Blue Mountains, the infant died and, wrapped in soft buckskin, was buried beside the trail. The sorrowing mother, intent on saving her other children, went on with her husband over the snow-covered range, and down the Columbia to the Pacific.

The next year, John Reed, a genial Irish clerk in Hunt's employ, induced the Dorion family and others to join in a trapping venture in the region of what is now Idaho.

A fur-hunter's post was built on Snake River near its junction with the Boise; but the threat of Indians caused Reed to give up this post and build another in what seemed a safer place, where they were joined by the three Kentucky hunters, Hoback, Rezner and Robinson. Mrs. Dorion cooked for the men, and helped take care of the skins. Everything went well until one day a friendly Indian came running with word that their first post had been burned by Indians. Reed and most of the trappers were off at their work when the message came.

Mrs. Dorion immediately put her two boys on a horse and hurried to find her husband. During the night she lost her way, and after two days of hiding from the hostile red men and searching for her husband, she finally neared the hut used by Dorion and his companions while trapping. Out staggered one of the trappers, wounded and faint from loss of blood.

A tragic story this man, LeClere, had for the Indian mother: Dogrib Indians had attacked them, killed her husband, the three Kentucky hunters, and two other trappers, and left him wounded. All their furs and weapons had been stolen by the red raiders.

Helping the wounded man on her horse and handing up the younger boy to him, Mrs. Dorion and the elder boy walked as they escaped from the scene of the tragedy to return to the greater safety of the winter camp, where there would be provisions if the Indians had not stolen them. That night LeClere died. She buried him as best she could under brushwood and snow.

A day later she reached the place, only to find Reed and the men with him murdered and scalped. Again she fled and remained in the cold all night with no food for her little ones or herself.

Wrapping the children in a buffalo robe, and tying her horse in a thicket, next morning she ventured to the top of a hill to observe whether any of the murderous Indians were still around the Reed post. All was quiet. The children were now so nearly frozen that she ran the risk of making a fire to save them.

After dark the mother rolled them again in the robe and stole back to the post, where she found a supply of fish. Gathering all she could carry, she hurried back to her children, and made another fire to warm them and to cook the food—the first they had tasted for three days.

Next night Mrs. Dorion ventured again to the trappers' post and carried off another load. This done she sank for a time with exhaustion from the terror and struggle. When she had recovered somewhat, she packed her horse with the remainder of the fish, and the robe and skins she had gathered. Then placing her two boys on the pack, she set out westward, leading the animal. For nine days, she kept on her journey through snow and woods, and over rugged paths.

At last, in the foothills on the eastern slope of the Blue Mountains, she stopped. Both she and her horse were exhausted. At the foot of a cliff which gave some protection, she selected a place to pass the rest of the winter. For shelter she built a hut of pine branches, long grass and moss, packed all around with snow like an igloo. Her buffalo robe, buckskins and a few furs added a little comfort.

For food she had no choice but to kill her horse. She smoked the meat and hung it on a tree to keep it from being eaten by prowling animals. Its hide was used to keep the wind out of the wickiup. Then for fifty-three lonely days she managed to keep herself and her two boys alive in that crude camp.

With the coming of a few warm days in March, Mrs. Dorion continued her westward journey. Painfully she and her boys went up and over the Blue Mountains. The glaring snow blinded her, and she was forced to wait three days until her sight returned enough for her to travel. The trip took fifteen days, during six of which they had nothing to eat.

At last, she saw smoke in the distance. Being unable to hurry with her boys, she again wrapped them in the robe, hid them, and went forward in desperation to get help. Part of the way she had to crawl, but finally she reached a band of Walla Wallas, who gave her welcome and food.

Indians immediately set off in search of the children, found them and brought them into camp that night. After a brief stay with the Walla Walla Indians, she went on with her boys to the Columbia to keep watch for trappers coming up the river. One day they came. The shouts of the Dorion boys brought them ashore, where they learned the fate of John Reed, Dorion and the others, who had gone into the wilds a year before, and heard the tale of the courageous mother.

Both Ezra Meeker and Nick Wilson often told me of the home life of the Indians as they had seen it day by day. Once when Meeker and his brother Oliver were cruising about Puget Sound in search of a new home-site, they camped ashore near a Chinook settlement. Two of the Indian mothers approached the young men with baskets of clams they offered to sell. The boys agreed to buy if the women would show them how to cook the clams.

Laughing, they cleared away the fire Oliver had started, and laid some smaller stones on the hot ones that served as a hearth. On these they placed a layer of clams, spread fine twigs over them, and covered the twigs with earth. The smoldering fire did the rest.

The boys shared the bread they had baked, and their boiled potatoes, with the visitors; then followed them to their own camp. Shy papooses hid behind their mothers' skirts and peeped out at the white men. The women reassured them with affectionate caresses and coaxed them forward to meet their new friends. The whole group proved helpful neighbors, teaching them how to avoid starvation by harvesting clams, teaching them Chinook, and giving them a haunch of venison as a parting gift.

The "Walker War" of 1853 grew out of the attitude of a different type of Indian, Chief Yellow Metal of the Utes. Here was a proud and haughty leader, fond of decking himself with brass, copper, and even gold ornaments. These he may have obtained from Spanish slave-hunters; at any rate they gave him his name. *Oker*, in the Ute language, means "yellow"; and the similarity of sound caused the whites to call this volatile Indian leader "Walker."

Chief Yellow Metal was not at all happy at the stopping of the Spanish slave trade that flourished on the trail between Sante Fe and Los Angeles, for he had been conniving with the Spaniards and was probably in their pay. It is, at any rate, a matter of record that the Utes made slaves of the weaker tribes; that is how Mamoots had been captured and brought to Fort Bridger by the Chief.

The conflict began with Indian raids on the settlements in southern

Utah. People were killed, and cattle and horses stolen. The Indians were well-mounted and had many horses to spare, whereas the settlers were fewer in number and had chiefly work horses. Consequently it was next to impossible to pursue the marauding Utes, or to anticipate their depredations. The only practical method of dealing with them was to inveigle the Chief and other Indian leaders into a powwow, make them gifts, entertain them as lavishly as was possible in a frontier economy. My maternal grandfather was one of the most successful of the "peace chiefs" appointed by the pioneers to deal with the Indians, and the Utes often came to counsel with him. They were never turned away hungry, or without kindly advice.

Once Chief Yellow Metal and his band paid a surprise visit on the settlers at Parowan, one of the campsites on the slave-trading route. There was anxiety and tension among the pioneers as the Indians made their camp nearby, but the white peacemakers arranged a friendly powwow and ordered a feast for all.

While they were eating, Chief Yellow Metal said, "Me hear Mormons dance. You show me."

In response, the pioneer fiddlers tuned up their instruments, and couples made ready for a square dance on the open space within the fort. Lively tunes with a caller for the changes had the dance going merrily.

Suddenly the Indian chief stopped the fun by shouting, "Ka-wino" (No good). "Injuns show how to dance." With a sharp command to his braves, he had them line up promptly. Then with tom-toms and chanting, they went through some of their native dances with vigorous rhythm while the white folk applauded heartily. The tension was eased, and the next morning before sunrise, the Indians were on their way northward.

A grand powwow, complete with generous gifts, was finally arranged to bring an end to the war. As a first gift to the Indians, one of the white leaders tossed plugs of tobacco to those in the circle. Chief Walker did not even look at the one that fell at his feet. Sensing the feeling of the Chief, the white leader, General Wells, quickly rose, and picking up the tobacco, presented it to the Indian leader. The situation was eased, and the group "made medicine"—that is, talked together successfully.

PLATE TWENTY

Labonte Creek in Wyoming, with Laramie Peak in the background.

PLATE TWENTY-ONE

Echo Canyon, the gateway to Utah.

PLATE TWENTY-TWO

The Mormons descending Little Mountain into Salt Lake Valley,
their new homeland, in 1847.

PLATE TWENTY-THREE

Handcart pioneers.

PLATE TWENTY-FOUR

Independence Rock, on the Sweetwater River, fifty miles west of Casper, Wyoming, called by Father de Smet "the great registry of the desert" from the hundreds of names inscribed on it by early travelers into the West.

PLATE TWENTY-FIVE

Old Fort Hall, built by Nathaniel Wyeth in 1834 near the junction of the
Snake and Portneuf Rivers in Idaho.

PLATE TWENTY-SIX

Fort Laramie, built as a trading post in 1834 and taken over by the government for an Army post in 1849, on the trunkline of western trails.

PLATE TWENTY-SEVEN

Pioneers fording the South Platte River at California Crossing, near Julesburg, Colorado.

PLATE TWENTY-EIGHT

Fort Kearny, on the Platte River in central Nebraska, established in 1848.

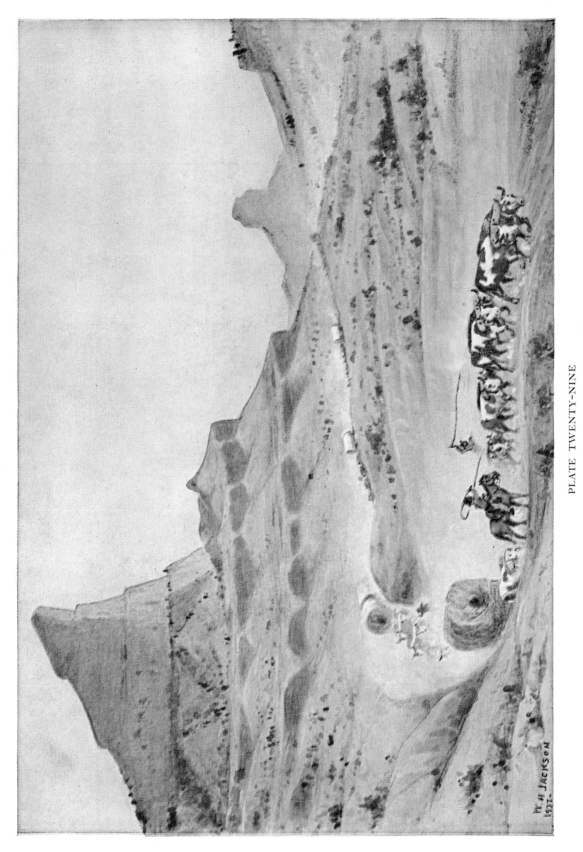

PLATE TWENTY-NINE

Mitchell's Pass, near Scott's Bluff, Nebraska. William H. Jackson sketched this picture in 1866, showing his own ox-team in the foreground, as he crossed the plains.

PLATE THIRTY

A Pony Express rider passing Split Rock in the Sweetwater Valley.

PLATE THIRTY-ONE

Rock Creek Station in Nebraska, a spot closely connected with the careers of Kit Carson, John C. Fremont, "Wild Bill" Hickok, the Pony Express and the Overland Stage.

Chief Yellow Metal kept the peace. During the few years he lived there was no further fighting; indeed, he grew friendly with the white settlers. His hope was to win one of the pioneer girls for his wife. When he expressed this desire, he met with no objection, provided he could find a white girl who would be willing to marry him.

One summer day nearly all the settlers of one of the Mormon outposts were out in the fields taking care of the crops. One old lady, however, was so crippled with rheumatism that she had to stay home with someone to wait on her. Mary, her granddaughter, one of the prettiest girls in town, worked about the house while the old lady sat in the rocker.

Suddenly the door was quietly opened, and into the room stepped Chief Yellow Metal, looking every inch a chief. His headdress of eagle feathers, his white buckskin shirt, and his leggings fringed and ornamented with bead designs made him a striking figure as he stood erect in his beaded moccasins. Pendants of gold hung from his ears. He carried no weapons; he had come to make love.

Even before he began to speak, Mary knew. She stepped quickly beside her grandmother, keeping the table between them and their uninvited guest. Then the Chief, in Indian tongue, made his plea for her hand: He wanted her to be his squaw; he had many ponies; he would build her a white man's tepee; she would have Indian women to do all her work for her. Would she consent?

Mary knew little of the Ute language, but she understood. She paused a moment, then with desperation, or inspiration, said: "I can't. I'm married already."

"Who?" demanded the Chief.

Put to the sudden test, Mary named the man to whom she was engaged.

Yellow Metal whirled on his heel, and stalked out of the room. The trembling girl and her grandmother waited until those in the fields returned home, then told the story. The leaders of the town were called to a council, for it was uncertain what the chief might do in revenge for being spurned.

Finally came a decision: Mary's word would have to be made good. That night there was a wedding ceremony; then the pioneer girl and her husband left under escort for Salt Lake City, to stay until the injured feelings of Chief Walker subsided. Gifts of flour and beef helped appease him, and he remained friendly until, two or three years later, he went to the happy hunting grounds, and was buried in the hills amid lamentations of the tribe.

Another of the "peace chiefs" was Jacob Hamblin, a God-fearing man. During the Walker War he and other angered white men gave chase to a band of raiding Indians. At daybreak the posse discovered their camp, surrounded it, and made ready to attack. Suddenly the leader of the camp came forward, making signs of friendship.

"I never hurt you," he said in his own tongue, "and I do not want to. If you shoot, I will. If you do not, I will not."

"I was not familiar with his language," Hamblin said in telling the story, "but I knew what he said. Such an influence came over me that I would not have killed one of them for all the cattle in the valley." The running of the women and children and their crying also aroused his sympathies. He tried to keep his men from shooting any of the Indians, but before he could prevent them, some shots were fired. Fortunately none of the Indians were injured. At Hamblin's command the firing ceased.

A powwow was held, and Hamblin asked some of the Indians to go back to the settlement with them. They were afraid, but upon the assurance of the white leader that they would not be harmed, they eventually consented to go. On their arrival at the village, the leader there was about to brush aside the promise Hamblin had given, and have the trustful Indians shot. Hamblin, however, calmly told his superior that if anyone was to be shot, he would be first; his promise of protection for Indians who had come with peace in their hearts must not be broken. He placed himself in front of the red men. The threat ended there. The Indians were fed, given presents and set at liberty. No further trouble came from this band of desert natives.

Jacob Hamblin was successful in dealing with other Indians, and the feeling grew in him that he was not to kill the red men but to be a messenger of peace to them. "It was manifest to me by the Holy Spirit," he said, "that if I would not thirst for the blood of the Indians, I should never fall at their hands."

This became a lodestar throughout his life. How it was repeatedly tested is revealed in the tales told of the frontiersman, such as the story of his placing his life at stake to defend the honor of his people and to keep the Navajos, a justly angered tribe, from going on the warpath.

The Navajos would often make forays across the Colorado River against the Piutes and sometimes against the pioneers as well. Hamblin went among them to counsel against fighting and promote trade between them and their white neighbors, and finally induced some to visit the settlements. These overtures led to the Indians bringing colorful blankets, decorated belts and bridles, jewelry of silver and turquoise, and other articles to trade for what the whites had to offer. Good fellowship and fair dealing followed. Through his understanding of Indian nature, and his justice, Hamblin won the confidence and affection of the Navajo leaders and their people. Whenever any difficulty arose, he was called into council to help resolve the trouble, and it usually was settled quickly and satisfactorily to all.

Through nearly ten years these friendly relations continued. Then abruptly the peace was broken by a rancher—a newcomer into southeastern Utah. Knowing little of the earnest efforts of the pioneers to keep peace with the red men, the unknown rancher acted rashly and cruelly.

Four young Navajos, two of them sons of a chief, had crossed the Colorado on a trading venture. Making their way into a valley of the upper Sevier River, not far from Bryce Canyon, they were caught in a snow storm and ran short of provisions. To save themselves from cold and hunger, they took shelter in an empty cabin on the ranch of the new settler, and killed a yearling calf for food.

The irate rancher gathered others of his spirit, and without seeking an explanation, shot three of the young Navajos to death. The fourth, wounded, managed to escape. For thirteen days he struggled until he finally reached home. Naturally his story roused wrath in the tribe. Young braves wanted to take the warpath at once and launch an attack on the pioneer settlers, who, they wrongly concluded, were responsible for the tragedy. Older ones counseled curbing justified anger and waiting until they could talk with Jacob Hamblin. Chief Tuba rode to Lees Ferry to urge that a messenger be sent to their trusted friend, then living at Kanab, Utah. The Lees—father and son—immediately rode on with the message.

Hamblin quickly responded to the call of the Indian leader, and against the advice of his friends, rode away on the trail to the Navajo country. Arriving at Lees Ferry, he found two men who proved good friends in time of need—brothers named Smith, non-Mormons, who had been trading with the Indians. Seeing Hamblin's tired horse, they brought another mount for him, and volunteered to ride on with him in his dangerous mission. There was a pause for the weary man to get something to eat; then away the three went to try first to find some of the Navajo leaders whose friendship Jacob had made.

One friendly Navajo was found who welcomed the three white visitors, and bade them come into his lodge. After they had eaten food prepared by the Indian women, older men of the tribe came to hear what Hamblin had to say about the tragedy that had befallen the four young Navajos. He told them his friends were not guilty of the outrage. Others with mean hearts had committed the crime. They should be found and punished. These older Indians, knowing Jacob, seemed to believe his earnest words, and listened in respectful silence; but all they would say when he had finished was: "We are not yet ready for a council. When the relatives are all in, we will talk."

About noon the next day they told Hamblin they were ready. A large lodge had been cleared for the council. Indians—most of them young Navajos, insolent and threatening—began to gather, but only four of the councilors of the nation assembled with the group.

Jacob and his two friends were seated at the end of the crowded room in the center of which was a fire. There was only one entrance, far from the three white men, so that they were virtual prisoners. Without the slightest trace of agitation Hamblin communicated to his companions what they all believed to be their death warrant.

Then he began his reply, reminding the Indians of his long acquaintance with their tribe and his many friendly dealings with them. "When," he demanded, "have I ever spoken with a forked tongue?"

Insolently the Navajos asked if he was afraid.

"Why should we be afraid of our friends?" Hamblin answered. "Are not the Navajos our friends, and we theirs? Else why did we place ourselves in your power?"

He spoke for a long time, and although he was frequently and rudely interrupted, his patience and nerve never gave way. When he ceased, it was apparent his reasoning had not been without effect in their stubborn bosoms, but the good influence was of short duration.

A young Indian, son of a chief, and brother of two of the slain Indians, addressed the assembled warriors, and the tide turned fearfully against the white men. He wound up his impassioned harangue by springing to his feet and, pointing to an Indian who had not yet spoken, called to him to come forward. The Indian came and knelt before him. With one hand he turned back his hunting shirt, revealing the mark of a recent bullet wound. With the other he pointed to the fire, uttering or rather hissing a few emphatic words, which were a demand for instant death of the whites by fire.

The sight of the wounded brave roused the Indians' passion to fury. The erect, proud athletic figure of the young chief as he stood pointing his finger at the kneeling figure before him; the circle of crouching forms; their dusky and painted faces animated by every passion that hatred and ferocity could inspire, and their glittering eyes fixed with one malignant impulse upon the whites; the whole partially illuminated by the fitful gleam of the firelight was a terrifying scene.

The suspense was broken by the Navajo host, who once again raised his voice in the ambassadors' behalf. After a stormy discussion, Hamblin finally compelled them to acknowledge that he had been their friend; that he had never lied to them and was worthy of belief now.

Thwarted in their determination to have Hamblin killed, the vengeful young Navajos next demanded that the pioneers pay for the killing of the young braves with one hundred head of cattle for each slain Navajo, and fifty for the wounded one. They asked Hamblin to give them a promise in writing that such would be done.

Hamblin was now in another critical situation. By agreeing to the proposition, he could go home free; but he would have to acknowledge that his people were guilty of the crime. He calmly replied that he would not sign any such agreement.

One of the Indians, pointing to the fire, suggested that if he were stretched over the coals he would accept the terms. "Let the ones who committed the crime, pay for it," Hamblin said. "I will not agree to pay, or have my people pay, for a wrong they never committed."

When they saw that he was not afraid of them, they began to soften in their feelings toward him. He was asked if he knew Hastele—one of their chiefs. "Yes," he replied. "In the great peace talk at Fort Defiance, it was agreed that all important difficulties between you and our people should be brought before Hastele for settlement. This trouble could have been settled if it had been brought before Hastele. My mission is one of peace. Let Hastele and as many more of you as wish come to our country and learn the truth as I have told it to you."

Hastele did come—and with him a peace party, including a representative of the United States government. With Hamblin and other leaders they went to the scene of the tragedy and learned the true story. Finally Hastele said: "I am satisfied. I know our friends, the Mormons, are true friends. They have taken the trouble to show us the truth. I believe they have good hearts. Here is Jacob. He has been traveling about to do good all winter and spring, and is going yet. When I get home I do not intend that my tongue shall lie idle, until the Navajos learn the particulars of this affair."

Jacob Hamblin spent his life working for peace and good among the pioneers and their Indian neighbors. The promise given him by the Lord, as he ever felt, was surely fulfilled. He did not thirst after the blood of the Indians; he never fell by their hands.

# CHAPTER NINE

# WYOMING WARPATH

On a hot day in August 1854 a covered-wagon train was making its way along the dusty trail toward old Fort Laramie. The mothers in the wagons with their babies, the boys and girls walking with their fathers beside the laboring oxen, were excited and a little frightened as they passed along the way some hundreds of Indians in tepee camps, who had come to receive blankets, cloth, utensils and other commodities in payment for the white man's use of the Big Medicine Road, as the Indians called the Oregon Trail.

The Indians did not molest the train. A band of their young bucks, however, galloped about it on ponies; and children and older red folk gazed curiously at the ox-drawn covered wagons as they passed by.

Some hundreds of yards behind the caravan came a lame cow driven by a boy trudging through the dust. Here was a chance for the reckless young Indians to have wild sport. As the last wagon disappeared beyond a hill, they let out a yell and circled around the lone boy. Scared out of his wits, he sped for his life toward the train, leaving the cow to her fate. The animal broke into a limping run, but not for long; for the bucks on their ponies staged a make-believe buffalo hunt, and shot a dozen arrows into her before she dropped on the trail. Then out came the squaws to get the meat for a tepee feast.

Meantime the boy had reached the caravan and told the captain what had happened. When the wagon train reached Fort Laramie, the captain reported the affair to the commander of the Army post, who assigned Lieutenant Grattan to take a detachment of soldiers and settle the matter with the offending Indians.

Grattan, new to the frontier, led his men to the tepee of The Bear, head of the tribe, who was awaiting gifts from the government. The chief came out with dignity to parley with the lieutenant, who demanded that the young bucks who had killed the cow be given up for trial.

Disgusted at such treatment for what he considered a mere killing in sport of one lame cow, the chief turned to stalk back to his lodge. Grattan ordered his men to fire, and The Bear fell dead. The burst of savage fury that followed had the lieutenant and his men fighting for their lives, and within a few moments it was all over for them. One soldier may have survived. The essential facts of the tragedy remained in the memory of the Indians, but they did little talking, except perhaps to the mountain men who had Indian wives.

Joe Wilde, who lived at that time in the barracks of Fort Laramie, was given the assignment of finding the graves of soldiers who had been killed along the trails; the bodies were to be exhumed and taken to the Fort McPherson military cemetery, or some other burial place for reinterment.

"We went first to the place where those killed in the Grattan fight had been buried in one large grave," Wilde told me. "Of course, only the bones remained, but it was easy to see the fury of the Indians in this battle. Skulls were split open with tomahawks or war clubs, and there were many arrowheads still in shoulder blades or other bones. We gathered up all we could find, and brought them to these barracks, where we did our best to assemble them on the long porch in front. It wasn't easy," the old scout concluded, "and I'm afraid some of the boys will have hard work getting themselves together on the morning of the resurrection."

I asked whether anyone in the fight ever told him just what had happened.

"No," he replied, "but I did hear from some old-timer that the Lieutenant acted unwisely and made the old chief angry. Then the shooting began. It was a wild fight. Only one soldier, I was told, lived to tell the tale. The story goes that an Indian girl, in love with him, threw a buffalo robe over him, though I don't know how she could, in that mad mix-up. Whatever happened, it was a bloody business. There was more killing of emigrants along western trails, and fighting between soldiers and Indians for a good many years."

Some of The Bear's tribe subsequently appeared threateningly before Fort Laramie, but were driven off with cannon shots from the "Barking Dogs," as the red men called the big guns. Tepees along the trail were struck, and the Indians disappeared for a time. War was on, however, and Indian fighting was to persist intermittently for more than twenty years.

In 1857, General William Harney made an attack on a Sioux village at Ash Hollow eastward on the old Oregon Trail, which he regarded as retaliation for what had come to be known as the Grattan massacre. Indian men, women and children were killed, deepening hate in the hearts of the red men along the Big Medicine Road.

Old Fort Laramie, on the trunkline of western trails, was a center for mountain men, Indians, emigrants, and soldiers. Founded as a fur-trading post in 1834, and purchased by the Government for an Army post in 1849, it saw stirring drama for half a century. In earlier years, Indians were constantly camped about the fort; trappers were always coming and going; covered wagon trains streamed by during the open months. It was a home station for the Pony Express and the first Overland Stage line, and finally for a main telegraph office on the transcontinental line.

During the Civil War, the garrison at the fort was held down to just a few companies of soldiers, but when Indian war flared up, volunteers from Kansas and Ohio were sent to reinforce the garrison and protect the mail and telegraph lines. Then as the Civil War was brought to a close, there was a waxing of hostilities on the old trails out West. More troops could be sent to quell the tribes, and fiercer fighting resulted. General Pat Connor, who had led a regiment from California and Nevada to Salt Lake, was made commander of the combined forces in the Rocky Mountain section. It was vital that the telegraph line be protected. Indians had become less credulous about the "talking wires" as a device of the Great Spirit, and were regarding them as a weapon and a spy, and were destroying them.

When Colonel William Collins, with his Ohio regiment, came to Fort Laramie, he was accompanied by Caspar Collins, his seventeen-year-old son. This high-spirited young man was happy to be in the wilds of the West, and his enthusiastic letters to his mother were filled with vivid descriptions and drawings of Indians, animals, Army life, and scenes along the trails. At eighteen, he enlisted as a soldier, and was assigned first to Sweetwater Station, near old Independence Rock in central Wyoming, though his father was sent with his troops into Colorado.

The Cheyennes, whose tribe had been brutally mistreated in the Chivington massacre, on Sand Creek in Colorado, were on the warpath. Sioux and other tribes, filled with avenging wrath, were also menacing the trails. General Connor called Caspar Collins to Fort Laramie to be commissioned a second lieutenant. Afterward, the young officer was to return at once to Sweetwater Station, but telegraphic reports of increasing danger to lone travelers along the trail, and advice from officers that he wait a day or two for others to accompany him, delayed his departure.

When he met Collins, Connor inquired why he was still at Fort Laramie. "Are you afraid?" the General asked.

Stung by the question, Caspar saluted and in a few moments was on his horse riding westward. No Indians molested him along the way to the Platte Bridge Fort, because the warriors had already staged an attack on that outpost, which was manned by Kansas volunteers, and then had withdrawn to the other side of the North Platte River to gather fighters for further attacks on the fort or anyone caught near it.

Just as the young lieutenant rode up on his tired horse, word came of a pending attack on Sergeant Amos Custard and the twenty-four men he had led out to repair the telegraph line that had been torn down by Indians some miles to the west. Captain Bretney, who had ridden with a detachment of soldiers from Independence Rock, found Sergeant Custard preparing to camp at Willow Springs, and advised him to ride on to the fort in the night, but his advice was not heeded.

Off to the west, the soldiers could see Custard and his men coming over a barren hill. Then Indians were sighted surrounding them. Major Anderson, in command at the Platte Bridge Fort, had been advised by Bretney to send a detachment of his Kansas volunteers in the night to escort the line-builders to the post, but the Major waited until morning. When Caspar Collins arrived, Anderson ordered him to lead the detachment to relieve Custard.

Captain Bretney told Caspar that it was not his duty to lead the Kansas soldiers. John Friend, the telegraph operator, also tried to dissuade the young lieutenant from plunging into the horde of savages, but Caspar asked only for a fresh horse. To him it was a call of duty; the question, "Are you afraid?" echoed in his mind. Across the Platte Bridge he led his men, and a few moments later they were in the thick of a battle with hundreds of Indians.

What happened during that fight on the hills no one could exactly know. Those at the fort could catch glimpses of the soldiers among the yelling, swirling Indians, and see some being shot down. Caspar was outnumbered ten to one, and ordered a retreat. As he was heading back to the fort, he saw one of his boys reaching for help. Reining his horse, he tried to get the fallen soldier up behind him, but an Indian waving a blanket frightened the horse, and it carried the Lieutenant to his death.

Two days later his mutilated body was found lying by what has ever since been called Casper Creek. Likewise with spelling changed, nearby Casper Mountains, and also Casper, Wyoming, were named in his honor.

Only two of Sergeant Custard's men escaped from the fight on the hill above the Platte Bridge Fort. Taking a desperate chance, three sped down a draw to swim the Platte River. One was killed; the others managed to save themselves.

The Big Medicine Road became a trail of danger, and for years alertness was required to get the covered wagon trains through. Even so, there was stealing and killing by watchful Indians.

My uncles Appolos and Parley Driggs, teamsters in one of the 1866 caravans, told me: "We had stopped for a noon rest among the lower Black Hills. The oxen were turned out among the willows to graze, while we had a buffalo flapjack lunch. Fortunately some of the teams had their yokes on for quicker hitching when we got ready to move the wagons.

"There were families of emigrants with a few lively boys in the train. Three of these youngsters decided to swim, ran down to the creek, stripped off their clothes and began splashing around. Suddenly they saw two Indians on ponies moving about among the cattle, brandishing sticks with rattlesnake rattles which they were shaking to excite the oxen. The boys jumped out of the water and ran naked to the wagon boss.

"He thought the boys were just scared, but when he stepped up on the wagon tongue, he saw half our cattle leaving, with a dozen redskins behind them. Some of us teamsters grabbed our guns, leaped on horses and chased the devils to the top of the hill. We stopped there, because maybe a hundred Indians were on the other side. They yelled and waved for us to come on, but we'd never have come back, so we had to take our medicine.

"We had been tricked. All we could do was go on with half enough oxen, and when we came to hard stretches of the road, double up the teams. It took longer, but we finally got through with our scalps on our heads."

That same year, 1866, the pioneer artist William H. Jackson was with a freight outfit bound for Virginia City, Montana. Because of Indian troubles, the long route via Utah had to be taken. As the party went up the North Platte, they found that Indians had been molesting the telegraph stations. For protection from these raiders, one operator had dug a secret tunnel from the station into the hillside.

"We camped," Jackson said, "just beyond Deer Creek, about fifty miles from the Platte Bridge Fort. All went well that night, but the next morning, as we were pulling out, we saw the telegraph station on fire, and a little way up the trail, we passed several Army wagons loaded with soldiers hurrying to the station. We wondered how they expected to catch Indians on ponies, for at best they could only put out the fire and get the station working again." The Big Medicine Road across Wyoming had a good many of such hit-and-run attacks.

The real Wyoming Warpath, however, was along the Bozeman Trail, which ran from Fort Sedgwick, near Julesburg, Colorado, northwestward to Bozeman and Virginia City, Montana. John Bozeman had lost his life on the road he opened on the trail; for it cut through one of the finest hunting grounds of the Indians, and the tribes fought desperately to keep the white men out of that region, called Absaroka ("Land of the Crows"). Buffalo, deer, elk, antelope, bear, wolves, coyotes and other game were abundant along the trail.

Red Cloud, war chief of the Sioux, and the leaders of other tribes made their last stand in this region, precious to them for food, clothing and trading goods. Recognizing their rights, Army officers and others tried to placate the Indians with annuities and promises. A council was held at Fort Laramie, at which was discussed the matter of permitting the Bozeman Trail to be used as a short cut to the newly opened gold fields around Virginia City. Red Cloud was ready to agree, providing no Army posts would be built along the trail.

Unfortunately for the peacemakers, Colonel Henry B. Carrington and his command arrived at Fort Laramie just at this time, with orders to proceed along the Bozeman Trail and establish Army posts for the protection of those using the road. When Carrington appeared at the council, Red Cloud leaped up and shouted that the Colonel was the man who had come to rob the Indians by making a road through their land. Then ordering his followers to strike their tepees, he openly declared war on the palefaces. Young Sioux were quick to follow the dynamic Red Cloud, and soon he had a formidable force ready to fight for the realm.

Fort Phil Kearny, in the heart of the Indian country, in north central Wyoming became known as "the hated fort on the Little Piney," and around it centered the bitter hatred of Red Cloud and his warriors, who were determined to wipe it out.

For two years this frontier post was in constant siege. Indians were not always in sight, but as Jim Bridger, then an Army scout, said: "Where you don't see no Injuns, they're certain to be the thickest." Every move of the workmen in enlarging the fort, which had been established in 1865, and all the activities of the soldiers, were under the eyes of Red Cloud's warriors, who never missed an opportunity to strike.

Men were not allowed to go for logs without an escort of soldiers, yet even with this protection they were often attacked. One of the woodsmen employed at the fort later told me: "We never knew whether we'd get back when we went out for logs or wood. The Injuns were laying for us all the time. One day when I was driving my mule team to the post on the hill, from half a mile away a bunch of redskins on ponies came whooping after us. My team was scared by their yells, and stung by my lashing. We were on the dead run. Arrows were flying round me and the other teamsters. I got to the fort first, but as bad luck had it, I was so excited I half missed the gate, and my wagon swung round and blocked the way. There was a pile-up until we got things straightened out so all the teams could go into the stockade. Of course the soldiers, seeing us coming, were out popping at the Injuns, but they kept out of gunshot."

Red Cloud's war parties kept things hot for the fort and its comparatively small garrison. Wood for the winter, and hay for the horses and mules had to be gathered under heavy guard. Cattle were in constant danger of being run into nearby canyons. There was never a moment, day or night, when the post was not on the alert.

When a wood train within sight of the fort was about to be attacked by Indians, Lieut. Colonel William Fetterman was sent with eighty-one men to protect the wood-haulers and bring the train through. Colonel Carrington, his superior, gave specific orders to Fetterman that if an attack was made no soldiers should cross the Lodge Pole Ridge, but should keep well within sight of the fort. However, when Fetterman and his men neared the wood train, the Indians attacked, and fell back of the Lodge Pole Ridge. Disregarding orders, Fetterman led his force after them.

Those at the fort, hearing heavy firing, knew that a battle was raging out of view, and Lieutenant Ten Eyck with fifty-four soldiers rushed to reinforce Fetterman. Before they reached the crest of the ridge, the firing had ceased, and they found every white man dead and mutilated. The exultant Indians had disappeared.

With such an appalling loss, there was grave danger that the rest of the garrison at Fort Phil Kearny would be slain, and the hated post consigned to flames. Colonel Carrington asked for a volunteer to go to Fort Laramie with a call for reinforcements. John Phillips—"Portugee" to his associates —volunteered.

"I'll go, Colonel, if I may ride your horse."

"Take him, of course," replied the commander. "God bless you."

It was 236 miles to Fort Laramie. Snow was three feet deep around Fort Phil Kearny, and the temperature thirty-five degrees below zero that December night; yet the blizzard which arose was welcomed as some protection from the Indian foes who formed a cordon around the fort. The civilian volunteer, protected with a fur cap, buffalo coat and fur-lined boots, rode into the storm after dark, with the prayers of all the mothers and the men at the fort for his safety and success.

How Portugee ever made the hazardous journey no one can tell with exactness, but Major Alson B. Ostrander, then a young Army clerk stationed at Fort Reno, a post on the way to Fort Laramie, gave me a glimpse of it.

"A few days before Christmas I was sleeping in a bunk of a room near the stockade. The Bozeman Trail ran just outside. Every night I could hear the sentry at the gate call the hours.

"Around midnight, I was wakened by a clear call of the guard. At the same time I heard hoofbeats and a shout. I could not distinguish the words, but as they were in English, I was relieved of an Indian scare.

"In a few seconds I heard a mounted horse passing along the trail at a smart trot, then through the gate and to the headquarters. There was some unusual commotion and talking. Then the hoofbeats again, as the horseman rode out into the night. I decided it must be the mail-carrier, and fell asleep.

"Next morning I heard at the adjutant's office that the midnight messenger was Portugee Phillips, who had brought the news of the Fetterman massacre and a plea for help to the hard-pressed garrison at Fort Phil Kearny."

Meanwhile Phillips was riding toward Fort Laramie. At the first telegraph station he reached, the operator made an attempt to get a message through, but the wires must have been down. Every mile brought Portugee and his steed closer to exhaustion.

On Christmas Eve they reached their goal. Lights were ablaze in the barracks, and at "Old Bedlam," the club for officers, a gay party was in progress with the ladies of the post in bright dresses and the officers in their best uniforms. Music of violins and laughter cheered the night. Suddenly the voice of a sentry broke into the gaiety.

The door was flung open, and into the room staggered Portugee Phillips. He gasped out the story of the tragedy at Fort Phil Kearny, then swayed and fell to the floor, overcome with exhaustion and cold. The messenger was carried to a comfortable bed, where he spent days convalescing, but Colonel Carrington's fine Kentucky-bred horse did not recover. Many years later a monument was dedicated to mark the end of that heroic ride.

Reinforcements for the beleaguered fort on the Little Piney were speedily on their way, and the garrison was saved. Red Cloud's vow had been made good so far as that spot was concerned. The great war chief of the Sioux did not succeed, however, in driving the white men out of the land of the Absaroka. No further attacks were made directly on the post, but there were to be bitter battles before the Indian fighting was over, many of them along the Wyoming Warpath.

In the Wagon Box Fight, the score was somewhat evened with Red Cloud and his warriors. Here breech-loading Springfield rifles enabled the soldiers within the fortification they had quickly made of wagon boxes to hold off the Indians and inflict heavy losses. The usual method of the red men was to dash up within range of the white men, risking their first shots; then while the old muzzle-loading guns were being reloaded, the warriors would close in for the kill. This time, however, the loading was done in a flash; and when the second charge of the Indians came, the soldiers were ready for it. Red Cloud couldn't understand this. After losing heavily of his best fighters, he held back to figure out the magic of the palefaces. The Wagon Box Fight was "bad medicine" for the red men.

At Fort Phil Kearny, the Major Ostrander who had heard Portugee Phillips dash into Fort Reno, had close views of Army life on the frontier. Once a band of Crow Indians, then at peace with the whites, appeared on Lodge Pole Ridge, and told a messenger sent to parley with them that they had come to do some swapping at the post. Jim Bridger advised that they be permitted to carry on the trading outside the fort.

Eager to possess a buffalo robe or two and some beaver skins, young Ostrander induced Bridger to do the swapping for him. The mountain man and Army scout agreed. "Buy some plugs of tobacco from the sutler's store," he told Ostrander, "and I'll see what I can do for you. But don't let any of the bucks see you put them in my pocket."

"When I returned to the tepee village," Ostrander said, "I found Bridger holding up a large fine robe, and under cover of it, I managed to slip three plugs of tobacco into each of his side pockets. He palavered for a few minutes with the buck who owned the robe, then made the swap while I was looking over other robes. Finding a smaller one, with long silky hair, evidently from a calf, I pointed to it. Jim was not long in getting the robe for me.

" 'Hold out your arms,' he said, 'and hide these away quick.' I took the two robes he had folded, and ran with them to the bunkhouse. He had made a good swap for me."

I asked Ostrander what Bridger looked like.

"When I first saw him," he said, "he was tilted back in a chair, with one arm on the counter of the sutler's store. His once light-colored hat, then dingy and smoky, was pulled down till it hid part of his face, which was tanned by the Wyoming winds, and was somewhat wrinkled. He wore a stubby beard, and his square-set jaw and keen eyes showed courage and intelligence.

"Nearly everyone who came in would say, 'Hello, Jim.' His response was generally, 'Howdy,' or merely a nod of acknowledgment."

Ostrander, promoted from Army clerk to second lieutenant, was ordered to report to the commander at Camp Stevenson, near Julesburg. A detachment of twenty men and civilians were to go under Major Van Voast to Fort Laramie in a few days, and Lieutenant Ostrander was told to be ready for this trip back along the Bozeman Trail, which still was a warpath. "As I was leaving Fort Phil Kearny," said Ostrander, "Jim Bridger, bidding me good-by, drew from his pocket a beaded buckskin pouch filled with tobacco. He handed it to me saying, 'Here, boy, is something for you to smoke on the way down.'"

Ostrander rode with Jack and Sam, two scouts at the head of the troops. It was not long before they saw signs that Indians were on the trail, and at the crossing of Clear Creek, fresh pony tracks showed that redskins were not far away. Jack judged there were about forty in the band.

When the commander received this report from the scouts, he ordered the wagons to close up, and the escort divided to ride alongside of them. It was timely preparation, for when the command reached the open prairie, the redskins appeared. Riding just out of rifle range, they began to dash back and forth parallel to the column of soldiers; but they evidently decided it was not wise to attack and finally disappeared over a ridge to the east.

About fifteen miles from Fort Reno, suddenly from around a hill about three-quarters of a mile ahead of the company, a bunch of Indians came on the dead run, yelling like fiends. Their object was to confuse and stampede the outfit.

Without a word, the ambulance driver stopped and sprang to the head of his mules. The head wagon swung round and came back for about a hundred feet; then turning, crossed the trail and stopped. Second and third wagons double-quicked to the right and the left in position. The fourth swung around quickly to complete the square. Meanwhile, twenty cavalry men had flung a line across the trail facing the Indians. Passengers jumped from the wagons into place with them, ready for action.

This corralling was all done in about two minutes, so that by the time the Indians reached a point where a quick dash would have brought them right among the soldiers, the outfit was ready to give them a warm welcome. A few scattering shots made the dirt fly at the feet of the Indians' ponies. The redskins swerved, but kept on the dead run in single file, circling just out of rifle range.

The command had not traveled very far before they came to the place where Van Volzah, a mail-carrier for the Army posts, had been killed a short time before by the Indians. An acre or more was still strewn with mail. Wind had blown letters and papers about, and snow or rain had loosened those that were sealed. As many of the letters as could be found were gathered and placed in a gunnysack to be taken on to Fort Laramie for delivery.

As no Indians appeared farther down the trail, the soldiers and civilians began to relax. Suddenly one night, shots were fired into camp. Confusion followed. Someone poked the embers of a fire.

"Sam called the one who did it every mean epithet in the dictionary," said Ostrander, "and he used the same words on me when I tried to get up. Grabbing me by the collar, he brought me down with my face in the dirt, and held me there while he gave me advice about making a target of myself for lurking Injuns. My nose was sore for days, but I deserved the lesson."

"When I was scouting for the Army, right after the Civil War," one frontiersman told me "the plains and the mountains were jest alive with redskins itchin' to lift white scalps. Never knew whether we'd come back with our hair."

Through the 1860's and 1870's there was a general Indian uprising, and fighting continued over much of the West for about twenty years: Kiowas and Comanches on the southern plains; Apaches in the mountains of New Mexico and Arizona; Cheyennes and Sioux in the Wyoming, Montana, Nebraska and Dakota regions; Nez Percés in Oregon and Washington; Modocs among the Oregon lava beds; Utes in Colorado and Utah. Even after the Army of the West was greatly reinforced, it took years to bring the hostile red men to terms. Thousands of them died fighting for their homelands, and thousands of white civilians and soldiers fell before the Great Plains and the valleys of the Rocky Mountains were made peaceful.

For the tribes, though greatly outnumbered, held their own. They knew the canyons, streams, valleys, and deserts of the West intimately, and they seized every opportunity to strike, then get back into the fast-nesses. Always they were preparing for larger victories. Seasoned generals, such as Crook, Terry, and Gibbon, and their soldiers, fought hard; but the Indians defended their homelands desperately.

Their great day came on June 25, 1876, about ten years after Fetterman and his force were wiped out behind Lodge Pole Ridge, near Fort Phil Kearny.

General George A. Custer, who had been relieved of his command because of his criticism of the Indian agencies and other acts that smacked of insubordination, was ordered by President Grant at General Phil Sheridan's demand, to return to his Seventh Cavalry at Fort Abraham Lincoln, near Bismarck, North Dakota.

That cavalry had been built up with pride. Each company in the regiment had its own color of horses; one was dapple gray, another black, another bay, another sorrel, another roan, or of some other color. Stepping to military music, the steeds with their blue-clad riders, made a stirring picture on the western trails. Custer himself added animation and color, with his carefully curled golden locks and his broad-brimmed hat. The Indians called him "Long Hair." He had incited their anger in wiping out Black Kettle's village on the Washita in Kansas. Determined to a point of recklessness to win a victory that would add luster to his Army career, he led his famed Seventh Cavalry from Fort Abraham Lincoln over the Dakota Hills into what was to be his last battle.

"I am going to clear my name," he told the telegraph operator at Fargo, North Dakota, where he had detrained to spend the night en route to the fort, "or leave my bones on the prairie." His army career had become tarnished; he desperately needed new laurels.

Custer led his command into an Indian hornet's nest. Major Reno, one of his officers, who was leading part of the cavalrymen, had struck the Indians first, and been driven back with serious loss; then had had to shoot down some of his mules to make a barricade to hold back the maddened warriors. Captain Benteen, with his detachment, took a roundabout way to attack from another point, and was so delayed that he did not get into the battle.

Custer, with the main body of the cavalrymen, rode to the top of the hill overlooking the Little Big Horn River. There was the great Indian encampment stretched for miles along the stream. John Martini, trumpeter, last white man to see "Long Hair" alive, told Captain Benteen that the General exclaimed: "Custer's luck! We've got them this time!"

Dismounting his men, he sent the horses behind the hill, and deployed the soldiers along its top to meet the onslaught of the Indians with rifle fire.

Led by Crazy Horse of the Sioux, a masterful Indian chief, and by Chief Two Moons and Chief Gall of the Cheyennes, the warriors swarmed up the hills and ravines for the fight. Their first winning stroke was made by stampeding the horses of the cavalrymen. Then they closed in for the kill.

Many of the yelling, shooting Indians who swirled around were dropped from their ponies, but there seemed no end of them. Custer's men gradually were killed until only a few were left on the hill for the last stand.

Colonel George W. Stokes, then in the Black Hills, told me: "We had the shocking news of the battle even before it reached the telegraph office nearest the scene of the fight. A relay of Indian runners had passed the story on to the Spotted Tail Indian Agency via the Black Hills. One of the runners told it to the Indian wife of a miner, who passed it along."

All that night there were wild expressions of victory through the Indian encampment along the Little Big Horn. Next day the attack was renewed on Major Reno and his men, but behind their barricade, they managed to hold back the Indians. Then the great encampment disappeared in the darkness.

Dust along the trail next day brought fear that the red men were coming back, but it turned out to be caused by the arrival of General Gibbon and General Terry and their men. The disappearance of the Indians was explained, but where was Custer?

Scouts riding over the battle ground soon found the startling answer.

Bodies of all the men Custer had led were scattered over the hillside, most of them mutilated. Custer, his brother Tom, Captain Keough, Captain Yates and other officers were among the victims.

"It was not a massacre," one of the women of the Sioux tribe told me. "It was a fair fight, and we won."

No human beings, except possibly Curley, a Crow scout with Custer, survived the fight waged by Custer's immediate command. One of the animals came through alive, however—Comanche, the horse of Captain Miles W. Keough, which was found wounded and wandering over the scene. Taken to Lawrence, Kansas, Comanche was cared for until he died. Then, stuffed and mounted, he was placed in a museum of the University of Kansas.

From an old sergeant at Fort Abraham Lincoln I learned of Rusty, a dog who also survived. Some days after the fight at Little Big Horn, Rusty returned limping to the fort on the Missouri, where he was given the best of care until he died. "It was part of my duty," the sergeant said, "to feed the dog, and keep him comfortable. We didn't mind this at first, but he got mangy and smelly, and I was tempted at times to kill him before he died. It would have been a mercy to the poor old fellow, but we couldn't do it, seeing what he'd been through."

After the disaster on the Little Big Horn, more soldiers were ordered to subdue the warring tribes. Generals Sheridan, Crook, Terry, Gibbon, Howard and Miles led armies. In addition destruction of the buffalo, winter campaigns, and other relentless measures, brought the Indian leaders to terms of peace. The plains and valleys were relieved of the strain of conflict. The tribes were settled on reservations, and efforts were made to provide for their needs.

# CHAPTER TEN

# MAIL AND MESSAGES
# FOR THE FRONTIER

Brave young men on their lean mounts were riding hard along the trail that linked East and West—from St. Joseph on the Big Muddy; then up through the Rockies, fighting blizzards in high mountain passes where earlier men had died; on across the heat and dust of the flatlands of Utah settled by the Mormons; through Nevada and on into the Sierras, clattering into canyons where unfriendly Indians might lurk, following the trails blazed by pioneer families seeking new land, missionaries bringing the word of God, and adventurers lured by gold; and down at last to Sacramento and San Francisco. These were the men of the Pony Express, who traveled fast and traveled light—but who carried a heavy responsibility in the leather pouches of mail that were slung across their saddles.

During the scant two years that the Pony Express flourished, it was one of the most dramatic institutions of the old West. "One object we were momentarily expecting," wrote Mark Twain about his stage trip west in 1861. "In a little while all interest was taken up in stretching our necks and watching for the pony rider—the fleet messenger who sped across the continent from St. Joe to Sacramento, carrying letters nineteen hundred miles in eight days."

Somehow or other all that passed us, [Mark Twain continued in *Roughing It*] and all that we met, managed to streak by in the night. We heard only a whiz and a hail, and the swift phantom of the desert was gone before we could get our heads out of the window.

But now we were expecting one along every moment and we would see him in broad daylight. Presently the driver exclaims "Here he comes!" and every neck is stretched further, and every eye strained wider. Away across the dead level of the prairie a black speck appears against the sky, and we can see that it moves.

In a second or two it becomes a horse and rider, rising and falling, rising and falling, sweeping towards us nearer and nearer, and coming plainer, till soon the flutter of hoofs comes faintly to the ear. In another instant a whoop and hurrah from the upper deck of our coach, a wave of the rider's hand, but no reply, and man and horse burst past our excited faces, and go winging away like the belated fragments of a storm.

Of all the methods used to carry the mail in the old days of the West —and several others were tried—the Pony Express was probably the most efficient, and certainly the most colorful. Letters were delivered by coach and wagon, on mule and even camel back, and sometimes in extremities, carried through deep snow and bitter cold over rough trails on the backs of men. But the pony riders, often dressed in red shirts, blue trousers, decorated boots and buckskin jackets, got the mail through dependably and regularly.

An old forty-niner told me, when I was a boy, of the heartache and loneliness even the roughest of the miners suffered far from home, friends, family and loved ones. The gold-seekers were not all so successful as is sometimes thought, nor was the precious yellow metal come by easily. Sometimes a whole ton of sand and gravel would have to be shoveled and washed by hand before a single nugget was extracted. Much of the gold dust found went for meat, or for flour to keep the sour dough jar filled for flapjacks, and more passed into the hands of the bartenders or into the pockets of gamblers. But the miners minded the toil and the disappointing rewards less than they did the homesickness.

For the men at the diggings there was then no regular mail. Friends going West by ox-team brought letters, but it would be months before they got through, and sometimes they didn't make it. Other mail went by ship—down to the Isthmus of Panama and across it by mule back, then up the coast. Once in a while a bag of letters got to a mining camp, where the storekeeper would dump them into a box and the miners would finger through the heap, taking what belonged to them and perhaps some that was addressed to boys they knew. In 1851 it was reported that more than a ton of undelivered mail was scattered around the camps in the Sierras.

Nearly half a million Americans—mostly young men—had dared the hardships and dangers of overland travel, or a rough voyage in crowded ships from the Atlantic seaboard to San Francisco Bay, to reach the gold fields, where wealth, they hoped, would soon be theirs. Many died on the way from hardship or illness and never reached the Eldorado on the American River; those who did had to suffer from not only the scramble for gold but from the loneliness that came with thoughts of the folks they left behind. *Bring us letters from home* was their constant plea.

In 1850, when California was made a state, and Utah a territory, there was some action by Congress to meet the demand for more efficient mail service to bring the country into closer communication. An overland mail along the shortest route from the Missouri River to California was established, and in May, 1851, a train of pack mules left Sacramento for the first trial of what the mining camp boys called "the jackass mail." Major George Chorpenning, Jr., an Indian fighter, was in charge, who, with Captain Absalom Woodward, had won a contract to carry the mail from Sacramento via Carson Valley to Salt Lake City. It was to run monthly each way for $14,000 annually—small pay for the hard work and the dangers of getting back and forth across the defiant desert.

Long stretches of sagebrush and alkali flats lay between the infrequent oases. Canyons inviting ambush by Indians were the only passes through mountain ranges. Yet Chorpenning took his men and mules over the high Sierras and into the desert with determination to get the mail through, and they did. June, July, August, September and October saw them make the journey safely.

November had a different story to tell.

At Willow Springs, about 150 miles west of Salt Lake City, Captain Woodward, who was leading the eastbound mule train, drew up his mount and signaled to his four muleteers to halt. Through the dust of the trail ahead came the men driving the mules of the westbound mail.

The second caravan came to a halt. Captain Woodward rode over to talk to its leader. "There may be trouble ahead," he warned. "We sighted a large band of Indians yesterday."

The two trains whipped up their mules and parted.

There was trouble ahead, but not for the westbound train, which reached Sacramento safely. Captain Woodward and his men were never seen again by their friends. The following spring a leader of a train from the East reported that they had been murdered by Indians, who made off with their animals and supplies.

Before this news reached California, in February, 1852, another party of mail-carriers, headed by Edson Cody, had started for Salt Lake City. Fifty-three days they had taken for the trip, and every one of the ten horses and the ten mules in the caravan froze to death in the bitter weather. Strapping the bags of mail to their backs the men walked for two hundred miles, feeding on mule meat until it gave out; then for the last six days of the terrible journey they trudged through the snow without food. But they delivered all the mail.

Major Chorpenning in Salt Lake City found no one willing to face the rigors of the next trip westward, which had to be made to fulfill the terms of his contract. When no one would agree to take the risk with him, the Major set out alone. How he managed to dodge the murderous To-soinitches, a group of the Paiutes, who killed Captain Woodward and his men, no one knows; he must have traveled the lonely trail by night. At any rate, Chorpenning made good.

The Major negotiated a second contract with the government in 1854, but this time he chose a safer trail. The new route detoured the short cut from Salt Lake City to Sacramento and went southward through the chain of Utah settlements over the old Spanish trail, to Los Angeles. Thence the mail was taken by boat through the Golden Gate and across San Francisco Bay to Sacramento. Pack mules carried it inland to the deep snows of the high Sierras, where a sturdy Scandinavian called "Snow-shoe Thompson" took it over the crest and down the eastern slope to Genoa and Carson City.

Regular weekly mail was taken from Los Angeles to Salt Lake City on mules, with a lone muleteer in charge. On one of his northward trips in 1856, this carrier welcomed an eighteen-year-old pioneer lad as a companion on his journey. The young man was Ben Driggs, my father.

Mail-carrying over the Independence-to-Salt-Lake route was hazardous too—with the threat of Indians in the plains and snows in the Rockies. Colonel Samuel H. Woodson, of Independence, Missouri, contracted in 1850 to put through a monthly mail over the route at an annual compensation of $19,500, for four years. Mountain storms that blocked his way in winter, kept Salt Lake City without mail for six months at a time, and caused the death of one of his men in the bitter cold of South Pass, finally forcing Woodson to give up the struggle.

Another man, W. M. F. McGraw, attempted, in 1857, to get the mail from Independence over the Oregon Trail into Utah. His men took coaches as far as Devil's Gate in present central Wyoming, where, because of heavy snow, they transferred the mail bags to pack mules and struggled on. Baffled by a blizzard in the South Pass, they had to turn back, go a hundred miles down the trail and winter on the North Platte River; and it was not until the next March that the McGraw mail reached Salt Lake.

Jefferson Davis, when secretary of war in the Cabinet of President Franklin Pierce, recommended that camels be used as carriers on the deserts. After the failure of two earlier bills, Congress made an appropriation of $30,000, with which seventy-five Arabian camels were bought and turned over to the Army, with Lieutenant Edward F. Beale in charge of the project in 1857.

Enthusiasts for the plan hoped that the herd would soon increase and provide a means of solving problems of transportation in the West. It was asserted that the camel was swifter than the horse, stronger than the mule, and could go long stretches without need of refilling his "water pouch." Alas for the hopes!

The camel caravan panicked horses and mules into running away. Worse, still, the camels' feet became sore. These natives of eastern deserts that could glide over the sands of the Sahara without limping had to be shoed with leather boots in order to traverse our rocky wastelands. In that clumsy gear they were easily outrun by horses and mules. Camelteers brought from Arabia were baffled, and managed only to get the caravan out to Bakersfield, California, where the herd was turned onto a ranch to await an official decision.

Most of the camels were finally sold to managers of circuses. The rest wandered away from the ranch to lead lonely lives in the wide open spaces of the Southwest. Stories of how they scared both Indians and white folk cropped up for time; then eventually all the beasts disappeared.

Efforts to establish an overland mail line went on, as Californians in Congress kept up the fight, led by their Senator W. M. Gwin, who had been born in Tennessee, looked like Andrew Jackson, and had something of the vigor of "Old Hickory." As a result, a bill was put through, late in 1857, providing $600,000 for a semi-weekly mail from St. Louis to San Francisco, that was to be carried in coaches which might also carry passengers.

The direct central route along the Oregon and Mormon trails and straight across the "Great American Desert" offered the shortest route for the mail service. Postmaster General Aaron V. Brown opposed it, however, because of the snow which made the trail impassable from four to six months in the year, and southern senators backed the postmaster general in his own plan to run the service over a trail through the Southwest. Opponents called it the "Oxbow Route"—a fitting title, for it swung down from St. Louis to Fort Smith, Arkansas; then across what was Indian Territory (now Oklahoma) to El Paso, Texas; over southern New

Mexico to Yuma, in present Arizona; thence to Los Angeles, and northward to San Francisco. It was fully 1,000 miles longer than the central route, which Californians and Utahans hoped would be followed, but it was finally approved by Congress.

John Butterfield, who had won his spurs managing a stage line along the Old Mohawk Trail, across his native New York, was given the contract for the service along the "Oxbow Route," later to be called the Butterfield Trail, as John put the coaches through, carrying mail and such passengers as dared the risk.

"The stations in Arizona," wrote the special post-office agent who took the initial trip, "are at the mercy of the Apache, and the Comanche may, at his pleasure, bar the passage of stages in Texas." Only four military posts were along the more than three-thousand-mile route. Butterfield added stage stations and equipped the line with coaches and lithe mules (*cuddies,* as they were called). Station-keepers who could fight Indians, and tough drivers who could handle the lines as well as guns, were set to rolling and bumping along the rocky trail. It took twenty-three days to make the first trip from Missouri to San Francisco. The one eastward—at about the same schedule—ended at St. Louis on October 9, 1858, with John Butterfield driving the coach.

President Buchanan, in response to a telegram announcing its arrival, sent a message to Butterfield, congratulating him, and saying:

> It is a glorious triumph for the Union. Settlements will soon follow the course of the road, and the East and the West will be bound together by a chain of living Americans, which never can be broken.

This was enthusiastic prophecy, though the part as to settlements was still largely to be fulfilled. Long stretches of the old Butterfield Trail are today as they were in 1858, just open desert country. Of course, paved roads with occasional service stations and a railroad paralleling the faded trail bring modern passengers whizzing along in a few minutes over the route where the little mules with coaches rolling behind them took hours. Within about two years after Butterfield drove the first eastbound stage into frontier St. Louis, his mail-carrying venture over the "Oxbow

Route" was stopped by the Civil War. It was not long, however, before he had transferred his equipment to another route—the Smoky Hill Trail which was opened from Leavenworth, Kansas, to Denver, Colorado.

Discovery of gold along Cherry Creek, where Denver sprang up, had touched off the "Pikes Peak or bust" rush for these new diggings in 1858 and 1859. Another stage line, called the Leavenworth and Pikes Peak Express, had been started by William H. Russell and John S. Jones. Passenger service received the emphasis in this new venture. Each coach could carry nine persons inside, and more—if they were willing to cling to the rails around the top, or take a seat beside the driver. Mail bags filled the "boot," or great leather receptacle beneath the driver's seat. They could be lashed on top too, or piled in unoccupied seats inside. The Pikes Peak Express, however, proved to be a losing game, and it was eventually expanded into the Overland Stage operated by William H. Russell, Alexander Majors and W. B. Waddell.

This great organization had its ox-team trains loaded with freight operating over the Santa Fe, the Oregon and other trails. Majors, with Waddell assisting him, directed the field activities of the firm, while Russell spent most of his time in Washington, getting contracts. While there he joined forces with Senator Gwin to work for a direct and speedy mail service from the Missouri to the Pacific Coast. Ox-teams were slow. Ships via Cape Horn and the Isthmus of Panama had not met the demand. Coaches over the tedious and uncertain "Oxbow Route" were not the answer.

But there was an answer, and like many of the solutions of other perplexing problems it came out of the homely principle that what man has done, man can do. Xerxes, the Persian emperor, had kept in touch with his bases during his invasion of Greece, by means of a chain of riders. Genghis Khan linked the parts of his vast empire together through a relay of messengers mounted on swift horses. And, closer to home, there was the 850-mile ride of the French-Canadian François Xavier Aubry from Santa Fe, New Mexico, to Independence, Missouri, accomplished so recently as 1853 in five and a half days. Why not link the East with the Far West in the same way?

One big objection, of course, was the Indians. War had broken out between them and the white men, and the natives had begun seriously to resent the incursions of the whites into their country, killing the animals on which they depended for food, and casually settling on their choicest homelands. Recently the gold-diggers had been even less considerate; their animals ate the Indians' grass, and the men sometimes shot a redskin or two just for fun. Then, too, there were the snow packed mountains and uplands in winter, and the parching deserts in summer, to contend with.

The solution was to establish stations all along the line, with keepers to take care of the fresh ponies, and with plenty of guns to hold off the redskins. It began to look like a winning idea. Gwin was all for it, and Russell, in enthusiasm, is reported to have said, "I'll bet $10,000 I can put the mail through in ten days." Whether he made such a wager or not, he must have offered the services of his freighting company. Although Majors feared it would not succeed financially, both he and Waddell agreed to the plan. Their company went bankrupt carrying through the patriotic enterprise, but the three will always be remembered in the history of their country as the founders of the Pony Express.

It took nearly a hundred American youths to do the riding. They had to be between fifteen and twenty-two years old, wiry and tough. A hundred and twenty-five pounds was the weight limit. It was a hard job, jumping on a horse and pounding away full tilt for ten miles; leaping on another and pounding the same distance again; then more jolting on still another mount, and another and another. Sometimes the boys thought the blood in their heads would come bursting through their skulls, and many of them had to lay off a while between runs until they got hardened to the job. They took a pledge that they would neither drink, nor swear, nor fight amongst themselves, and that they would be faithful in their duties—meaning they would get the mail through. Each was given a small, leather-bound Bible.

Among the first of the riders to be engaged were John Frey, who had been a jockey; William Richardson, who had been a sailor; Gus and Charley Cliff, Jack Keetley, Don Rising, George Towne, Alex Carlisle and Henry Wallace. But probably the most picturesque of all was Bill Cody, who at the age of fifteen was first given a short run of only forty-five miles west from Julesburg, Colorado. Later he was assigned to the run from Red Buttes to Three Crossings, on the Sweetwater River, which ran through hostile Indian country. Many times he nearly lost his life to the enemy Sioux, but through daring, endurance and resourcefulness he survived to become world-famous later as "Buffalo Bill."

Three hundred men, generally older than the riders, were hired to tend the stations along the trail, and keep them stocked with supplies. Some four hundred horses, likewise strong and wiry, were provided to make the runs. Stations were planted ten to fifteen miles apart, at ranches and military posts, or built of logs or stone at oases on the desert. By late March of 1860, the setup was in readiness for the first run east and west.

On April 3, 1860, the Pony Express was touched off at St. Joseph, Missouri. After speeches by Mayor Jeff Thompson and Alexander Majors, and the firing of a homemade cannon, the pony rider, probably Johnny Frey, leaped on his horse, galloped down to the wharves where a steamboat, the *Denver*, ferried him over the Big Muddy, and dashed away across the northeast corner of Kansas. In San Francisco there was another celebration. A brass band accompanied a make-believe rider and a decorated pony (on which an enthusiastic lady had put her flowered bonnet) to a waiting boat. The mail was taken over the bay and up the river to Sacramento, where about midnight the rider took off into the rainy night.

Ten days passed with only one brief report of progress—printed in the *Deseret News*, Utah's pioneer paper. The two riders east and west had passed through Salt Lake City on schedule. About five days later Sacramento and St. Joseph staged excited welcomes to the boys who had brought the mail through, and soon a ringing shout went up all over the nation.

For sixteen months longer the riders and their ponies put the letters and messages through on schedule. Once they even cut down the time for the 1960-mile run from ten days to seven days and seventeen hours, when they carried Lincoln's first Inaugural Message from St. Joseph to Sacramento.

PLATE THIRTY-TWO

Devil's Gate, near Independence Rock, in Wyoming, described in many of the journals of the pioneers.

PLATE THIRTY-THREE

A herd of bison incited by Indian hunters to stampede around a covered wagon train.

PLATE THIRTY-FOUR

Texas longhorns being driven northward over the Chisholm Trail to supply
industrial centers with beef and to stock northern ranches.

PLATE THIRTY-FIVE

Virginia Dale, in Colorado, one of the most famous stations of the Overland Stage.

The boys who rode the ponies, like the pioneers themselves, had little notion of their own heroism. Experiences that took sheer grit were all in the day's work to them. Most of them were full of fun and deviltry, and they played many a trick of a rough and tumble sort on one another. Breaking in a tenderfoot was the principal diversion. The new hand was likely to find his bunk full of cactus, his coffee well salted, his pants missing. Or his horse would be sent bucking by a burr hidden in the *mochila*.

A *mochila* was a leather covering for the saddle tree, which was left loose so that it could quickly be lifted off and thrown on the saddle of a waiting fresh horse. It had two leather pockets on each side for letters, fastened with small padlocks. One of these was the "way pocket," for which the station keeper had the key so that the mail for his depot could be removed and fresh mail inserted; the others were for "through mail." The saddles themselves, which were scarcely more than skeleton, were not easy riding, and as the riders got further west, the horses were often hardly more trained than wild broncos.

But the boys remained boys at heart even many years after their last trip, and when I found them at their various homes all the way from St. Joseph to Oakland, California, their youth vibrated as they recalled their days on the Pony Express.

Billy Fisher, crippled with arthritis, sat with me by the kitchen stove of his Oxford, Idaho, home, and told me of having got lost in a blizzard.

"Just couldn't see where I was going," he said, "so I got off my horse and sat under a cedar tree to think things over. Must have dozed off, which ain't so safe in a snowstorm. Suddenly something jumped on my legs. I woke in time to see a jack rabbit bouncing off into the sagebrush. Always felt it saved me from freezing there. Anyway, I got on to my pony, and turned it over to him. Managed to reach the home base about four o'clock in the morning."

At St. Joseph, Missouri, I found Charley Cliff, last of the Pony Express riders in that town, playing cards at the fire station. He took me to see the Pikes Peak Stables where the Pony Express horses were kept, the place where they picked up the mail bags, the spot on the Missouri where rider and horse boarded the ferry. After his Pony Express days, when he was trading on the trail in 1864, his train was attacked by Sioux, and Charley was shot in the back with an arrow. Fortunately it did not penetrate deeply, but he had to jolt along in the wagon back home.

"What did you do to cure the wound?"

"Had the boys pour some turpentine in it. The treatment was a little rough, like the old days."

Bill Streeper told me that though he wasn't a regular Pony Express rider, he hauled the heavy "mule mail" over the same route. This service was slower and less expensive and carried most of the personal mail, accommodating people who couldn't afford to pay the rate of $5.00 for one half-ounce that the Pony Express charged its customers, who were chiefly business men.

Bill told me that sometimes he had to pinch-hit on the Pony Express if one of the boys got sick. Once he said that he took the mule mail and the pony mail through together, because of a pony rider's encounter with some of the potent raw whiskey that was sold by saloons in outpost areas. Bill explained that occasionally a rider or a station-keeper didn't live up to his pledge to stay away from liquor.

Coming through Nevada, Bill told me, he had passed the saloon and seen the pony rider drinking. "I'll ketch up with your—ole—mules 'fore you get—a mile," the rider called. As Bill was jogging along the trail, he heard the Pony Express rider whooping behind him and a minute later he shot past. About a half-hour later, as they were passing through a canyon, his mount's ears began to prick up. Bill was worried because there were a lot of rocks and trees along the trail, and he was afraid of an Indian ambush. Riding ahead cautiously, at a bend in the path he suddenly came upon the pony rider stretched out full length with his horse standing beside him. At first Bill thought he had been shot by Indians, but he hadn't been. "He was dead drunk," Bill said.

Bill couldn't leave the man there, but he wasn't able to arouse him, though he shook him, pinched him, shot off his revolver a couple of times, and even kicked him. Finally he lassoed the unconscious man and with great difficulty hoisted him across the back of his pony, with his head hanging on one side of the saddle and his feet on the other. Then he jumped on his mule Muggins and, leading the horse with the pack-mules following, went jogging down the trail.

Before they reached the next station, the Pony Express rider revived and pleaded with Bill to untie him. But Bill only said, "No, you darned cuss, I've had trouble enough with you for one day; you're goin' into the station just as you are." And he jolted him harder than ever. The man was severely reprimanded when he got to the station so far behind schedule. "That was the last time I ever saw him on the Pony Express," Bill said.

When the mule mail was discontinued, Bill took up freighting along the trail from the Missouri to Salt Lake. By that time he had six fine mules and two wagons.

One day he was clipping off the miles to the West at good speed with his double load of freight when two hikers on the way to California asked for a lift. Bill was in a hurry because his sweetheart Mary was waiting for him, and he expected that what he earned on that trip would make it possible for them to build a home and get married. However, the two boys promised to help, so he took them on.

Up in the Sioux country they stopped for noon, and Bill asked the boys to take the mules to the Platte River to drink and graze, telling them to keep sharp watch. But the weather was hot and the boys yielded to the temptation to take a swim. The first thing Streeper knew they were dashing back naked, and he looked up to see the mules with Indians behind them running off into the hills. He grabbed his revolver and shot at the redskins, but they were too far away.

It was a serious loss. How could he get his loaded wagons into the Salt Lake Valley? How could he tell Mary about their ruined plans?

The eastbound stage drove up, and one of the passengers recognized Bill, who had once befriended him. When he heard the story, he had Streeper go back East with him, leaving the two boys to guard the wagons. A week or so later Bill was back with several yoke of oxen his friend had helped him get. Though greatly delayed, he finally reached Salt Lake City and delivered his freight. Then he went to Mary and told her of his loss.

"I'm afraid it means we can't get married this year."

Mary put her hand in his and shyly looked up into his eyes. "Why, Bill," she said, "I didn't want to marry your mules."

The Pony Express, though certainly not a financial success, performed an important role in the making of the West. First it took the terror out of the Great American Desert. It proved that mail could be carried across that arid region, and over blizzard-swept Rockies and Sierras summer and winter. Indian tribes, though troublesome at times, did not seriously hamper the riders and station-keepers who put the pony and mule mail through. Important messages were sped across the continent with the help of this first fast mail. It opened the way too for the first transcontinental telegraph.

October 24, 1861, marked the close of its dramatic service. On this day, the wires from the East and the West were linked at the old telegraph station on Main Street in Salt Lake City. A few moments afterward this message was flashed over them:

To ABRAHAM LINCOLN, PRESIDENT OF THE UNITED STATES:

In the temporary absence of the Governor of the State, I am requested to send you the first message which will be transmitted over the wires of the telegraph line which connects the Pacific with the Atlantic states. The people of California desire to congratulate you upon the completion of the great work. They believe that it will be the means of strengthening the attachment which binds both the East and the West to the Union—and they desire in this—the first message across the continent—to express their loyalty to the Union and their determination to stand by its government on this its day of trial. They regard that government with affection and will adhere to it under all fortunes.

STEPHEN J. FIELD,
CHIEF JUSTICE OF CALIFORNIA.

The building of the last 1900-mile link of the first transcontinental telegraph had begun back in 1844, when Samuel F. B. Morse flashed his historic first message, "What hath God wrought!" from Washington, D. C., to nearby Baltimore. During the next decade larger cities over the

East were connected with telegraph lines. By 1861 one had been stretched to old Fort Kearny in central Nebraska. California too had built its telegraph lines with one reaching eastward as far as Carson City, Nevada.

How to build the line over the plains, the Rockies, the Great Basin, was the challenging problem. Hiram Sibley, president of the Western Union Telegraph Company, determined to see the line through, had gone to President Lincoln to win support of the government for the enterprise, and to ask for military protection during its construction. The President was ready to give what support he could to assure its success, but he feared that the Indian tribes along the route might tear down lines and destroy the poles. With the nation doing its utmost to get soldiers to hold the Union together, it would be difficult to find enough to patrol the long route, but all that could be done to encourage and protect the telegraph line, so desperately needed in the crisis, would be done.

Hiram Sibley, through the Western Union, went ahead. The Pacific Telegraph Company was organized for the construction work from Omaha west to Salt Lake City. Edward Creighton was in charge of that division. Another similar company, with James Gamble as its leader, was organized to do the line-building from Carson City west to the Utah capital. In April, 1861, the race started, with an extra reward promised to the group that was first to reach Salt Lake City.

The work went forward feverishly. Ox-drawn wagons distributed poles and other supplies over the treeless plains and the Rockies. Mormon pioneers undertook to get the poles and wires along the Pony Express Trail across the desert, though with ox-teams and poor wagons and no improved roads, they found it an all but impossible task. Some gave up, and the rest were ready to do so. In the emergency James Street, the foreman of the line builders, went to see Brigham Young, who called the discouraged men into his office and faced the situation frankly with them. An open agreement had been made; it must be fulfilled. They agreed.

"Mr. Street," said the pioneer leader, "your poles will be delivered even if it makes paupers of us. The Mormon people will not break a contract."

The poles were delivered and the western line was brought up to the telegraph office of Salt Lake City on October 22, 1861. Two days later the first transcontinental telegraph line was in operation.

For two or three years the Indians did not interfere with what they called the "talking wires," but regarded them with awe. Usually, it is said, they would ride their ponies under them on the run. White men encouraged this superstitious regard by saying that the wires singing in the wind were carrying the voice of the "Great Spirit." Chief Washakie cooperated in an experiment, by giving a message to be transmitted to another chief, arranging to meet that chief on a certain day at a place he named. When the two came together, they both were ready to believe the message had been carried by the Great Spirit.

Then, too, other experiences inculcated into the savages' hearts a superstitious fear of the system. Braves would pick up live wires and be thrown to the ground with the shock. Indians mistook the acid in the batteries for whisky and were jolted into respect.

But when the Indian wars broke out, three or four years after the transcontinental line had been set up, the red men dared to take measures against the white man's talking wires which could carry the Indians' secrets to distant ears. Wires and poles were torn down, stations burned, operators killed—one by an arrow in the midst of clicking out the message that his post was about to be attacked.

President Lincoln requested volunteers from the Mormon people to help guard the line of communications, and two companies were enlisted and placed under command of General Pat Connor, who had brought a regiment of volunteers from the California and Nevada mining fields. Fort Douglas was established near Salt Lake City in 1862 as headquarters for these troops.

Telegraph lines were later run from Salt Lake City north and south through Utah. My mother became an operator on this so-called Deseret Telegraph Line, and when a telegraph office was set up in our home, she taught me to click out and to receive messages in Morse Code.

With the linking of the "talking wires," the Pony Express came to an honorable close, though boys and ponies still carried messages on branch trails to mining camps or settlements accessible only on horseback. The "mule mail" on the main line was discontinued too, heavy mail being carried by the Overland Stage, with some of the former pony riders as stage drivers.

Russell, Majors and Waddell—bankrupt through financing these pioneer ventures—relinquished the Overland Stage business to ambitious Ben Holladay. Palmy days followed. Virginia City, Nevada, came into its glory as the greatest silver mining camp in the world. Hard-rock mining in the Rocky Mountains to the west of Denver likewise was booming. Other mining camps in Utah, Montana and Idaho began to flourish. Holladay spread his stagecoaches over many lines. Following him the Wells Fargo Company took over the expanding business.

There were other dangers besides those of crazy roads in stagecoach traveling. Indians through the 1860's staged attacks on the coaches and the stations. Some of these were incited by overt acts of travelers. Nick Wilson, who was a driver, told me that one passenger took a shot at an inoffensive Gosiute who was just above the road trying to trap some gophers to feed his family. The Indian's body rolled down into the road after the stage clattered by. Other Indians came upon the dead man and were incensed. Near Eight-Mile Station, just west of the Utah-Nevada line, a stage driver was shot and killed by some of the angered red men. A judge riding beside him grabbed the lines and raced eastward to the Deep Creek Station, with the passengers and mail.

Farther to the east in Nebraska, another race for life was made by George Emory, alert driver of a stage heading west. Dr. A. E. Sheldon, Nebraska historian, reported the incident as the result of interviews with Emory and the passengers.

Rounding a turn on the trail, Emory caught sight of a band of Sioux coming toward him. In a moment he had swung his four-horse team completely around and, laying the lash on the animals, had them on the dead run toward the station some miles away.

The Indians on their fleet ponies were closing the gap between them and the flying stage, making their arrows fly at the target as they came yelling close after it. Some stuck in the stage coach. One clipped the rosette from a bridle on a wheel horse. Inside the rocking coach, the passengers were wild with fright.

Emory kept a cool head, making the turns with care, then going full speed along straight stretches. Soon he sighted a wagon train coming west. The captain of the train, sensing the situation, whirled his wagons in a circle. Teamsters grabbed their rifles and began to shoot at the redskins. The Indians finally turned and sped away while Emory drove the team and coach into the corral made by the wagon train. Saved, the passengers leaped from the coach. Some of the women threw their arms about the neck of the heroic driver and petted the foam-specked horses that had brought them through to safety.

Not all the attacks on stage coaches came from red men. Thieves, murderers and other criminals flocked to the West in gold-rush days. Bands of hard-riding, sure-shooting, white brigands ambushed the stages and stole the mail. Road agents, as the highwaymen were called, sometimes worked with crooked sheriffs, who passed the word along as to which stages out of the mining camps carried gold. The transportation companies fought back. Armed guards rode the stages, sometimes disguised as travelers, to catch the desperadoes. Strongboxes were used to protect the valuable cargo of gold dust or ingots. Sometimes the local citizens took the law into their own hands. Through the year 1864 twenty-five or more of the road agents who had ravaged the state of Montana were tried and hanged by vigilantes. In the Black Hills of South Dakota, robbery of the Deadwood-to-Denver Stage was almost an everyday affair. After a particularly brutal holdup in which Johnny Slaughter was shot down while saving his coach and passengers, outraged citizens took Slaughter's blood-spattered vest, nailed it to the door of the stage office with an invitation for law-loving folk to enroll to help put outlawry out of business in the Black Hills. Colonel George W. Stokes, a young adventurer from Missouri who was a reporter on the *Denver Tribune* for a time, commented: "I do not recall any hangings that followed, but a list of undesirables was posted, and a good many faces that had haunted saloons and gambling dens became memories."

It was this sort of drama that accompanied life along the lines of communication until the development of the railroads toward the end of the century.

But the mail went through.

# CHAPTER ELEVEN

# WILD LIFE STORIES
## OF THE WEST

"*Suddenly there was a sound like an approaching storm. Our cor-ralled cattle sprang to their feet, and men, women and children wakened from sound sleep, were quickly up and dressed. The coming roar we heard was like that of a heavy railroad train passing close by. 'It's a buffalo stampede!' someone shouted.*

"*All stood trembling. Fortunately the big animals streamed by our wagons without doing damage. How long they were in passing we did not know. It seemed an age. When daylight came, only a few stragglers were left. Our hunters shot some of these, so we had a good feast on buf-falo steaks and roasts. All had ended happily. Another train not far away was not so lucky . . .*"

This is the story Ezra Meeker told me about a night encounter with a herd of buffaloes. Such tales and many others of wild life are woven into every first-hand record of the making of the West, for in the conquest of that vast realm, animals, tame and wild, had important parts. For Indians and white folk they provided motive power, food, clothing, and sometimes shelter. They also brought adventure out of which stories grew.

The Journals of Lewis and Clark and their men reveal the riches of wild life along the route they followed. The country was full of game. Ducks, geese, turkeys, and other fowl kept the streams and air alive. At one place on the river, as Sergeant Floyd recorded, "twelve men went to the creek a fishen—caut 709 fish, different coindes." Another entry tells that three fat bucks were killed that evening. Later they came to the buffalo country, and the hunters brought to camp an abundance of its good meat.

Their band of about fifty men had to have plenty of food. Nature provided generously for them in buffalo roasts and steaks, elk, antelope, deer, and other large game. Prairie chickens, sage hens, rabbits, and beavers added variety to the frontier menu. Along the Columbia, salmon was so plentiful that they tired of eating it. There were times of food scarcity, yet on the whole the exploring party fared rather well on their long journey.

Grizzly bears, which do not yield the right of way to any man, gave the pathfinders several close calls. Captain Lewis had so narrow an escape from one of the "silvertips" that he remarked he'd rather fight two Indians than one grizzly bear.

Stories of the wealth of fur-bearing animals the Lewis-and-Clark party brought back from their great adventure started hundreds of Americans in quest of the furs of the far West. Through the decades of the 1820's and the 1830's, courageous mountain men combed most of the Rocky Mountain valleys and the Great Basin for the beavers, minks, otters, martens, and other creatures with precious coats on their backs. In so doing, they not only charted the West, but greatly increased the wealth of our country.

These riches were not easily won; for the fur-bearing creatures also prized their soft, warm coats, and used every device to keep them from the trappers. Beaver lodges, for instance, were skillfully constructed, with many hidden ways into and out of them. The sharp teeth of a beaver could cut through a sapling to which the trap had been tied, and the animal could make off with his life and the trap. If a beaver could not thus free itself, he would sometimes bite off the leg that was caught. Wading through icy waters to capture the sleek rodents, the trapper frequently found both beast and trap gone, and traps were almost impossible to replace.

Competitors in the fur game, Indians and white men, were constantly warring, with losses of life on both sides. In addition, British fur companies found it advantageous to promote ill feeling between the American trappers and the Indians by arming the red men and encouraging them to raid American outposts up near the Canadian territory. In July, 1832, one of the worst battles between mountain men and the Blackfoot Indians was fought in Pierre's Hole—now called the Teton Basin, in Idaho. American trappers, meeting there at a rendezvous, found a chance to even their score against the Indians.

Over the Teton Divide, down what is now called Trail Creek Canyon, came a large band of Blackfeet. Evidently they were not expecting trouble, for they had their women and children along and were led by a chief bearing a pipe of peace. Suddenly, Antoine Godin, whose father, an Iroquois hunter, had been killed by the Blackfeet, and an Indian of the Flathead tribe, which had suffered at the hands of the Blackfeet, took aim and fired. The chief fell dead. Caught by surprise, the Blackfeet retreated into a grove bordering the nearby stream and threw up a barricade. Trappers under the leadership of William Sublette and Robert Campbell, heads of the American Fur Company, and Alexander Sinclair, leader of the free trappers, charged into this. Sinclair was killed and Campbell severely wounded. Many of the braves of the Blackfeet fell in the battle. Their women and children, retreating into the protecting hills, escaped harm. The battle of Pierre's Hole was a turning point in the fierce rivalry for the fur riches of the West.

For the nomadic Indians of the plains, and the slopes of the Rockies, the buffalo had been the mainstay of the tribes. Roving herds provided good food, skins for their tepees, robes and articles of heavier clothing. The buffalo, or bison, was a migrating animal, moving to southern ranges in the fall and winter, and following the growing grass of the far-spread plains in spring and summer.

Pioneers told many stories about buffaloes. "One day on the plains," said my Uncle Fred, "we had to stop our covered wagon train for six hours while a big herd of brown buffaloes trailed across the road. Mothers and children got pretty excited. Some of us boys and men wanted to start shooting for meat, but the captain of our train said, 'No killing until most of them get by. We don't want any buffalo stampede.' He was right—a buffalo stampede could mean death for anyone who got in the path of the excited beasts."

In well-organized caravans of pioneers special men were designated as hunters to provide buffalo and other meat for the families. There was danger in letting just anyone shoot the wild animals along the way. Members of the train might be accidentally killed, a stampede might occur, or the Indians might attack the train for shooting down their game. Through a treaty with the tribesmen, general permission had been gained for the emigrants to follow the Big Medicine Road. The migrating settlers had little time to kill game on the road; so on that score the red men had few worries.

Colonel Tom Majors, last commander at old Fort Kearny, gave me some idea of the great herds of buffalo when the pioneers of the 1860's were crossing the plains. "I was leading my command," he said, "from the fort on the Platte River southward to the Republican River, when we struck the largest herd of buffalo I ever saw. It was several miles wide, and so long we just couldn't see the end of it. As the beasts came lumbering along steadily, there was danger they would crush our supply train, so I had the men load some cannon and fire cannister into the moving mass. Finally the herd took the hint and parted so that our wagons could get through. It was just part of the mighty migration of the animals made each year from the southern to the northern ranges."

Francis Parkman, in *The Oregon Trail*, brings to life a buffalo hunt he experienced on the Arkansas River. A shout from one of his attendants, Henry Chatillon, directed the attention of Parkman and Quincy Adams Shaw, his companion, to a dark mass passing rapidly over "swell after swell of the distant plain."

It was the hunters of the Arapahoe camp pursuing a herd of buffalo. Shaw and I hastily caught and saddled our best horses, and went plunging through sand and water to the farther bank. . . . From the river bank on the right, away over the swelling prairie on the left, and in front as far as the eye could reach, was one vast host of buffalo. The outskirts of the herd were within a quarter of a mile.

"Keep down in that hollow," said Henry, "and then they won't see you till you get close to them."

The hollow was a kind of wide ravine; it ran obliquely toward the buffalo, and we rode at a canter along the bottom until it became too shallow; then we bent close to our horses' necks, and, at last, finding that it could no longer conceal us, came out of it and rode directly towards the herd. It was within gunshot; before its outskirts, numerous grizzly old bulls were scattered, holding guard. They glared at us in anger and astonishment, walked towards us a few yards, and then turning slowly round retreated at a trot which afterwards broke into a clumsy gallop. In an instant the main body caught the alarm. That countless multitude of powerful brutes, ignorant of their own strength, were flying in a panic from the approach of two feeble horsemen. To remain quiet longer was impossible.

"Take that band on the left," said Shaw; "I'll take these in front."

He sprang off, and I saw no more of him. A heavy Indian whip was fastened by a band to my wrist; I swung it into the air and lashed my horse's flank with all the strength of my arm. Away she darted, stretching close to the ground. I could see nothing but a cloud of dust before me, but I knew that it concealed a band of many hundreds of buffalo. In a moment I was in the midst of the cloud, half suffocated by the dust and stunned by the trampling of the flying herd; but I was drunk with the chase and cared for nothing but buffalo. Very soon a long dark mass became visible, looming through the dust; then I could distinguish each bulky carcass, the hoofs flying out beneath, the short tails held rigidly erect. In a moment I was so close that I could have touched them with my gun.

Suddenly, to my amazement, the hoofs were jerked upwards, the tails flourished in the air, and amid a cloud of dust the buffalo seemed

174

to sink into the earth before me. One vivid impression of that instant remains upon my mind. I remember looking down upon the backs of several buffalo dimly visible through the dust. We had run un-awares upon a ravine.

It was impossible to stop; I would have done so gladly if I could; so, half sliding, half plunging, down went the little mare. She came down on her knees in the loose sand at the bottom; I was pitched forward against her neck and nearly thrown over her head among the buffalo, who amid dust and confusion came tumbling in all around. The mare was on her feet in an instant and scrambling like a cat up the opposite side.

At length I was fairly among the buffalo. They were less densely crowded than before, and I could see nothing but bulls, who always run at the rear of a herd to protect their females. As I passed among them they would lower their heads, and turning as they ran, try to gore my horse; but as they were already at full speed there was no force in their onset, and as Pauline ran faster than they, they were always thrown behind her in the effort. I soon began to distinguish cows amid the throng. One just in front of me seemed to my liking, and I pushed close to her side. Dropping the reins I fired, holding the muzzle of the gun within a foot of her shoulder. Quick as lightning she sprang at Pauline; the little mare dodged the attack, and I lost sight of the wounded animal amid the tumult. Immediately after, I selected another, and urging forward Pauline, shot into her both pistols in succession.

For a while I kept her in view, but in attempting to load my gun, lost sight of her in the confusion. Believing her to be mortally wounded and unable to keep up with the herd, I checked my horse. The dust and tumult passed away, and on the prairie, far behind the rest, I saw a solitary buffalo galloping heavily. In a moment I and my victim were running side by side. My firearms were all empty, and I had in my pouch nothing but rifle bullets, too large for the pistols and too small for the gun.

Riding to a little distance, I dismounted, thinking to gather a handful of dry grass to serve the purpose of wadding, and load the gun at my leisure. No sooner were my feet on the ground than the buffalo came bounding in such a rage towards me that I jumped back again into the saddle with all possible despatch.

Bethinking me of the fringes at the seams of my buckskin panta-

175

loons, I jerked off a few of them, and, reloading the gun, forced them down the barrel to keep the bullet in its place; then approaching, I shot the wounded buffalo through the heart. Sinking to her knees, she rolled over lifeless on the prairie. To my astonishment, I found that, instead of a fat cow, I had been slaughtering a stout yearling bull. No longer wondering at his fierceness, I opened his throat, and cutting out his tongue, tied it at the back of my saddle. . . .

Then for the first time I had leisure to look at the scene around me. The prairie in front was darkened with the retreating multitude, and on either hand the buffalo came filing up in endless columns from the low plains upon the river. The Arkansas was three or four miles distant. I turned and moved slowly towards it.

Parkman's trip, in 1846, was along the old Oregon Trail, to Fort Laramie, south on the trail of Indians and mountain men to Bent's Fort, on the Arkansas, and eastward over the Santa Fe Trail to Independence. This took him into a region where countless buffalo roamed, their main range extending over the great plains from Texas into Canada.

How many of these American bison were in the vast herds no one can tell. Estimates by Army personnel who covered much of the range in the course of their duties vary from sixty million to one hundred million. Martin S. Garretson, secretary of the American Bison Society, quotes dependable men who saw some of the vast herds. One buffalo hunter told Garretson:

Picture in your mind an open grassy valley a mile wide and straight westward for many miles. . . . Early one morning in 1851, I stood on an eminence overlooking this valley. From bluff to bluff on the north and the south and up the valley to the westward, as far as the eye could reach, this was literally blackened by a compact mass of buffalo. . . . It looked as if not another buffalo could have found room to squeeze in, and a man might have walked across the valley on their huddled backs. . . . This herd was on the move and was many hours in passing.

On a steamboat trip up the Missouri to Fort Benton in 1867, Captain Le Barge ran into an immense drove of buffalo crossing the river. For four miles, he relates, the water was a living mass of brown animals pouring down from the high banks. It took four hours for the steamboat to get into the clear again, and at times the engines were stopped to give the deck hands a chance to push the struggling buffalo away from the bow.

Colonel Charles Goodnight, for whom Martin Garretson worked as a cowboy, told of a buffalo stampede that split a herd of 1300 cattle Goodnight and his men were driving westward to the Pecos River. Luckily the cowboys were about equally divided when the bison crashed through. By hard riding, they managed to round up what had become two herds of longhorns, and bring them together again when the crazed buffaloes had passed. For more than a hundred miles farther, it took constant alertness to prevent another mix-up; buffalo by the thousands were all along the trail.

In after years when there was danger of the destruction of all buffalo, the Colonel at the suggestion of Mrs. Goodnight started a herd on his ranch in the Texas Panhandle. He captured two wild calves, a male and a female, as a beginning. Cowboys roped others; and the herd gradually increased to help save the buffalo from extinction.

Indians regarded the buffaloes as their herds of cattle, a gift from the Great Spirit. Before going into a hunt they usually performed ceremonies to the Great Spirit symbolizing the hunt as the sacrifice of the animals to supply the needs of the tribe. Care was taken not to kill too many, and what came from the chase was judiciously used.

Food was first among the necessities. Since buffalo meat was a major part of the daily diet, what was not eaten fresh was preserved. Sometimes it was cut in strips and hung to cure in the sun, during which process there was a "jerking" of the drying flesh resulting in what was known as "jerked" meat. Another method of preserving was to cut the meat into small pieces, pound and pack it with its own fat or tallow, and store it in bags to provide nourishment during the snowy moons of the long winter.

Clothing and shelter also came from the buffalo. Warm coats and cozy sleeping robes for winter were made from buffalo skin with the hair left on. A summer blanket was provided by removing the hair and tanning both sides to softness. Dressed hides were used for moccasins, leggings, shirts and dresses. Coverings of tepees were made from cow skins.

Braided strands served as lariats, or ropes. Bullboats were made by stretching several buffalo hides over a frame. Bags for carrying small articles on the travois were shaped from the large skins. And from the tough hide around the neck of the bull could be made a sturdy shield that would turn an arrow or even a musket ball.

It is small wonder that the relentless destruction of the buffalo met with such bitter opposition from the tribes—especially on the Great Plains. The day the buffalo all but perished from the earth was soon to follow the great covered-wagon migration to the valleys of the mountains. It seems inconceivable, but within about two decades—the 1860's and the 1870's—all but a scattered few of the millions of these animals were destroyed.

Various factors contributed to the mass killing. Indians continued to get their food and other supplies from the herds, but their annual kill was more than balanced by the natural increase of the animals. It was wanton shooting by sportsmen, some of them from Europe, who killed for excitement, that started the extermination. Building of the railroads brought many of these "big game" men into the West. There also was deliberate destruction by our Army, a measure to bring hostile tribes under control. Hide-hunters, who flocked on to the Great Plains with their repeating rifles were the worst destroyers of all. When buffalo skins were in growing demand on the eastern markets, out went these killers to slay, to strip off the coats of the fallen animals and sell them, leaving the carcass where it lay. Shipping records show that hundreds of thousands of the hides were sent eastward over the railroads.

Indians were incensed over this greedy destruction of the herds from which they derived their livelihood. Following the intervention of their chiefs, in 1867 a treaty was made between peace commissioners; Army officers, including General Sherman; and heads of some of the tribes of the Southwest. Under this agreement, the hide-hunters were forbidden to go south of the Canadian River, in which territory buffalo-hunting was reserved for the Indians.

Unprincipled white men, however, were not long in breaking the agreement. As a result, the Comanches under Chief Quanah Parker, who had white blood in his veins, attacked twenty-eight hide-hunters in June 1874 at Adobe Walls. One hunter was killed and the others were literally held prisoner inside their shelter for about two months, until rescued by Army troops. This put an effective check on buffalo-hunting in that area.

Destruction of the bison, however, went on elsewhere. For a decade more it continued, until only a few of the animals survived. Bones of the multi-millions that had perished whitened the Great Plains, where Indian women and children were crying for food that their braves could no longer bring.

As early as 1822 a Pawnee chieftain who had gone to Washington to represent his people said to President Monroe: "There was a time when we did not know the whites—our wants were then fewer than they are now. They were always within our control—we had seen nothing we could not get. There was a time when we could lie down and sleep and when we awoke we could find buffalo feeding around our camp—but now we are killing them for their skins, and feeding the wolves with their flesh to make our children cry over their bones."

The following prayer by an unknown Indian poet expresses the magnitude of this tragedy which had befallen his race:

### Sioux Prayer—Ghost Dance

Father, have pity on us
We are crying for thirst
All is gone!
We have nothing to eat,
Father, we are poor.
We are very poor.
The buffalo are gone,
They are all gone.
Take pity on us, Father,
We are dancing as you wished
Because you commanded us.
We dance hard,
We dance long—
Have pity.

Father, help us
You are close by in the dark
Hear us and help us.
Take away the white men
Send back the buffalo
We are poor and weak
We can do nothing alone
Help us to be what we once were—
Happy hunters of buffalo.

While the government did not leave the Indians without food and shelter, they were no longer hunters of the buffalo with freedom of the unfenced plains. Instead, they were settled on reservations, given annuities of beef, canvas for their tepees, and other commodities to help them take care of themselves. Besides deer, antelope, elk, bear and other big game, there were various kinds of smaller game. The streams were still alive with fish, the leafy swamps with wild fowl.

When the Indians of the plains were placed on reservations, settlers who had come to develop farms and ranches over the vacated land discovered it was strewn with buffalo skeletons. One enterprising man started to garner this harvest of sun-bleached bones, and daily drove his team and empty wagon out for a load; then returned to a siding of the newly built Santa Fe Railroad.

"What the deuce is that old fellow doing?" queried one of the farmers.

"Must be 'teched in the head,'" suggested another. "The idea of piling up heaps of bones looks funny to me."

Though frequently ridiculed and even nicknamed "Old Buffalo Bones," the settler continued his strange occupation. One day the citizens of the new town saw the train switch some empty flat cars onto the siding, and not long afterward they were loaded with bones and taken eastward to factories, where the bones were ground and made into potash. The best of it was used in sugar refining; the poorest, as fertilizer, to enrich the lands of run-down farms.

When word got around that "Old Buffalo Bones" had received from six to eight dollars a ton, his neighbors speedily followed his lead, and whole trainloads were soon being shipped to the potash factories. This first "cash crop" of the plains brought millions of dollars to the pioneer farmers. Records show that from 1868 to 1881, the income from shipments of buffalo bones amounted to $2,500,000 in Kansas alone. Nearby states profited similarly. Even as late as 1886, travelers across Dakota could still see great ricks of the skeletons piled along the sidings of the railroads.

Fortunately, a few buffaloes survived the reckless slaughter. On December 8, 1905, a group of sixteen individuals met in a room of the Lion House in Bronx Park, New York, and organized the American Bison Society. One of the first activities of the society was taking a census of the living buffalo. Because of his work as a cowboy at the Goodnight Ranch in the Texas Panhandle, and on the cattle trails and other western ranches, Martin S. Garretson was chosen to make this census. Although he traveled far over the plains and mountains of the West and into Canada, he found fewer than one thousand buffalo still alive. Part of these had wandered into Yellowstone Park, where there was some protection from poachers.

Finally, companies of the United States Cavalry were sent with instructions to protect the buffalo.

Today, thanks to the efficient staffs of Stephen Mather, Horace M. Albright and other leaders in the National Park Service, these natural reservations have become a haven for wild animals and birds of great variety. Those who saved the fine animal from extinction were intent upon improving the stock. Another objective was to distribute the buffalo over the country, when possible to place them on natural ranges, and to have small herds in parks, under good conditions. Today buffalo may be seen virtually in every part of our land.

# CHAPTER TWELVE

# LONGHORNS AND SHORTHORNS

During the summer of 1855, Major Howard Egan bought a herd of 1500 well-fed shorthorn cattle from settlers in the Utah valleys and struck out westward for California's gold fields, where the settlers and prospectors were calling for beef. Two Salt Lake City business men had backed the adventurous Irishman and outfitted the train with 15 wagon-loads of supplies, 100 horses and mules.

As the cloud of dust made by hundreds of hooves moved slowly across the plains and along the old Humboldt River Trail blazed by the forty-niners, Egan and his thirty-five cowboys kept always on the alert. In this business a man had to be ready for anything.

One day as Egan rode quietly along, his sharp eyes roving the land-scape, he spotted the feathers of a sage cock off in the brush. Something about the bird's movement bothered him, though. Then he realized it didn't look exactly like a sage cock. Quickly Egan spurred his horse and rode over to have a look.

Partly concealed by a shrub was a crouching Paiute Indian with bow and arrow ready.

"Huh!" exclaimed the Major.

"Huh, huh!" blurted the scared Indian, jumping to his feet to face the white man's revolver.

Instead of putting a bullet through him, the boss of the cattle herd motioned for the Indian to throw down his bow and arrow and go with him. The cowed Indian walked ahead.

It was customary for the hungry red men to lurk along the trail waiting for the chance to shoot arrows into a passing steer or cow, which naturally would fall behind, and the drivers could do nothing except leave it, giving the Indians a chance for a feast on "white men's buffalo."

Egan's men soon pitched camp, near the Humboldt. When supper was ready, the Major fed the Indian flapjacks and beefsteak, then gave him a bag filled with leftover food. The redskin left gratefully.

Next morning the herd was rounded up and started on the trail. At a narrow point where the route passed through a gulley, the Major posted some of his cowboys, and they counted the passing animals. Ten were missing. Looking around, the men saw the Indian they had fed the night before and two others watching them from the bushes. When the red men came up, Egan held up ten fingers, and with signs made them understand that ten cattle were lost. Then he motioned for them to go find the animals. They hurried away. Within about two hours, the Indians were back, driving fifteen!

The Indians remained with the Major's train until the herd was safely through the Paiute country and were paid with food and provisions. The one Major Egan had spotted in the brush the first day stayed with him all the way to California, and for years afterward. The Major called him Tecumsee.

Major Egan, who became superintendent of the Pony Express, and later of the Overland Stage, is remembered today through Egan Canyon in Nevada, which was named in his honor. He was one of the adventurous frontiersmen who came to Utah with Brigham Young and pioneered in the cattle business.

Beef was in constant demand at mid-century. The California gold rush brought half a million men to the "diggings," and they had to be fed. Soldiers at Army posts throughout the West also called for beef. And the Indians sought to replace the vanishing buffalo with beef. In addition, there were steadily increasing calls from industrial centers in the East. Railroads, pushing their way into the plains states opened an opportunity for large shipments of meat back to the Atlantic coast.

On the other hand, residents in the Lone-Star State at the close of the Civil War were "cattle poor." There were literally millions of longhorns over the region. There were good supplies of beef in the North too, in the thousands of short-horned cattle the pioneers had driven into Oregon and Utah.

Cattle and sheep could transport meat on the hoof. So the migration of great herds of longhorns of Texas and shorthorns from the north began.

Sheep as well as cattle played a great part in the story of the gold rush to California. New Mexico, whose story roots deeply into the Spanish in the Southwest, had gone far in the sheep industry, and thousands upon thousands of these wool-bearing animals roamed the arid Sierra Madre ranges and desert stretches.

Colonel Edward N. Wentworth, eminent authority on the sheep and cattle industry in America, relates that when the rush for California came, Judge Antonio Jose Otero, of New Mexico, saw the opportunity to market sheep in the gold fields. In 1849 he started his younger brother with Antonio Jose Luna, a business associate, on the trail to California with 25,000 sheep. Divided into smaller bands, each attended by three herders and dogs, they followed the approximate route of the Santa Fe Railway across Arizona, moved up the Mohave River in California, crossed Tehachapi Pass, and drove down the valleys to the north. At the "diggings" the sheep brought ten to twenty-five dollars per head, depending on the hunger of the prospectors, and the supply of gold dust.

Another drive of 9,000 sheep was made by "Uncle" Dick Wootton, keeper of a toll road through Raton Pass from Colorado into New Mexico. He lost only 100 animals in getting his flock of "woolies" through to California and had a gross return of $50,000. Kit Carson, famed frontiersman, and Lucien Maxwell, his partner, took 13,000 sheep from the Rio Grande valley below Santa Fe, to San Francisco, where they sold the herd to a merchant at $5.50 per head and netted $60,000.

In many ways sheep were less difficult to transport than cattle. They would not stampede; on the contrary, if frightened, they rushed together in a huddle. They could do without water longer than cattle, horses, or mules. They moved more slowly on the trail, however, because they stopped to nibble the herbage along the way, a habit that enabled them to "bed down" and sleep at nights. Because they could live on the sage and other desert growth, they kept fat through the snowy months, and they met changing weather conditions better than cattle, for by growing their warm coats on their backs, they were generally able to endure the blizzards.

Sheep also presented a serious problem. When pastured in the high grasslands, moving in flocks as they did, they would beat to earth the grasses and flowers on the hills and dells where cattle liked to graze, thus causing trouble between the cattlemen and sheepmen. The war continued until laws were passed to restrict the ranges for flocks and herds. Sometimes the rivalry broke out into open hostility, as in the case of a schoolmate of mine, Willie Limb, who herded sheep. Grudge-bearing cattlemen one night fired into the tent where he and a Mexican herder slept. The Mexican was killed, and Willie's arm was so badly wounded that it had to be amputated.

After the days of the buffalo, there was a steady stream of longhorns out of the vast ranges of Texas. Their ancestors had been seven calves of Spanish breed shipped from Santo Domingo to Mexico in 1521 by Gregorio de Lilalobos, who saw that the gold-hungry Spanish conquistadors would need meat, and started with this tiny herd. In time the cattle industry was to bring in far more wealth than all the mines of the new dominions of the Spanish Empire.

The United States inherited a share of this industry. Longhorns by the thousands were scattered over the wide plains and foothills of Texas. How these cattle, wild as deer, were gathered out of the thorny brush of that untamed region and taken northward to the military posts, the Indian reservations and the shipping centers along advancing railroads is a story of adventure, bravery and hardship that makes portrayals of the cowboy's life in modern Westerns seem tame and unconvincing.

Captain James Cook, a direct descendant of the British Captain Cook who sailed around the world, played a real role in the drama. When Cook's mother died, he and his younger brother were left by their father, also a Captain in the British Navy, to be reared by a Michigan pioneer family. Alden Brown, a gunmaker, trained the boy to shoot.

Finding the life of a sailor on Lake Michigan not to his liking, Jim went with a pal to Kansas. Near Fort Ellsworth, he was given the job of herding longhorns which had just been driven up from Texas over the old Chisholm Trail. Later, with some fellow cowboys, Jim rode back over the trail to San Antonio, where the boy, still in his teens, was hired as a "brush popper" by Ben Slaughter, a cattleman. This meant tough, dangerous work gathering longhorns out of the brush. Jim worked with Mexican *vaqueros*—the only American beside himself was the *caporal*, or boss. The pay was $10.00 a month with board.

Each of the men was given four or five saddle horses, some of them only half broken. Their food was mainly beef, which they obtained by killing cattle as they needed it. Jim had just started with the band when the caporal selected a critter in the herd and fired at it, but failed to bring the animal down. It charged, breaking the lariat a vaquero had thrown around its horns, and was making straight for Slaughter on his horse. Young Jim leveled his gun, aimed at the steer six feet away, and dropped it—shot through the forehead.

"I reckon you'll do to help fight Comanches," Slaughter said. Alden Brown's training had won a place for the boy in the wilds.

Brush popping was hard. One way they caught the cattle was to wait until a moonlit night when they came out to graze in the open. Then at a signal from the caporal, the vaqueros, hidden in the brush, burst on to the prairie and rode with lassos twirling to catch one of the wild critters before it got back into the thicket. Thrown and tied by an expert on a trained horse, the longhorn would be left until some of its fight was gone; then it would be taken to the corral or pasture where the herd was being gathered for branding.

Another method was to drive partly tamed decoys into the brush to mingle with the wild ones. With careful handling they might be brought into the open and driven to the enclosures.

Roping wild cattle while they were in the brush was a job for the expert. Mexican vaqueros, trained from childhood, became so skilled they usually could master it. "For a young novice such as I," said Captain Cook, "it often meant disaster."

One time when he was out working he heard a faint lowing on a cow trail close beside him. Getting his rope ready, young Cook waited. A few seconds later, a sleek bull dashed by. "I was ready for him and threw my loop over his head just as he passed," he said. "There must have been an extra spring in that bull's body, which he used at that moment, for when he came to the end of the rope my saddle girth parted with a loud snap. I went sailing through space with my feet still in the stirrups, and my head bumped the ground.

"I never heard from that bull or that saddle again, but I had a big lump on my head as a souvenir of the occasion."

What was known to Texans as the "brush" country, Captain Cook described as the most difficult of regions. Mesquite, varying in size from bushes to trees, with long, sharp thorns, and many other plants with protective spikes, heightened the danger. Prickly pear, and rattail cactus annoyed the vaqueros.

Their leather chaps, jackets, *tapaderos* (toe protectors), heavy boots, leggings and gauntlet gloves were necessary. Ten-gallon hats were worn not just for style, but protection, though in later years, the well-to-do wore them for fun, as they do today.

Jim went back to the age of rawhide, and he and his Mexican companions were adept in making their lariats and quirts from the skins of longhorns and other animals. A poncho, or leather cape, helped to shed the rain, but otherwise they lived through storms and sun with about as little shelter as the cattle they chased and herded. "Sometimes, as we stood with rain dripping off us," remarked Captain Cook, "I felt the longhorns had the advantage, so far as shedding water was concerned."

Beautiful mustangs that roamed the ranges of the West, were of special interest to young Cook. These wild horses usually were buckskin, cream or mouse colored. A black stripe along the back from mane to tail and a few black marks above the knees were characteristic.

Properly broken, they made excellent saddle horses. They were clean-limbed, and with perfect hoofs they could stand the roughest trails. They found food on the ranges. Jim, who wanted a mustang, once set out to capture a stallion. Secreting himself near the bank of a stream, the young cowboy waited his chance to "crease" the prize—that is, to stun him with a pistol shot, then rope and tie him. As the stallion trotted by, the bullet struck too low, and the beautiful animal fell dead. "I could have cried," said the Captain. "Probably I did." Later, however, Cook did capture a mustang, and trained him to be a fine saddle horse.

Experiences on the cattle trails were different, but just as hazardous; for stampedes, storms and Indians, called for alertness and courage every mile of the long way. Always a reliable companion if there was trouble in the air was MacNeil Stewart, the caporal. "Caporal Mac" shared cheerily the ups and downs of the trail. At the outset, before the herd of about two thousand jittery cattle was "trail broke," there was a stampede, started by Jim Cook when he touched with his stirrup a seemingly gentle cow. She jumped to her feet, and the whole herd was up like a shot and off in the darkness. All night the cowboys rode like mad to turn the leaders and get the scared cattle milling, or going in a circle, yet morning came with about five hundred missing, some of which were picked up later.

Farther up the trail, the Comanches staged an attack, wounding one of the night herders and running off with some of the cattlemen's horses. Jim joined a few others to retrieve the loss, caught the Indians off guard a day or so later, and made them pay the price—a few killed. The horses, plus some Indian ponies, were driven back to the cattle camp.

At the Red River, bank full from storms, there was "big swimming" for cattle. On the way across on a raft, Caporal Mac lost a boot, and threw the other after it. Young Cook also lost his footgear, and both had to make do with Indian moccasins until they reached one of the few supply posts.

During a tornado on the plains, hailstones pounded men, horses and cattle, scattering them in every direction. After a few hours, the outfit was reassembled. The next day the sun smiled again. *Stay with the herd* was the main slogan of the cowboys, and stay with it they did, storm or shine, Indians or no Indians. Finally they reached the end of the trail, and after a little celebrating, went back to Texas to trail other herds into the Northland.

The miners' continuing demand for meat brought more longhorns out of Texas. With the discovery of new diggings, it rose. The "Pikes Peak or bust" rush of 1859, opened a rich market for beef in Colorado. On the heels of this came another scramble for gold in the vicinity of Virginia City, Montana.

Nelson Story, an adventurer from Ohio, was one of the many who struck it rich in Alder Gulch. Weary of prospecting, he sold out his claim and left to make money in a different way.

Off he went to Texas and spent $10,000 for longhorns. About forty range-hardened cowboys were hired to help him get the steers over the long trail to Virginia City. It meant dodging redskins across the Indian Territory, then following the Wyoming Warpath through the cherished hunting realm of the Sioux and allied tribes.

When he reached Fort Laramie, officers tried to talk him out of his plan to take the Bozeman Trail. Story listened but still was determined to try the short cut to the Montana diggings. His cowboys filled their cartridge belts, and started out; their breech-loading rifles would shoot faster than the guns of the Indians. But before they reached Fort Kearny, Sioux charged the herd, killed two men and stole some cattle. At the fort, Colonel Carrington ordered Story not to go through, saying that Red Cloud and his warriors would be waiting for them.

Story's men built a corral to protect the herd by night. Through the day the cattle grazed on good grasses, while the men, watching, looked toward the north, and itched to be going. Finally Story had a night meeting with his Texas hands. Would they risk a getaway in the dark and drive the herd on, Indians or no? All but one agreed, and he was held, so that no word of the plan reached the nearby Army post.

The break was made that night. Most of the driving was done in the dark. With a few of his men, Story made a strike at the Indians who had attacked them earlier and chased the red raiders into the Badlands, where he gave them bullets for arrows, and got back his longhorns. There might be tougher fighting ahead, but they were determined to get to Virginia City.

In the daring adventure only one of the boys was lost; caught alone, he was shot and scalped. There was no attack on the group, and little loss of cattle. The rich returns from the sale of the beef might have tempted others to follow Story's lead, but by this time Red Cloud had closed the Wyoming Warpath, and Montana had to look elsewhere for meat.

Farther south the longhorn drives were increasing, to fill the needs of mining camps in Colorado and needy Indians, crowded on reservations, from whom buffalo had been largely cut off.

Colonel Charles Goodnight enlisted Oliver Loving, an older man, to get a large herd from Texas across the arid stretches into New Mexico. The most direct way was over waterless plains, and the men decided to take it rather than a greener trail to the north, which led through the Comanche country. The drive was begun in June 1866 with a large water wagon drawn by ten yoke of oxen and an escort of Confederate veterans to ward off Indian attacks.

At the last stream the water wagon was filled. Cattle were given a chance to feed and rest and quench their thirst before they were headed west over the parched plain. Through the long day the cowboys, with faces masked by kerchiefs to ward off some of the blinding dust, kept the herd moving, moving. Weaker animals dragged behind. Tired drivers could not escape the heat that pressed down from above nor the light that blinded their eyes, but the third day found the men and most of the herd struggling on.

On the fourth day came cooler breezes, and they saw the green fringe along the Pecos River. Cattle, smelling the water from afar, took on new life, and in the end stampeded toward the welcome stream. The daring venture ended in victory.

At Fort Sumner there was rejoicing and feasting among red and white men. Rations were given to soldiers and the half-starved Indians whose tepees were pitched around the frontier post. The longhorns could be brought through from Texas. A new way had been blazed—the Goodnight-Loving Trail, as it was afterward called.

Youthful Joe McCoy, of Illinois, had a bright idea as he watched the longhorns streaming out of the Southwest. Fearful of the "tick fever" the animals might bring to their stock, Missourians strenuously objected to their coming on the hoof. Kansas farmers were raising similar protests. Why not drive them over trails farther west, build shipping corrals on the Kansas-Pacific Railroad, and send the cattle east on trains?

The plan looked good to the drovers, and McCoy acted, choosing Abilene, Kansas, the center of the stock-buying, as the shipping point, and thereby putting the spotlight on that frontier town. A big corral was built, and Texas herds were diverted to it. Records show that nearly 40,000 longhorns were handled at the McCoy corral during 1867.

The first herd was brought over the old Chisholm Trail, the famed route opened by Jesse Chisholm, of Scotch father and Cherokee mother, who had used it to transport wagons and cattle in carrying on his trade with the Indians. Following a trace made during the Civil War by federal troops under Colonel Emory, this trail up from Texas ended at Abilene, which became a typical "Wild West" town. Its wildness, however, has been overplayed. Basically it was the center of a developing industry, with the stalwart working to provide food for the nation.

Holding herds in McCoy's stout corrals, and getting fractious longhorns into cattle cars called for hard work. Those who did it and the trail-tired cowboys craved entertainment; and saloons, gambling houses and dance halls lured many of them and their cash. In the hectic life there were clashings of will and tragedies. "Two-gun" sheriffs of the legendary "Wild Bill" Hickok type added notches to their guns, less often, however, than some storytellers would have us believe.

191

The millions of longhorns trailed out of Texas served well. After them came the shorthorned, red and spotted Durham breed, such as the pioneers had driven in ox-teams across the plains. In old Oregon and Utah these multiplied into hundreds of thousands, and trail-driving during the late 1870's and 80's was largely from these western regions.

Ranges in Wyoming and Montana grew a nutritious grass that would cure by itself. It was demonstrated that, except when occasional killing blizzards came, such as the disastrous one of 1886, cattle wintered on this forage.

In 1887 my brothers and I drove a herd of shorthorned cows and calves through Wyoming into the Teton Basin to start a ranch. Cowboys were having their roundups, branding and bronco-busting. But barbed wire fences were being stretched around the hay and grain fields, and preparations were being made to house the stock in barns through the wintry months, and to provide cured hay for feed, for the open range was disappearing.

It was a time of change. Pasture lands were being defined by law. Ranges were being fenced. The railroads were coming into greater use for shipping. Stockyards were built in various centers. Packing houses were developed to prevent waste of meat, and to process it for homes all over the country. In the cattle story, heroism was not usually spectacular, but of the quieter kind. Out of pioneer beginnings, men of stature and boys of dependability, such as Major Egan, Captain Cook, Nelson Story, and Joe McCoy, carried the great industry to success.

PLATE THIRTY-SIX

Three Crossings, on the Sweetwater River, an important station of the first
Transcontinental Telegraph, located in the heart of the Indian country.

1000 MILE TREE

Laying track for the Union Pacific in Weber's Canyon, Utah, one thousand
miles west of Omaha, Nebraska, the eastern terminus.

# CHAPTER THIRTEEN

# HOME LIFE IN PIONEER BEGINNINGS

The story of the new United States Steel plant on Utah Lake was to provide the theme for a radio broadcast over one of the national networks. The director of the program, who had come from Hollywood to Utah to make the arrangements, said to me:

"This Geneva Steel plant is a wonderful creation. It sprang up overnight."

"That's true," I replied. "But to me it seems more like the century plant. It blossoms overnight, but remember, it takes a hundred years to get ready."

Although present-day needs brought the Geneva Steel plant into reality, some such plant to make iron or steel was in the dreams of the pioneers when they came west almost a hundred years ago. They were desperately in need of iron and worked hard to make it in Utah.

The great Salt Lake City Tabernacle with its dome-shaped roof is a monument to pioneer ingenuity. Not an ounce of iron or steel was available for use in its construction, and its huge arching beams had to be put together with hard-wood pegs, and the joints reinforced with strips of rawhide, which in drying bound the timbers together with a lasting grip. So it was with many other buildings erected in the early days.

Transporting steel over plains and mountains by ox-drawn wagons from smelters in the East was too difficult. Consequently, metal was so scarce that every bit was made use of. For example, when my father was a boy, working as a blacksmith's helper in Wyoming, he drove sixty miles in a wagon along the Overland Trail to gather scraps of iron left along the way by the pioneer trains for use in the shop.

Primitive iron works were finally started in southern Utah, where there was a good supply of the main things needed—iron ore and coal. Pioneers from Wales, who had been trained in the job, were set to building a blast furnace to produce pig iron. When the furnace was finished, it was charged with iron ore and fluxing limestone. Before the fire was started, the people fasted and prayed for success. The next morning they gathered and the furnace was tapped.

When they saw the molten iron running out into the molds, they shouted, "Hosanna to the Lord!"

Ezra Meeker once told me how the pioneers lived in the woods in old Oregon. "Indoor life centered round the fireside," he said. "It gave us heat for cooking and light to see by. Our first hearth was made of float lava which had been washed down by floods from Mt. Rainier." Newspapers, which were then made of rag and more sturdy than now, were used to cover the walls. "It was from these papers," Ezra said, "that children learned their ABC's." When enough families had settled nearby, he said they pitched in and built a school—a large cabin with rough benches and a table for the teacher.

Meeker said that the children had to walk through the woods to school. "Our little daughter, Carrie, came running home one day out of breath," he recalled. "She told us she had seen a big pussy cat sharpening its claws on a tree. I took her back to the place and found the scratches on the bark. In the soft ground were tracks of a cougar or mountain lion. After that we were more careful. But we found that wild animals were neighborly if we didn't start trouble."

There were food shortages sometimes; when the fish weren't running in the streams, families were known to live on potatoes. If a hunter dropped a deer, it was shared by all.

Clothing presented more of a problem. Meeker recalled that one winter they didn't have enough money to buy shoes, so they spent what they had for leather and made their own. Rough lasts were hewn from an alder log; wooden pegs were whittled out and dried in the Dutch oven. A pig was killed to get bristles for the wax-ends. The shoes were clumsy but they kept their feet warm, and his family were luckier than some of the neighbors who had to go barefoot in cold weather.

Pioneers were on their own. Food and clothing had to be provided with nature's help, for there were no railroads to bring these necessities overland. Manufactured articles such as tools and utensils were scarce. Yet somehow they managed to get along. They planned their own schools and recreations and conducted their own home worship before churches were established.

Animals provided settlers with much of their food and clothing. Well-tanned skins of deer and elk, which the Indians brought to swap for flour, tea and other things, provided materials out of which nimble-fingered mothers made shirts, leggings and even fringed dresses. Moccasins were obtained from the Indians, who knew best how to make this comfortable footwear.

"Buckskin had its faults, though," Meeker said. "When it got wet it stretched. I remember one newcomer who came in from a soaking rain and discovered his trousers were a foot too long. So he took his shears and cut off the extra length. After he had dozed by the fire awhile, he woke up and discovered he was wearing short pants."

195

Wool helped solve the clothing problem for many pioneers. Sheep that were brought with the covered-wagon caravans multiplied into flocks scattered among the settlements. Spinning wheels and home looms were active, and before long people were wearing their own homemade woolen clothing. I have a photograph of my mother at the age of nineteen wearing an attractive dress made of wool from sheep her father raised in Manti, Utah. She washed, dried and spun the wool, colored it with homemade dye, wove the material on an old hand loom, and sewed up the dress.

Sheep from Hawaii were brought to Oregon in the 1830's by the Hudson's Bay Company with a view to producing wool, hides and tallow for the British market. It is possible that John Jacob Astor may have imported them as early as 1811 on the ship *Tonquin*, which stopped in the Islands for cargo en route to establish the fort at Astoria. Dr. John McLoughlin, head factor, helped settlers stock their farms with cattle and sheep.

Dr. Marcus Whitman and the Reverend Henry H. Spalding, who established missions in old Oregon Territory in 1836, made sheep- and cattle-growing part of their service to the Indians. They felt that it was their Christian duty to train the Indians in the arts of peace. These lines from a letter Dr. Whitman wrote in 1838 to a fellow missionary in Honolulu are revealing:

> Five of the six sheep [sent from Honolulu] reached here in safety, for which we feel very thankful, as we value them highly.

What the Doctor wanted to see in the beautiful Walla Walla valley was farmhouses, not "squalid Indian huts, near which stalked abroad a few broken-down Indian horses cropping the rich grasses of the surrounding plain, but grazing there the cow, the ox, the sheep of a happy Yankee community."

At the Whitman mission, near present Walla Walla, Washington, Mrs. Whitman used a homemade wheel to spin wool sheared from her own sheep. A hand loom made by a Mr. Munger supplied the family with cloth. In 1854, Dr. Whitman wrote:

. . . we have about 80 sheep, a large part ewes, as we kill the wethers. . . . A good many have been given to the Indians. . . . We shall have more than 100 when the spring lambs come.

Because his sheep had increased by 1840 to twenty-six head, Reverend Spalding requested the Mission Board "for weaving equipment with which to work up the wool." In the meantime, the "ingenious missionary had made a spinning wheel, the yarn from which was woven by native girls into 23 yards of flannel and 14 yards of carpeting and also knitted leggings and stockings." Native hand looms were employed at the Spalding mission, on the Clearwater River near present Lewiston, Idaho.

What is believed to have been the first sugar processed in Utah was made by my grandfather Shadrach Driggs, a wagon-maker who needed hard wood to keep the wagons of the pioneers in repair. In March, 1853, he and my father, then in his teens, made their way up the side of a steep canyon with a yoke of oxen, axes and chains, prepared to cut scrub oak and maple. As they began to cut the maple, they noticed sap dripping down the stump. Grandfather let some of it fall on a finger and tasted it. "Ben," he announced, "these are sugar maples. Taste the sap."

Next day they were back, with auger, spiles and pails. Holes were bored into the trunks, the spiles set in to guide the sap down to the pails hung below. After two days they had collected enough for maple sugar.

"We had enough to make nearly two pounds," my father said. "It was a treat—the first sugar we'd had since leaving Iowa. Back East we could get maple sugar and syrup, and we had a good deal of New Orleans molasses, shipped up the Mississippi and Missouri on steamboats, and there was honey from the bees too. Sometimes in Iowa we discovered a hollow tree in the woods that a runaway swarm of bees had filled with honey. We'd build a smoking fire, stupefy the bees, and take the honey."

But there were no bees in the West until, with difficulty, some pioneers managed to get hives of bees into the valleys of the West. Hen Brown, of Pleasant Grove, Utah, liked to brag about "drivin' a whole swarm from the Mississip' to Californy without losin' one." In later years Utah had plenty of bees to make choice honey and help pollenize the blossoms of fruit trees.

After a careful study of the manufacture of sugar from beets in France, John Taylor laid before Governor Brigham Young, and other leaders in Utah, his plan to establish similar factories in that faraway territory. The plan was approved, a company was organized, and money provided. Philip Delamare, a young Frenchman, and Elias Morris, a Welsh mason and millwright, joined Taylor in the enterprise.

Machinery for the sugar factory was made in Liverpool and shipped to New Orleans. Since much of this equipment was of wrought iron, it was too heavy for the standard wagons provided to haul it over plains and mountains; so forty ponderous Sante Fe wagons, each drawn by multiple ox-teams, were substituted. After fifty-three days of hardship, with losses of cattle, the caravan finally rolled down the canyons into the valleys of Utah.

Truman O. Angell, architect of the Temple and the Tabernacle in Salt Lake City, designed the building in which the machinery was placed. Sugar beets were grown, and processing tried. However, all the earnest effort and the more than $100,000 gathered for the venture at real sacrifice did not result in one pound of sugar. It just didn't work; the product that was forthcoming was not palatable. Every effort to make it failed. Lack of certain equipment and knowledge of chemistry seemed at the root of the failure, and the project was given up.

About one-third of a century later the dream came true. In 1890 a new sugar refinery was opened at Lehi, Utah. Trainloads of sugar beets poured in, and refined sugar of highest quality came forth. As a boy clerking in a store, I sold three pounds for a quarter. It was a boon to the housewives of the community for preserving their berries, apricots, peaches, pears and other fruits for the winter time—popular, too, with the children in the form of stick candies, chocolates, gum drops, and candy canes for the Christmas tree.

How to start gardens and orchards in the arid valleys was another problem. It was not so easy to get good seed, and there was difficulty in bringing the choicest cuttings of fruit trees and roots of berry plants across the plains. But these finally were transported, and the valleys began to bloom and produce fruits, vegetables and flowers.

One story suggests the beginning of gardening in a town in Utah. Just after the advent of the pioneers in Salt Lake Valley, Peregrine Sessions moved away from the fort and built his cabin ten miles to the north. A few covered wagons once passed that way en route to California. Standing by his lone cabin, Peregrine hailed the travelers and watched the caravan roll down the dusty road. When it had passed, he picked up his shovel and started across the trail to irrigate a small field of wheat on the other side.

Something green in the dust caught his eye. It was the seed of a pea. Looking more closely, he found others along the road. Evidently there was a hole in the bag and the peas had dribbled along the way. The pioneer followed the wagon tracks, picking up the peas. When Sessions was two miles from his cabin, he had gathered enough to plant two or three rows. That was the start of luxuriant gardens in Sessions Settlement. This thriving village, now aptly called Bountiful, has for more than a century been a rich source of garden stuffs for nearby Salt Lake City and other markets.

With hard work and inventive skill, pioneers managed to get food, clothing and shelter from natural resources. Their needs were simple, but their desires grew for something more than the homemade suits and dresses, tallow candles, rag carpets, wooden dishes and mixing bowls. Grandma's wedding dress and other finery had served two or three generations. Grandfather's broadcloth coat and trousers was at last worn out. Young folk were calling loudly for new "store clothes."

Railroads, bringing East and West closer together, were the answer. The need had been foreseen and action taken way back in the 1850's when the Army charted the routes for the steaming, whistling engines with their trains of laden cars. Jefferson Davis, secretary of war under Franklin Pierce, is to be largely credited with these Pacific Surveys. In 1853, Isaac I. Stevens, governor of the Territory of Washington led surveyors safely through hostile Indian country on a hazardous expedition from the headwaters of the Mississippi to Puget Sound. Further to the south, Lieutenant A. W. Whipple, assisted by Lieutenant Ives, charted a route from Memphis westward to Albuquerque, New Mexico, and over the Sierra Madre Mountains and the California Desert to San Diego. The present Santa Fe Railroad in large part follows this route over the southwest.

Captain J. W. Gunnison and his party made a survey of another route farther north, crossing the Colorado Rockies into the valley of the Green River in Utah. The Captain found a way through the mountain barrier, but he and his entire party were murdered by Indians in reprisal for the slaying of some of the tribesmen by gold-seekers. The Gunnison route is followed most of the way by the Denver and Rio Grande Western Railroad.

It was along the central route, however, that the first transcontinental railroad was built, authorized by an act signed by President Lincoln July 1, 1862. Construction was started in 1863, delayed by the Civil War, and completed May 10, 1869. On that day, lines from East and West were linked at Promontory Point north of Great Salt Lake, and Governor Leland Stanford of California drove the famed Golden Spike. A crowd of railroad officials and workers witnessed the ceremony. Telegraph wires carried news of the event across the continent.

Longed-for new clothing, a wider variety of food, chinaware, glassware, shining silverware, and bright utensils came to the pioneer homes. Parlor organs and other musical instruments brought pleasure. Farmers and laborers could get more and better tools. A new day had come for the people of the West.

In the years that followed, other transcontinental railroads were built along historic trails. Toward the close of the century, William A. Clark, a frontier freighter who had struck it rich in the mines of Montana, decided to build a railroad from Salt Lake City to Los Angeles. The new line ran over the route followed by Fathers Escalante and Dominguez in 1776, and the Spanish trail, where Jedediah Strong Smith had later led his trapping expeditions. When the road was completed, Mr. Clark invited pioneers of the region to be his guests on a Pullman trip over the railway. There was researching by newspapermen to make a list of those still living who had gone over the road by ox team or other means in pioneer days. Finally the roster was printed with a special article telling the story of the old trail.

Next day Joshua Terry, last of Utah's mountain men, clad in his fringed buckskin jacket, smoke-darkened by a hundred campfires, appeared at the office of the newspaper.

"What's the matter with you newspaper fellows?" he said. "Don't you know the real history of the West?" He held up the newspaper clipping. Tapping it with a finger, he continued: "The fellow who wrote this piece has a lot to learn."

The writer, Isaac K. Russell, young veteran of the Spanish-American War, was called in. "What's wrong with my story?" he asked Terry.

"It doesn't mention the real trail-blazers of this desert. Gives the credit to pioneers who followed afterwards. It's all right to praise these later folks for what they did, but don't forget the men who took the risks ahead of them."

Russell urged the mountain man to go on. The gray-bearded visitor spoke of Jed Smith, Jim Bridger, Joe Meek, and others he had known. In a word, he lifted a curtain on a little-known drama of the old West.

It is this part of history that I have attempted to set down in these pages—Josh Terry's stories of his life as a mountain man, and those of his close companions in trapping and fur-trading. Others—Indians, covered-wagon pioneers, gold-miners, Pony Express riders, Overland Stage drivers, frontier freighters, cowboys, and soldiers who played a part in the building of the West.

It is hoped that here some of the drama in which they had such colorful roles is preserved in lasting form. As the Indians say: "White Man's book never forgets."

# BIBLIOGRAPHY

The following readable and dependable books are suggested for readers who wish to get closer to the epic of the West in its making.

Bidwell, John, *Echoes of the Past in California*. Chicago: Lakeside Press—Donnelley, 1928.

Bratt, *Trails of Yesterday*. Lincoln: University Publishing Co., 1921.

Brown, John, *Autobiography*. Salt Lake City: Stevens and Wallis, 1941.

Chapman, Arthur, *The Pony Express*. New York: G. P. Putnam's Sons, 1932.

Clayton, William, *Journal of the Pioneers*. Salt Lake City: Deseret Book Co., 1921.

Clemens, Samuel L., *Roughing It*. New York: Harper & Brothers, 1934.

Dimsdale, Thomas J., *Vigilantes of Montana*. Helena: State Publishing Co., 1915.

Driggs, Howard R., *The Pony Express Goes Through*. Philadelphia: J. B. Lippincott Co., 1936.

Driggs, Howard R. and Sara S. King, *Rise of the Lone Star*. Philadelphia: J. B. Lippincott Co., 1936.

Egan, Howard R., *Pioneering the West*. Richmond: Howard R. Egan Estate, n.d.

Garretson, Martin S., *The American Bison*. Bronx Park: New York Zoological Society, 1938.

# BIBLIOGRAPHY

Gudde, Erwin G., *Sutter's Own Story*. New York: G. P. Putnam's Sons, 1936.

Hafen, LeRoy R., *The Overland Mail*. Glendale: Arthur H. Clark Co., 1926.

Hebard, Grace Raymond, *Sacajawea, Guide of Lewis and Clark*. Glendale: A. H. Clark Co., 1933.

Hulbert, Archer B., *The Forty-Niners*. Boston: Little, Brown & Co., 1931.

Irving, Washington, *Astoria*. Portland: Binfords & Mort, 1950.

—— *Adventures of Captain Bonneville*. Portland: Binfords & Mort, 1954.

Jackson, Clarence and Lawrence Marshall, *Quest of the Snowy Cross*. Denver: Denver University Press, 1952.

Jackson, William H., *Time Exposure—An Autobiography*. New York: G. P. Putnam's Sons, 1940.

Larpenteur, Charles, *Forty Years a Fur Trader*. Chicago: Lakeside Press—Donnelley, 1933.

Leonard, Zenos, *Adventures*. Chicago: Lakeside Press—Donnelley, 1934.

Linderman, Frank, *American*. Yonkers: World Book Co., 1930.

Lockley, Fred, *Oregon Trail Blazers*. New York: Knickerbocker Press, 1929.

Lyman, George D., *John Marsh, Pioneer*. New York: Charles Scribner's Sons, 1930.

Manly, William Lewis, *Death Valley in '49*. Chicago: Lakeside Press—Donnelley, 1927.

Nibley, Preston, *Brigham Young—the Man and his Work*. Salt Lake City: Deseret News Press, 1936.

—— *Exodus to Greatness*, Salt Lake City: Deseret Book Co., n.d.

Osborne, Kelsie Ramey, *Peaceful Conquest—The Story of Lewis and Clark*. Portland: Oregon Sesquicentennial Commission and Old Oregon Trail, Inc., n.d.

Palmer, William R., *Pahute Indian Legends*. Salt Lake City: Deseret Book Co., 1946.

Pancoast, Charles, *A Quaker Forty-Niner*. Philadelphia: University of Pennsylvania Press, 1930.

Parkman, Francis, *The Oregon Trail*. Philadelphia: John C. Winston Co., 1931.

Pike, Zebulon Montgomery, *Southwestern Expedition*. Chicago: Lakeside Press—Donnelley, 1925.

# BIBLIOGRAPHY

Porter, Clyde and Mae, *Ruxton of the Rockies*. Norman: Oklahoma University Press, n.d.

Pyper, George D., *Romance of an Old Playhouse*. Salt Lake City: Deseret Book Co., 1928.

Richardson, Marvin M., *The Whitman Mission*. Walla Walla: Whitman Publishing Co., 1940.

Rollins, Philip Ashton (ed.), *Discovery of the Oregon Trail*. New York: Charles Scribner's Sons, 1935.

Ross, Alexander, *Adventures on the Oregon*. Chicago: Lakeside Press—Donnelley, 1923.

Stookey, Walter M., *Fatal Decision—The Story of the Donner Party*. Salt Lake City: Deseret Book Co., n.d.

Victor, Frances Fuller, *The River of the West*. Published by subscription, 1870.

Wellman, Paul I., *The Trampling Herd*. New York: Carrick and Evans, 1939.

——*Death on Horseback*. Philadelphia: J. B. Lippincott Co., 1947.

*Note:* The American Pioneer Trails Association, 4828 217th St., Bayside 64, New York, publishes the following brochures, illustrated with maps and pictures, in *The American Trails Series*.

Brayer, Garnet and Herbert O., *American Cattle Trails*.

Driggs, Howard R., *Mormon Trail*.

Fletcher, R. H., *American Adventure*.

Meacham, Walter, *Old Oregon Trail*.

Vestal, Stanley, *Wagons Southwest*.

# INDEX

## A

Abilene, Kansas, 191
Absaroka Indians *see* Crow Indians
Absaroka ("Land of the Crows"), 141
Adobe Walls, Indian attack on, 178-179
Agreda, Mary Coronel de, 67
Alamo, Mexican attack on, 66-71
Alamo Mission, built by Franciscans, 67
Albright, Horace M., 181
Alcove Springs, 87
Allen, James, 97
Alvarado, Juan Bautista, 82-83
American Bison Society, 176, 181
American Board of Foreign Missions, 43, 196
American colonies in Texas, 66
American Falls, Astorians at, 124
American Fur Company, 172
American River, fur trapping, 47, 48
American River, gold mining, 89, 153
Angell, Truman O., 198
Apache Indians, 147, 157
Applegate, Jesse, 54, 57
Applegate, Lindsay, 57
Applegate Trail, 57
Arabian camels, for mail-carrying, 155-156
Arapahoe Indians, 52, 174
Archer, Patience, 111
Arkansas River, buffalo hunt, 173-176
Arkansas River, Cimarron Crossing, 49-50
Arkansas River, Pike encampment, 33-34
Army of the West, 80, 86, 97, 98, 147

# INDEX

Ashley, William, 37, 46, 47, 53
Ashley-Henry expedition (1823), 37, 46, 47
Astor, John Jacob, 51, 52, 196
Astoria, Fort, 51, 52
Astorians, 52, 124
Aubry, François Xavier, 158
Austin, Moses, 66
Austin, Stephen, 66
Austin, Texas, 66

## B

Baagshaw, Captain, 79
Baptiste, 27-30, 86
Barlow, Kimbrough, 58
"Barlow Cutoff," 58
Bartelson-Bidwell group in New Helvetia, 83
Basil, 29-30
Battle Lakes, massacre at, 77, 80
Bay of Monterey, 49
Bay of San Francisco, 83
Beale, Edward F., 155
The Bear, Indian chief, 136-137
Bear River, 38-39
Bear River Bay, 39
Beaver hats, 40
Beaver trapping, 19-20, 172
Beaverhead River, 28
Bees, brought to West, 197
Beet sugar, in pioneer Utah, 198
Benteen, Captain, 148
Bent's Fort, 176
Bidwell, John, 83
Big Blue River, 87
"Big game" hunters and buffalos, 178
Big Hole River, 28
Big Horn River, 31
Big Medicine Road, see Oregon Trail
"Big Mountain," 102
"Big Muddy," see Missouri River
Big River, 55
Big Sandy, Mormon raid at, 116-117
Bigler, Henry, 89
Biles, James, 59
Bird Island, Great Salt Lake, 104

"The Bird Woman," see Sacajawea
Bison, see Buffalo
Black Hawk, Chief, 81
Black Hills, road agents in, 168
Black Kettle, Indian chief, 148
Black Rock Desert, 57
Blackfeet Indians, 31-32, 44, 52, 172
Black's Fork, 41-42, 108
Blast furnaces, pioneer, 194
Blue Mountains, 51, 53, 59, 124, 126
Boats, leather, 101, 178
Bodega Bay, 83
Bonneville, Benjamin Louis Eulalie de, 53, 77
Boise River, 53
Boone, Daniel, 52
Bordeaux, James, 100
Borden, Gail, 71
Borden County, Texas, 71
Bountiful, Utah, 199
Bowie, James, 67-70
Bowie knife, 67
Bozeman, John, 141
Bozeman Trail, 141-146, 189
Brannan, Sam, 89, 101-102
Breech-loading rifles, 144-145
Bretney, Captain, 139
Bridger, Jim, 31, 38-45, 61, 101, 122-123, 142, 145-146, 201
Bridger, Mary Ann, 43, 45
British competition in fur trade, 37, 49, 60, 77, 78, 172
*Brooklyn*, Mormon emigrant ship, 85, 95, 101, 110
Brown, Aaron V., 156
Brown, Alden, 186
Brown, Hen, 197
Brown, John, 102
"Brush" country, Texas, 187
"Brush popping," 186
Bryce Canyon, 131
Buchanan, James, 113, 117, 157
Buckskin clothing, 195
Buenaventura River myth, 38, 40
Buffalo
    hunt, 24-25, 173-176

Buffalo (cont.)
    number of, 176, 181
    slaughter of, 178-180
    stampedes, 58, 170
    uses of, 25, 56, 172-173, 177-181
"Buffalo Bill," *see* Cody, William
"Buffalo chips," 56
Buffalo Creek, 20
Bullboats, of buffalo hides, 178
Burnett, Peter, 54, 57
Butterfield, John, 157
Butterfield Trail ("Oxbow Route"),
    156-158

C

Caldwell, Matthew, 88
California
    admitted to Union, 105
    Americans in, 81, 82, 88-91
    Gold Rush, 47, 89-91, 152, 153, 182,
        184
    Mormons in, 88-90, 101-102
    Spanish in, 36, 48, 77
California Trail, 100
Cameahwait, Chief, 29
Camels, Arabian, used as mail carriers,
    155-156
Camp Floyd, Utah, 120
Camp Stevenson, 146
Campbell, Robert, 172
Canadian River, boundary for hide-
    hunters, 178
Cannon, Sutter's fort, 83, 90
Carlisle, Alex, 159
Carrington, Henry B., 141-144, 189
Carson, Kit, 84, 85, 185
Carson Valley, Nevada, 48, 108
Carthage, Ill., 91
Carthage Grays, 92-93
Cascade range, 59, 60
Casper, Wyo., 139
Casper Creek, 139
Casper Mountains, 139
Cass, Lewis, 81
Catholic missionaries, 35-37, 67, 79, 99,
    200

Catlin, George, 121
Cattle, 182-192; *see also* Sheep
    herding, 186-187
    longhorn, 185-186, 190
    ranges, 192
    shipped on trains, 191
    shorthorn, 182, 192
Cattlemen and sheepmen, war between,
    185
Cayuse Indians, 43, 45, 61, 62, 63
Cedar River, Mormon camp at, 110
Celilo Falls, 29
Census, buffalo, 181
Charbonneau, Toussaint, 27
Chatillon, Henry, 174
Cherry Creek, gold discovery, 158
Cheyenne Indians, 138, 147, 149
Chimney Rock, 100
Chinook Indians, 127
Chisholm, Jesse, 191
Chisholm Trail, 186, 191
Chivington massacre, 138
Cholera, and emigration to West, 100
Chorpenning, Jr., George, 153-155
Chouteau, Jr., Pierre, 41, 46
Church of Jesus Christ of Latter-Day
    Saints, *see* Mormons
Cimarron Crossing, Arkansas River, 49-
    50
City Creek, 102, 103
Civil War, 120, 137-138, 158, 200
Civilization and Indians, 122
Clark, William, 22, 27-33, 37, 51, 123
Clark, William A., 200
Clearwater River, mission on, 197
Clemens, Samuel L., quoted, 152
Cliff, Charley, 161
Cliff, Gus, 159
Clothing, cowboy, 187
Clothing
    homemade woolen, 196
    in pioneer Oregon, 195
Clothing and shelter, buffalo used for,
    177
Cochran, Augusta Joyce, 85-86
Cody, Edson, 154

Cody, William ("Buffalo Bill"), 116, 160
Collins, Casper, 138, 139
Collins, William, 138
Colonies, American, in Texas, 66
Colorado River, 35, 36, 72
Colorado River, Navajo forays across, 131
Colter, John, 30-32
"Colter's Hell," 31
*Columbia* (ship), 51
Columbia River, 29, 37, 51, 54, 57, 124, 126
Comanche (horse), survivor of Custer's stand, 150
Comanche Indians, 49, 81, 147, 157, 178-179, 188
Communication, transcontinental, 151-168
Competition, motivation of fur-trappers, 46
Congregational church, 43
Connor, Pat, 138, 166
"Contractor's War," *see* Utah War
Contracts, mail-carrying, 113, 153
Cook, James, 186-189, 192
Cooke, Phillip St. George, 86-87, 120
Cos, General, 66, 68
Covered Wagon Centennial (1930), 108-109
Covered wagons, 41
Covered wagons, Mormon, 95
"Cow column," 54
Cowboys, 186-191
Crazy Horse, Chief, 149-150
Creighton, Edward, 165
Cricket plague, Salt Lake City, 104
Crockett, Davy, 68-70
Crook, General, 148, 150
"Crossing of the Fathers," 37
Crow Indians, 24, 31, 145
*Cuddies*, 157
Cultural conflicts with Indians, 121-122
Cumming, Alfred, 114, 118, 119
Curley, Crow scout with Custer, 150
Custard, Amos, 139

Custer, George A., 148-150
Custer's last stand, 148-150

D

Davis, Jefferson, 155, 199
Deadwood-to-Denver Stage, robberies of, 168
Deaf Smith, 72
Deep Creek Station, 167
Deer Creek, handcart pioneers at, 111
Delamare, Philip, 198
*Denver*, steamboat, 160
Denver and Rio Grande Western Railroad, 200
*Denver Tribune*, 168
*Deseret News*, Utah newspaper, 160
Deseret Telegraph Line, 166
De Smet, Father, 99, 109
Diablo Ranch, 81, 83, 84, 90-91
Disease, among Indians and pioneers, 43, 45, 100, 122
Dogrib Indians, attack on fur-hunters post, 125
Dominguez, Father, 35-37, 200
Donner, George, 88
Donner Lake, 88
Donner Party, 87-88, 102
Dorion, Mrs., 123-126
Dorion, Pierre, 123-125
Driggs, Appolos, 140
Driggs, Ben, 155, 197
Driggs, Parley, 140
Driggs, Shadrach, 197
Driggs, Idaho, 19, 20
Drouillard, George, 31
Drummond, W. W., 113
Durham cattle, 192

E

Eagle Rock (Idaho Falls), 22
Echo Canyon, 87, 118
Education, pioneer, 194-195
Egan, Howar, 182-183, 192
Egan Canyon, 183
Eight-Mile Station, Indian attack at, 167
Emigration, Mormon, 95-106

# INDEX

"Emigration Canyon," 102
Emigration fund, Mormon's, 109
Emory, Colonel, 191
Emory, George, 167-168
Escalante, Father, 35-37, 200
Escalante Desert, 36
Esparza, Gregorio, 67-68
European mission, Mormon, 109
Evans, Robert, 45, 47, 48
Express and mail service, 112, 113, 151-168

## F

Fannin, Colonel, 71
"Father of Texas," 66
Fayette, N.Y., 93
Feather River, 91
Ferry boat across North Platte River, 101
Fertilizer, from buffalo bones, 180-181
Fetterman, William, 142-143
Fetterman massacre, 142-144
Field, Stephen J., 164
Fillmore, Millard, 105
Fisher, Billy, 161
Fitzhugh's mill, Independence, Mo., 54
Fitzpatrick, Thomas, 49
Flathead Indians, 172
Flores, Lt., 75
Floyd, Sergeant, 171
Food supply, pioneers' and Indians', 171, 177, 195
Fort Abraham Lincoln, 148, 150
Fort Astoria, 51, 52
Fort Bent, 176
Fort Benton, 176
Fort Boise, 53
Fort Bridger, 41-42, 43, 116-119, 122
Fort Defiance, peace talk at, 134
Fort Douglas, 166
Fort Ellsworth, 186
Fort Hall, 42, 53, 82
Fort Kearny, 141-146, 173, 189
Fort Laramie, 100, 111, 112, 135-147, 176, 189

Fort Leavenworth, 62, 88, 97, 114
Fort McPherson, 136
Fort Mandan, 29, 30
Fort Moore, 87
Fort Nonsense, 77
Fort Platte Bridge, 138-140
Fort Reno, 143, 145, 146
Fort Ross, 83
Fort Snelling, Minn., 80
Fort Sumner, 191
Fort Supply, 30, 116
Fort Sutter, 83-89
Fort Vancouver, 49, 61, 82
Fort Walla Walla, 54, 57
Fort Yerba Buena, 86
Fox Indians, 81
Frampton, William, 112
Franciscans, 67, 79
Frémont, John C., 84-85, 88, 99
Frey, John, 159, 160
Friend, John, 139
*Frontier Guardian* (newspaper), 105
Fruit trees in pioneer Utah, 198
Fur-traders' rendezvous, 47, 52, 53, 77, 172
Fur-trapping and trading, 19-20, 30-31, 37-53, 60, 77, 78, 171-172

## G

Gall, Chief, 149
Gallatin River, 28
Gamble, James, 165
Gantt, Captain, 84
Garden Grove, 96
Gardens, vegetable, in Utah, 198-199
Garretson, Martin S., 176, 177, 181
"Gates of the Mountains," 28
Geneva Steel plant, 193
Ghent, Treaty of, 60
Gibbon, John, 148, 149, 150
Gillespie, Lt., 85
Gobel, Silas, 45, 47, 48
Godin, Antoine, 172
Gold discovery, Cherry Creek, 158
Gold fields, Virginia City, Montana, 141, 189

# INDEX

Gold Rush, California, 47, 89-91, 152, 153, 182, 184
  Pikes Peak, 158, 189
Goliad, Texan defeat at, 71
Goodnight, Charles, 177, 190
Goodnight-Loving Trail, 191
Goodnight Ranch, buffalo herd on, 177, 181
Gosiute Indians, 23, 48, 167
Grand River, 96
Grand Ronde valley, Dorions at, 124
Granny Pokiboro, 27
Grant, Ulysses S., 25, 71, 148
Grantsville, Bishop of, 22
Grass, for cattle, 192
Grattan, Lt., 136-137
Grattan massacre, 136-137
Gray, Robert, 51
Great American Desert, 45, 47, 48, 156, 164
Great Basin, 36, 37, 38, 53, 87, 105
Great Falls Missouri River, 28
"Great Migration" (1843), 54
Great Salt Lake, 38-40, 87, 102-105
Green River, 35, 41, 42, 44, 46, 101, 116
Green River-Horse Creek rendezvous, 77
Green River valley, 53, 200
Grover, Thomas, 101
Gunnison, J. W., 200
Gunnison route, 200
Gwinn, W. M., 156-159

### H
Hamblin, Jacob, 130-134
Hamilton, Artois, 93
Hamilton, Squire, 92
Hamilton Hotel, 93
"Handcart pioneers," 108-112
Hand looms, pioneer use of, 196, 197
Harmon, Appleton, 100
Harney, William, 137
Harris, Moses, 101
Harrison, George, 111, 120
Harvard University, 80, 81
Hastele, Chief, 134

Hastings, Lansford, 99
Hawaii, sheep from, 196
Henry, Andrew, 37, 46, 47, 52
Hide-hunters, buffalo, 178-179
Himes, George, 58
Historical Museum, Portland, Ore., 58
Hoback, John, 52
Holladay, Ben, 167
Home life in old Oregon, 194
Homemade woolen clothing, 196
Honey bees, brought to West, 197
Horses, Pony Express, 161
  wild, 188
Houston, Sam, 71-74
Howard, Benjamin, 150
Hudson's Bay Company, 49, 60, 61, 196
Humboldt River, 57, 77, 80
Humboldt River Trail, 182
Hunt, Wilson Price, 124

### I
Idaho Indian encampment, 24
Inaugural Message, Lincoln's, carried by Pony Express, 160
Independence, Mo., 54, 81, 91, 113, 155, 176
Independence Rock, 108-109, 139
Independence-to-Salt-Lake mail route, 155
Indian Tribes
  Absaroka, see Crow
  Apache, 147, 157
  Arapahoe, 52, 174
  Blackfeet, 31-32, 44, 52, 172
  Cayuse, 43, 45, 61, 62, 63
  Cheyennes, 138, 147, 149
  Chinook, 127
  Comanche, 49, 81, 147, 157, 178-179, 188
  Crow, 24, 31, 145
  Dogrib, 125
  Flathead, 172
  Fox, 81
  Gosiute, 23, 48, 167
  Idaho, 24
  Mandan, 27

# INDEX

Indian Tribes (cont.)
 Minataree, 27
 Modoc, 147
 Mojave, 48
 Navajo, 130-134
 Nez Percé, 147
 Omaha, 97, 98
 Paiute, 37, 42, 131, 154, 183
 Pawnee, 33, 179
 Pottawatomie, 96-97
 Sauk, 81
 Shoshone, 21-30
 Sioux, 81, 138, 141-145, 147, 149-150, 162, 167-168, 179-180, 189-190
 Tejas, 67
 Tosoinitche, 154
 Utes, 22, 36, 122, 127-130, 147
 Walla Walla, 126
Indians
 attacks on pioneers, 61, 127-128, 153-154, 167, 188-190
 competition in fur trade, 172
 relations with Mormons, 96-97, 128-134
 reliance on buffalo, 25, 172-173, 177-180
 Reservations, 25, 150, 180
 and telegraph lines, 138-141, 144, 166
 wars, 81, 135-150, 159, 190
 women, 122-126
Intermarriage with Indians, 122
Iron and steel, pioneers need for, 193-194
Iron works, early, 193-194
Irrigation in Utah, 102, 106, 107-108, 199
Ives, Lt., 199

## J

"Jackass mail," 153
Jackson, Andrew, 77
Jackson, William Henry, 15, 140-141
Jackson County, Mo., Mormons in, 94
Jackson's Hole, 22, 31
Jefferson, Thomas, 27
Jerked meat, 177
Johnston, A. S., 118, 120

Jones, John S., 158
Jordan River, 87, 120
Journals of Lewis and Clark, 171
Justice, frontier, 54, 62-63, 87, 168

## K

Kane, Thomas L., 96, 97, 117-119
Kanesville (Council Bluffs, Iowa), 96, 98
Kansas-Pacific Railroad, 191
Kaw River, 55
Kearny, Stephen Watts, 80, 86, 97, 98
Keetley, Jack, 159
Keough, Miles W., 150
Keyes, Sarah, 87
Kimball, Heber C., 99
Kimball, Hiram, 113
Kimball mail contract, 113
King, Charles F., 65, 66
King, Sarah, 65
Kiowas, 147
Kirtland, Ohio, 93

## L

*Lagoda* (ship), 79
Land Donation Act of 1850, 63, 64
"Land of the Northern Mystery," 36, 37, 40
Lane, Joseph, 62
Laramie River, 100
Lariats, of buffalo hide, 178
Law, New York, in Oregon, 60
Law and order, frontier, 54, 62-63, 87, 168
Leather boats, 101, 178
Leavenworth and Pikes Peak Express, 158
Leavenworth-Denver mail route, 158
Le Barge, Captain, 176
Lee, Jason, 57
Lee, Orin, 116
Lees Ferry, 132
Lemhi Pete, Chief, 21, 22, 27
Leonard, Zenas, 77, 78
Lewis, Jo, 45

INDEX

Lewis and Clark Expedition, 22, 27-33, 37, 51, 123
Lewis and Clark, Journals of, 171
"Liberty Pole Camp," 99
Lilalobos, Gregorio de, 185
Limb, Willie, 185
Lincoln, Abraham
  Inaugural Message carried by Pony Express, 160
  signs railroad act, 200
  and transcontinental telegraph, 164, 166
Lion House, Bronx Park, New York, Bison Society organized at, 181
Lisa, Manuel, 31
Little, Jesse, 97
Little Big Horn River, battle at, 149-150
Little Blue River, 55
"Little Mountain," 102
Lodge Pole Ridge, 142-143, 145
Lolo Pass, 29
"Long Hair," see Custer, George A.
Longhorn cattle, 185-186, 190
Loretto, 44
Los Angeles, Calif., 37, 81, 87, 155
  in Mexican War, 86
Louisiana Purchase, 33
Loving, Oliver, 190
Luna, Antonio Jose, 184

M

McCoy, Joe, 191
McCulloch, B. M., 119
McGraw, W. M. F., 113, 155
Mackenzie, Donald, 37
McLoughlin, Dr. John, 49, 61, 196
"Mad River" (Snake River), 124
Madison River, 28, 32
Mail-carrying contracts, 113, 153
Mail and express service, 112, 113, 151-168
Majors, Alexander, 158, 159, 160, 167
Majors, Tom, 173
Mamoots, 122-123
Mandan Indians, 27

Manuel's Post, 31, 32
Maple sugar, in pioneer Utah, 197
Mapping of the West, 32, 38, 40
Mark Twain, see Twain, Mark
Markham, Stephen, 99
Marsh, Alice, 90, 91
Marsh, Charles, 81, 90-91
Marsh, Dr. John, 80-84, 90-91
Marsh, Marguerite, 80-81
Marshall, James, 47, 89, 90
Martini, John, 149
Marysville, Kansas, 87
Massanet, Father, 67
Mather, Stephen, 181
Maxwell, Lucien, 185
Measles epidemic, and Whitman mission massacre, 43, 45
Meek, Helen Mar, 43, 45, 54, 62
Meek, Joe, 43, 51-54, 60, 201
Meeker, Ezra, 63, 126-127, 170, 194, 195
Menchaca, Captain, 75
Methodist mission, The Dalles, Oregon, 57
Mexico, Revolution of 1821, 66, 81
Mexico, Texas Revolution against, 65-75
Mexico, War with, 85-87, 97
Micheltorena, Manuel, 84
Migration, buffalo, 173
Miles, General, 150
Miles, Edward, 71-75
Milk, preserving of, 71
Miller, Joseph, 52
Minataree Indians, 27
Miners
  demand for meat, 189
  hardships, 152-153
  mail deliveries to, 153
  relations with Indians, 159
Mining, gold
  California, 47, 89-91, 152, 153
  Pikes Peak, 158, 189
  Virginia City, Montana, 141, 189
Mining, silver, Virginia City, Nevada, 167
Mission, Mormon, in Europe, 109
Mission San Gabriel, 48

Missionaries, American Board of Foreign Missions, 43-45, 53, 54, 56, 63, 196-197
Missionaries, Catholic, 35-37, 67, 79, 99, 200
Missionaries, Methodist, 57
Missouri River, 27-29, 30, 31, 37, 46
Missouri River, buffalos on, 176-177
*Mochilas*, 161
Modoc Indians, 147
Mohave Desert, Calif., 37
Mohave River, 184
Mojave Indians, 48
Monroe, James, 179
Monterey, Calif., 35, 37, 49, 79, 85
Montgomery, John B., 85
Mormon Battalion, 88-90, 97-98, 120
Mormon Ferry, 101
Mormon Tabernacle, 103, 115, 118, 194, 198
Mormon Temple, 90, 198
Mormon trail, 41, 100, 156
Mormons
    in California, 85-90, 101-102
    emigrant ship *Brooklyn*, 85, 95, 101, 110
    emigration, first, 43
    "Handcart pioneers," 108-112
    mission in Europe, 109
    relations with Indians, 96-97, 128-134
    religious persecution of, 92-106
    tenth anniversary in Salt Lake, 107-108
    and transcontinental telegraph, 165-166
    "Water Pioneers," 85, 89, 95, 101
    war with U.S., 112-120
    Winter Quarters, 98-99, 103
Morris, Elias, 198
Morse, Samuel F. B., 164
Mt. Diablo, 81
Mt. Hood, 57, 58
Mt. Pisgah, 96
Mules, used for mail-carrying, 155, 157, 162
Museum, Portland Historical, 58
Mustangs, 188

N

Natches Pass, 59
Natchitoches, La., 34
National Park Service, 181
Nauvoo, Illinois, 94-96
Navajo Indians, 130-134
Nebraska, 30, 31
New Helvetia, Calif., 82-85, 87
*New Helvetia Diary*, 89
New Mexico, 33-34, 36, 184
New York law in Oregon, 60
Newell, Bob, 53-54
Newspapers
    *Denver Tribune*, 168
    *Deseret News*, 160
    *Frontier Guardian*, 105
Newspapers, pioneer use of, 194
Nez Percé Indians, 147
North Platte River, 100, 101, 111

O

Ogden, Peter Skene, 61
Ogden River, 47
Ogden's Hole, Utah, 47
Ohio regiment at Ft. Laramie, 138
"Old Buffalo Bones," 180
Old Mohawk Trail, 157
Old Ocean, Indian guide, 27
Old Tabernacle, Salt Lake City, 103, 115, 118, 194, 198
Omaha Indians, 97, 98
Oregon, 37, 49, 53, 54, 57, 58, 60-62, 194
Oregon City, 58, 62
Oregon Territory, opening and settlement of, 51
Oregon Territory, government of, 60-62
*The Oregon Trail*, 173-176
Oregon Trail
    blazing of, 52-54
    Ft. Bridger on, 41-42
    "Great Migration," 54-56
    Indian attacks, 135-141
    mail route over, 155-156
Osage River, 33
Ostrander, Alson B., 143-147
Otero, Antonio Jose, 184

Overland Stage, 137, 158, 167; *see also* Mail and Express Service
Overland Trail, 194
Ox team caravans, 54-60
"Oxbow Route," 156-158

P

Pacific Surveys, for railroad routes, 199-200
Pacific Telegraph Company, 165
Paiute Indians, 37, 42, 131, 154, 183
Pantsuk, 23
Parker, Chief Quanah, 178-179
Parkman, Francis, 173-176
Parowan, Mormon settlement at, 128
Pasture lands, defined by law, 192
Pawnee Indians, 33, 179
"Peace chiefs," 128, 130
Peace commission, Utah War, 119
Peace talk, Fort Defiance, 134
Pecos River, 177, 191
Peg Leg Smith, 42, 61
Phillips, John ("Portugee"), 143-144
Pied Riche, Chief, 96
Pierce, Franklin, 155, 199
Pierre's Hole (Teton Basin), battle at, 172
Pig iron, pioneer produced, 194
Pico, Pio, 84
Pike, Zebulon Montgomery, 32-34
Pike expedition of 1806, 33
Pikes Peak, 33
"Pikes Peak or bust" gold rush, 158, 189
Pikes Peak Stables, 161
Platte Bridge Fort, 138, 139, 140
Platte River, 30, 34, 55, 99, 140
Pokiboro, Granny, 27
Polk, James K., 61, 62, 90
Pony Express, 137, 151-166
Portland Historical Museum, 58
Potash, from buffalo bones, 180-181
Pottawatomie Indians, 96-97
Potts, John, 31
Powell, L. W., 119
Prairie-dog villages, 58
Pratt, Orson, 100, 102

Presbyterian church, 43
Promontory Point, transcontinental railroad linked at, 200
Provisional government, Oregon Territory, 60, 61
Provo, Utah, 107
Pueblo, Colorado, 33
"Puritan Pathfinder," 77

Q

Quanah Parker, Chief, 178-179

R

Raft River, 57
Railroads
    cattle shipments, 184, 191
    routes charted by U.S. Army, 199-200
    transcontinental, 199-200
Raton Pass, 185
Red Cloud, Chief, 141-145, 189-190
Red River, 34, 188
Redwood trees, 78
Reed, J. F., 87, 124-126
"Registry of the desert," 109
Rendezvous, fur-traders', 47, 52, 53, 77, 172
Reno, Major, 148, 149
*Revenue Cutter,* (ship), 101
Revolution of 1821, Mexican, 66, 81
Revolution of 1836, Texan, 65-75
Rezner, Jacob, 52
Richards, Franklin, 109-110
Richards, Willard, 93
Richardson, William, 159
Riders, Pony Express, 159-164
Rifles, breech-loading, 144-145
Rio de los Americanos *see* American River
Rio del Norte *see* Rio Grande
Rio Grande, 34, 66, 67
Rising, Don, 159
Rivers *see* Particular rivers
Road agents, 168
"Roadmeter," 100
Robinson, Edward, 52
Robison, Solon, 117

# INDEX

Rock Creek, handcart pioneer grave at, 109
Rock Island Railroad, 108
Rockwell, Porter, 112
Rockwood, A. P., 99
Rocky Mountain Divide, 25, 28, 29
Rocky Mountain Fur Company, 46, 47, 53
*Roughing It*, quotation from, 152
Russell, Isaac K., 201
Russell, William H., 158, 159, 167
Russian cannon, Sutter's fort, 83, 90
Russian competition in fur trade, 78, 79, 83, 87
Rusty (dog), survivor of Custer's stand, 150

## S

Sabine River, 72
Sacajawea, 27-30, 86, 123
Sacramento, Calif., 47, 83, 151-160
Sacramento River, 83
St. George, Utah, 90
St. Louis-San Francisco mail route, 156, 157
Saints *see* Mormons
Salmon River, 27
Salt Lake *see* Great Salt Lake
Salt Lake City, Utah
    founding of, 103-104
    in Gold Rush days, 105
    mail routes, 113, 153-155
    transcontinental telegraph link, 164, 166
    in Utah War, 112-120
Salt Lake City Tabernacle, 103, 115, 118, 194, 198
Salt Lake City Temple, 90, 198
Salt Lake-Los Angeles trail, 45
Salt Lake valley, 90, 100, 101
San Antonio, Texas, 66-67
San Bernardino, Mormons in, 108
San Diego, 47, 86-87
San Fernando, battle at, 84
San Francisco, mail routes, 151, 156, 157
San Gabriel, Mission, 48

San Jacinto, battle of, 72-75
San Joaquin River, 83
San Jose Mission, 49
San Pedro River, 86
Sand Creek, Colorado, Chivington massacre at, 138
Sandwich Islanders in New Helvetia, 83
Santa Anna, Antonio Lopez de, 66, 68-75, 83-84
Sante Fe, N. M., 34, 35, 37
Santa Fe Railroad, 180, 184, 200
Santa Fe Trail, 35, 37, 62, 81, 127, 158, 176
Sante Fe wagons, 198
Sauk Indians, 81
School for Indian and white children, Whitman mission, 43
Schools, pioneer, 194-195
Sequin, Captain, 75
Serra, Father Junipero, 79
Sessions, Peregrine, 199
Sessions Settlement, gardens in, 199
Seventh Cavalry, U.S. Army, 148-150
Sevier River, 131
Shaw, Quincy Adams, 174
Sheep from Hawaii, 196
Sheep industry, 184-185
Sheep, used for wool, 196, 197
Sheepmen and cattlemen, war between, 185
Sheldon, Dr. A. E., 167
Sheridan, Philip, 148, 150
Sherman, William Tecumseh, 178
Shields, buffalo hide, 178
Shoes, pioneer produced, 195
Shorthorn cattle, 182, 192
Shoshone Indians, 21-30
Shumway, Charles, 95, 101
Sibley, Hiram, 165
Sierra Mountains, 36, 47, 48, 76, 77, 88, 105
Silver mining camp, Virginia City, 167
Simpson, Lew, 116-117
Simpson's Hollow, U.S. Army supplies burnt at, 116-117
Sinclair, Alexander, 172

# INDEX

Sioux Indians
  attack communications, 138, 162, 167-168
  defeat Custer, 148-150
  on Bozeman Trail, 141-145, 189-190
Sioux Prayer—Ghost Dance, 179-180
Sioux village, attack on, 137
Skull Valley, Utah, 48
Slaughter, Ben, 186
Slaughter, Johnny, 168
Slave-trade, Spanish, 37, 127
Slavery, among Indians, 127
Sloat, Commodore, 85
Smith, Deaf, 72
Smith, George A., 102
Smith, Hyrum, 92-93
Smith, Jedediah Strong, 45-50, 77, 85, 200, 201
Smith, Joseph, 92-94, 96, 109
Smith, Lot, 116-117
Smith, Peg Leg, 42, 61
Smoky Hill Trail, mail route over, 158
Smoot, Abram, 112, 113
Snake River, 24, 29, 42, 52, 124
Snake (Shoshone) land, 30
Snow, Erastus, 102
"Snowshoe Thompson," 155
Sonoma, battle of, 85
South Pass, Rockies, 37, 46, 52, 53, 77, 101, 111, 155
Spalding, Henry, 53, 196-197
Spalding mission, 196-197
Spanish empire in Southwest, 33-37, 47-49, 77-79
Spanish slave trade, 37, 127
Spanish Trail, 37, 47, 67, 155, 200
Spotted Tail Indian Agency, 149
Spring Creek, 21, 22
Springfield rifles, used in Indian wars, 144-145
Stage lines, 137, 157-158, 167
Stanford, Leland, 200
Stanton, Charles, 87-88
Stevens, Isaac I., 199
Stewart, MacNeil, 188, 189
Stewart, Sir William Drummond, 82

Stockton, Robert F., 86
Stoddard, Judson, 112
Stokes, George W., 149, 168
"Store clothes," demand for, 199, 200
Story, Nelson, 189-190, 192
Streeper, Bill, 162-164
Street, James, 165
Stuart, Robert, 52, 53
Sublette, William, 49, 172
Sugar, in pioneer Utah, 197, 198
Sugar refining, 180, 198
Sutter, John August, 80-91
Sutter's Fort, 83-89
Sweetwater River, 108-109, 160
Sweetwater Station, 138
Sweetwater valley, 53
Sylvester, Lt., 73

## T

Tabernacle, Salt Lake City, 103, 115, 118, 194, 198
Taylor, John, 93, 100, 198
Tecumsee, 183
Tehachapi Pass, 184
Tejas Indians, 67
Telegraph lines and Indian wars, 138-141, 144
Telegraph office at Ft. Laramie, 137
Telegraph, transcontinental, 164-166
Temple, Mormon, Salt Lake City, 90, 198
Temple Square, Salt Lake City, 105
Ten Eyck, Lt., 143
Tepee village, 21
Terry, General, 148-150
Terry, Josh, 38, 42, 51, 103, 122-123, 201
Teton Basin, 19, 22, 31, 172, 192
Teton Canyon, 21
Teton Creek, 20, 21
Teton Divide, 172
Teton Peaks, 20
Teton River, 21
Teton Valley, 27
Texan defeat at the Alamo, 67-70
Texan treaty with Santa Anna, 74
Texas, American colonies in, 66

# INDEX

Texas, Franciscans in, 67
Texas Panhandle, Goodnight Ranch in, 177, 181
Texas Revolution of 1836, 65-75
The Dalles, Oregon, 29, 57, 58
Thimblerig, 68, 69
Thompson, Jeff, 160
"Tick fever," 191
*Tonquin* (ship), 196
Tosenamp, 22
Tosoinitche Indians, 154
Towne, George, 159
Trading posts, 52, 60
Trail-blazers, 53, 201
Trail Creek Canyon, 172
Trails, *see* Particular trail
Transcontinental railroads, 199-200
Transcontinental telegraph, 164-166
Travis, William, 68, 69
Treaty of Ghent, 60
Treaty, Texan, with Santa Anna, 74
Tuba, Chief, 132
Twain, Mark (Samuel L. Clemens) quoted, 152
Two Moons, Chief, 149

## U

Uintah Range, 41, 42
U.S. Army, destruction of buffalos, 178
U.S. Army, Seventh Cavalry, 148-150
U.S. Army, in Utah War, 112-120
U.S. Cavalry, protection of buffalos by, 181
U.S. Indian agents, 37, 106
United States Steel plant on Utah Lake, 193
University of Kansas museum, 150
Urrea, General, 71
Utah, bees imported into, 197
Utah, early iron works in, 193-194
Utah Lake, U.S. Steel plant on, 193
Utah militia, 116
Utah Territory, 22, 35-50, 105, 108
Utah Valley, 36
Utah War, 112-120
Ute Indians, 22, 36, 122, 127-130, 147

## V

Vallejo, Makiano G., 85
Van Vliet, Captain, 114-115
Van Voast, Major, 146
Vegetable gardens in pioneer Utah, 198-199
Virginia City, Montana, gold fields, 141, 189
Virginia City, Nevada, silver mining in, 167

## W

Waddell, W. B., 158, 159, 167
Wagon Box Fight, 144-145
Waiilatpu, mission at, 43, 53, 56, 61-63, 196
Wales, pioneers from, 194
Walker Chief, *see* Yellow Metal
Walker, Joseph Reddeford, 77, 78, 79, 80
"Walker War," 127-128, 130
Walker's Pass, 80
Walla Walla Indians, 126
Walla Walla valley, 196
Wallace, Henry, 160
War between cattlemen and sheepmen, 185
War of 1812, 37, 60
War with Mexico, 85-87, 97
Wasatch Mountains, 36, 87, 107
Washakie, Chief, 22, 24-26, 30, 123, 166
"Water Pioneers," 85, 89, 95, 101
Weber Canyon, 118
Weber River, 47
Wells, General, 114, 128
Wells, Emmeline B., 98
Wells Fargo Company, 167
Wentworth, Edward N., 184
Western Union Telegraph Company, 165
Whipple, Lt. A., 199
"White Foot," 22
Whitman, Marcus, 43-45, 53, 56, 63, 196-197
Whitman, Narcissa, 43-45, 54, 63, 196

# INDEX

Whitman, Perrin, 56
Whitman mission, 43, 53, 56, 196
Whitman mission, massacre at, 61-63
Wild-life reservations, 181
Wilde, Joe, 136
Willamette River, 60, 61
Willamette valley, 54, 57
Wilson, Nick, 21-27, 126, 167
Wind River Mountains, 53
Wind River Reservation, 25
Winter of 1888, 20
"Winter Quarters," Mormon, 98-99, 103
Wiser, Peter, 31
Woodruff, Wilford, 101, 103
Woodson, Samuel H., 155
Woodward, Absalom, 153, 154
Wool, use for pioneer clothing, 196

Wootton, "Uncle" Dick, 184-185
Wyoming Warpath, 141-146, 189, 190

## Y

Yagaiki, 25
Yakima River, 59
Yates, Captain, 150
Yellow Metal, Chief, 122, 127-130
Yellowstone Park, 25, 31, 32, 181
Yellowstone River, 30, 31
Yerba Buena, Calif., 82, 85
Yosemite valley, 77
Young, Brigham, 22, 30, 37, 94-106, 108-120, 165, 198
Young, Ewing, estate, 60-61
Young, Mahonri, 105
Y X Company, 112, 113